Building a
Scholarship
of Assessment

Building a Scholarship of Assessment

Trudy W. Banta and Associates

 JOSSEY-BASS
A Wiley Company
San Francisco

Published by

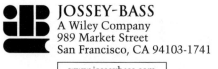

JOSSEY-BASS
A Wiley Company
989 Market Street
San Francisco, CA 94103-1741

www.josseybass.com

Copyright © 2002 by John Wiley & Sons, Inc.

Jossey-Bass is a registered trademark of John Wiley & Sons, Inc.

No part of this publication may be reproduced, stored in a retrieval system, or transmitted in any form or by any means, electronic, mechanical, photocopying, recording, scanning, or otherwise, except as permitted under Sections 107 or 108 of the 1976 United States Copyright Act, without either the prior written permission of the Publisher or authorization through payment of the appropriate per-copy fee to the Copyright Clearance Center, 222 Rosewood Drive, Danvers, MA 01923, (978) 750-8400, fax (978) 750-4744. Requests to the Publisher for permission should be addressed to the Permissions Department, John Wiley & Sons, Inc., 605 Third Avenue, New York, NY 10158-0012, (212) 850-6011, fax (212) 850-6008, e-mail: permreq@wiley.com.

Jossey-Bass books and products are available through most bookstores. To contact Jossey-Bass directly, call (888) 378-2537, fax to (800) 605-2665, or visit our website at www.josseybass.com.

Substantial discounts on bulk quantities of Jossey-Bass books are available to corporations, professional associations, and other organizations. For details and discount information, contact the special sales department at Jossey-Bass.

We at Jossey-Bass strive to use the most environmentally sensitive paper stocks available to us. Our publications are printed on acid-free recycled stock whenever possible, and our paper always meets or exceeds minimum GPO and EPA requirements.

Library of Congress Cataloging-in-Publication Data

Building a scholarship of assessment / [edited by] Trudy W. Banta.— 1st ed.
      p. cm. — (The Jossey-Bass higher and adult education series)
Includes bibliographical references and index.
  ISBN 0-7879-5945-6 (alk. paper)
  1. Universities and colleges—Examinations. 2. College students—Rating of. 3. College teaching—Evaluation. 4. Education, Higher—Evaluation. 5. Educational tests and measurements. I. Banta, Trudy W. II. Series.
  LB2366 .B85 2002
  378.1'66—dc21   2001008098

FIRST EDITION
HB Printing   10 9 8 7 6 5 4 3 2 1

Contents

Preface

The term *scholarship of assessment* has arisen spontaneously among outcomes assessment scholars and practitioners over the last three years. By late 1999 so many of the authors of chapters in this volume had begun to use this term that some of us proposed a session for the June 2000 American Association for Higher Education Assessment Conference with the title "The Scholarship of Assessment." In that session we acknowledged that there are many barriers to conducting scholarly work in outcomes assessment. Most of the individuals chosen to lead assessment initiatives on their own campuses are respected members of their campus communities whose communication skills figure more prominently in their selection than does their expertise in psychometrics, cognitive development, program evaluation, or one of the other areas most closely related to the intellectual domain of outcomes assessment in higher education. In fact, scholars in these allied fields generally have not chosen to become leaders in this new area.

Other barriers to the conduct of assessment scholarship include the fact that this work is not specifically recognized or rewarded on many campuses. Since most assessment leaders must spend time away from their primary disciplines when tapped to coordinate outcomes assessment campuswide, they elect to give up their administrative roles after a few years to return to their disciplinary roots. Finally, there are very few places in the country where one can pursue graduate studies that prepare one to become an assessment scholar. All of these factors combine to yield only a very small number of academics who are willing and able to carry out the scholarship of assessment.

In June 2000 we had no formal definition for the scholarship of assessment, though of course we recognized that we were building on Ernest Boyer's seminal work in *Scholarship Reconsidered* on the scholarship of teaching (1990) and on Glassick, Huber, and Maeroff's subsequent conceptualization in *Scholarship Assessed* (1997) of methods for evaluating the scholarship of teaching. Now, in part because of the distinction Hutchings and Shulman (1999) have made between scholarly teaching and the scholarship of teaching, we must distinguish between *scholarly assessment* and *the scholarship of assessment*. For the purposes of this book, we will define scholarly assessment as the work under way on hundreds of campuses across the country that is aimed at improving the day-to-day conduct of assessment. It involves selecting or creating assessment methods, trying them out, reflecting with colleagues on their strengths and weaknesses, then modifying the methods or trying new ones in the spirit of improving the effectiveness and impact of assessment continuously. The scholarship of assessment is systematic inquiry designed to deepen and extend the foundation of knowledge underlying assessment. It involves basing studies on relevant theory and/or practice, gathering evidence, developing a summary of findings, and sharing those findings with the growing community of assessment scholars and practitioners.

While we fervently wish it were otherwise, we acknowledge at the outset that the scholarship of assessment in higher education is still relatively rare. Marcia Mentkowski and colleagues at Alverno College have been engaged in some of the most outstanding work in this arena since the early 1970s. Dary Erwin's research at James Madison University (JMU) has been under way since the mid-1980s, and recently JMU became the first institution to offer a doctoral program in outcomes assessment. Although not considered a component of outcomes assessment until relatively recently, noteworthy activity in evaluating and improving teaching has been taking place in centers for teaching improvement at the University of Illinois, Syracuse University, and the University of California at Berkeley since the 1970s. Systematic studies of the effectiveness of out-of-class programs and services have been conducted by student affairs professionals at the University of Maryland, Iowa State University, and the University of Missouri for more than a decade. While all who conduct assessment on their own campuses benefit from the presentations at national conferences and the publications contributed by the individuals and institutions just mentioned, their number is insignificant when considered in light of the more than 3500 postsecondary institutions that educate students in the United States today and thus need to be concerned about conducting assessment as effectively and efficiently as possible.

We have undertaken to produce this volume on the scholarship of assessment for three principal reasons. First, we intend to provide a chronicle of the history and current status of the development of outcomes assessment in higher education at the beginning of a new millennium. Second, we wish to remind current faculty and administrators as well as scholars in training of the theoretical underpinnings of assessment and of the many avenues for future scholarship these foundation stones can support. And finally, we hope to provide our own piece of scholarship that can help to convince all the skeptics who still believe outcomes assessment is a fad and will fade away soon that, in fact, this is an interdisciplinary area with deep roots and developing stems that could support magnificent blossoms any day now!

In keeping with these purposes, we have created for faculty, academic and student affairs administrators, and graduate students who are preparing for these roles, a work in five parts. The chapters in Part One trace the history of outcomes assessment in higher education and bring it up to the current day with a summary of current status and impact derived from a national survey and follow-up visits to selected campuses. Chapters in Part Two suggest the range of disciplines that provide the underlying theoretical perspectives on which the scholarship of assessment has been, and will continue to be, based. Part Three contains descriptions of some of the basic methods and tools that can be employed in the scholarship of assessment. In Part Four the chapter authors describe applications of the methods of assessment, and they identify many of the sites across the country where scholarly assessment is under way. Part Five provides a summary of the principles of good practice derived from scholarly assessment to date and suggests some of the avenues for scholarship that are likely to bear most fruit in future years.

Indianapolis, Indiana   TRUDY W. BANTA
January 2002

To all of the wonderful people
at IUPUI
who assist on a daily basis
in
building the scholarship of assessment—
Linda and Karen
Patti, Angie, Michele, Julie, and Amy
Vic, Howard, James, and Susan

The Authors

Thomas Anthony Angelo is professor of education, associate provost, and founding director of the Institute for Teaching and Learning at the University of Akron. Prior to coming to Akron, he served as a faculty member, administrator, and/or researcher at DePaul University, the University of Miami, the American Association for Higher Education, Boston College, California State University, Long Beach, the University of California, Berkeley, and Harvard University. His publications include *Classroom Research: Early Lessons from Success* (1991), *Classroom Assessment Techniques: A Handbook for College Teachers* (with K. Patricia Cross, 1993), and *Classroom Assessment and Research: An Update on Uses, Approaches, and Research Findings* (1998). Angelo has held fellowships from the Fulbright Program in Italy and the Gulbenkian Foundation in Portugal and has served as visiting scholar for the Higher Education Research and Development Society of Australasia. He earned a B.A. in government from California State University, Sacramento, an M.A. in political science, an Ed.M. in TESOL from Boston University, and his doctorate from Harvard's Graduate School of Education.

Trudy W. Banta is professor of higher education and vice chancellor for planning and institutional improvement at Indiana University-Purdue University Indianapolis. Before coming to Indianapolis, she was a professor of education and founding director of the Center for Assessment Research and Development at the University of Tennessee, Knoxville. She is founding editor of the bimonthly periodical *Assessment Update*, which has been published by Jossey-Bass since 1989. Other published works include *Making a Difference: Outcomes of a Decade of Assessment in Higher Education* (1993), *Assessment in Practice: Putting Principles to Work on College Campuses* (with J. P. Lund, K. E. Black, and F. W. Oblander, 1996), *Assessment Essentials: Planning, Implementing, and Improving Assessment in Higher*

Education (with C. A. Palomba, 1999), and *Assessing Student Competence in Accredited Disciplines: Pioneering Approaches to Assessment in Higher Education* (with C. A. Palomba, 2001). Banta has received awards for her work from the American Association for Higher Education, the American Productivity and Quality Center, and the National Council on Measurement in Education. She received her baccalaureate and master's degrees from the University of Kentucky and earned her doctorate in educational psychology from the University of Tennessee.

Karen E. Black holds a B.A. in English and an M.S. in college student personnel from Indiana University Bloomington, where she is a Ph.D. candidate in higher education, with a minor in English. She manages the program review process for Indiana University-Purdue University Indianapolis, serves on the Program Review and Assessment Committee, and teaches in the technical communications department. Black has assisted in the development and coordination of ten national conferences and nine international conferences on the topic of assessing quality in higher education. In addition, she has written several articles and made invited presentations at national and regional meetings on program review and assessment in higher education. She coauthored *Assessment in Practice* with Trudy Banta, Jon Lund, and Frances Oblander (1996), and she serves as the managing editor of *Assessment Update,* a bimonthly periodical published by Jossey-Bass.

Victor M. H. Borden is associate professor of psychology and associate vice chancellor for information management and institutional research at Indiana University-Purdue University Indianapolis (IUPUI). He developed his interest in institutional research and assessment at the University of Massachusetts, Amherst, George Mason University, and IUPUI, within the divisions of student affairs, academic affairs, finance and planning, and planning and institutional improvement. He received his baccalaureate degree from the University of Rochester and his master's and doctoral degrees in social psychology from the University of Massachusetts, Amherst. With Trudy Banta, Borden edited *Using Performance Indicators to Guide Strategic Decision Making* (1994). Recent publications include *Measuring Quality: Choosing Among Surveys and Other Assessments of College Quality* (with J.L.Z. Owens, 2001) and a chapter in *Electronic*

Portfolios: Emerging Practices in Student, Faculty, and Institutional Learning (2001). Borden currently serves on the board of directors for the Association for Institutional Research.

Kathryn E. Daniels is a second-year master's student in industrial organizational psychology at Indiana University-Purdue University Indianapolis (IUPUI), and her research interests include team decision processes. She received her bachelor's degree in psychology at Indiana University Bloomington. She is currently working as a research assistant at IUPUI's Testing Center. She has coauthored (with Mark D. Shermis) *Automated Essay Grading for Electronic Portfolios* (2001), published in *Assessment Update,* and has authored *Norming and Scaling for Automated Essay Scoring* (forthcoming).

T. Dary Erwin is director of the Center for Assessment Research and Studies and professor of psychology at James Madison University. His previous institutional affiliations include Texas A&M University and the University of Tennessee, Knoxville. He received his bachelor's and master's degrees from the University of Tennessee and earned his doctorate in student development and measurement from the University of Iowa.

Peter T. Ewell is vice president of the National Center for Higher Education Management Systems (NCHEMS), an independent research and development center on higher education policy and management, located in Boulder, Colorado. He joined the staff of NCHEMS in 1981 and since then has led many multi-institutional demonstration projects on assessment and educational effectiveness, funded by major foundations. In addition, he has consulted directly with over 350 colleges and universities and twenty-three state systems on assessment-related issues. He has written broadly on assessment and has given invited addresses on the topic at national and international meetings. His awards include the Sidney Suslow Award of the Association of Institutional Research (AIR), the Leadership Award of the Association for the Study of Higher Education (ASHE), the Academic Leadership Award of the Council of Independent Colleges (CIC), and the Virginia B. Smith Award of the Council on Adult and Experiential Learning (CAEL). He received his baccalaureate degree from Haverford College and his master's and doctoral degrees in political science from Yale University.

Robert M. Gonyea divides his time at Indiana University Bloomington between his roles as project manager of the College Student Experiences Questionnaire and research analyst for the National Survey of Student Engagement. He is also a doctoral student in higher education and student affairs with a minor in educational inquiry. Gonyea is a Michigan native and earned his bachelor's and master's degrees from Michigan State University. His research interests include assessment of institutional quality, the contribution of student affairs to student learning, and the use of assessment in student affairs. He is a frequent presenter at professional conferences on assessment. Before coming to Indiana University, he worked for fourteen years in the field of student affairs, in the areas of residence life, student activities, and leadership development.

Peter J. Gray received his Ph.D. in educational psychology from the University of Oregon and has a master's degree in curriculum theory from Cornell University. His research interests include higher education assessment, course, curriculum, and program evaluation, and institutional research. As associate director of the Center for Support of Teaching and Learning at Syracuse University, his responsibilities include managing the design, implementation, and reporting of evaluation, research, and instructional development projects. Gray holds adjunct associate professor appointments in the higher education department and in the instructional design, development, and evaluation department at Syracuse University. With Trudy W. Banta, he coedited *The Campus-Level Impact of Assessment: Progress, Problems, and Possibilities* (New Directions for Higher Education, 1997). He was the editor and a contributor to *Achieving Assessment Goals Using Evaluation Techniques* (New Directions for Higher Education, 1989). He has been a contributing editor to *Assessment Update* since its inception. He is currently chairing the Middle States Association Commission on Higher Education's advisory panel on student learning and assessment, which is developing an assessment handbook to accompany its new *Characteristics of Excellence in Higher Education: Standards for Accreditation.*

Kimberly A. Kline is a doctoral student in the Higher Education and Student Affairs program and is also assistant coordinator of the Academic Support Centers at Indiana University Bloomington. She received a B.A. in political science from Slippery Rock University and an M.S. in student personnel administration from the State University of New York, College at Buffalo. Her research focuses on professional development, social justice issues, assessment, and adventure-based education. Kline is particularly interested in the use of reflection and action theories in the development of student affairs practitioners.

George D. Kuh is Chancellor's Professor of Higher Education at Indiana University Bloomington, where he directs the College Student Experiences Questionnaire project and the annual National Survey of Student Engagement, which is sponsored by The Carnegie Foundation for the Advancement of Teaching and is supported by The Pew Charitable Trusts. Kuh's research and scholarly activities focus on assessment strategies, campus cultures, and the out-of-class experiences of undergraduates. He has served in several academic administrative positions and is past president of the Association for the Study of Higher Education. Among his twenty books and monographs are *Student Learning Outside the Classroom: Transcending Artificial Boundaries* (1994), *Involving Colleges* (1991), and *The Invisible Tapestry: Culture in American Colleges and Universities* (1988). His work has been recognized with awards from the Association for the Study of Higher Education, the American College Personnel Association, the National Association of Student Personnel Administrators, the Association of Institutional Research, and the Council of Independent Colleges. He has also received the Tracy Sonneborn Award for Distinguished Scholarship and Teaching at Indiana University. He holds a B.A. from Luther College, an M.S. from St. Cloud State University, and a Ph.D. from the University of Iowa.

Georgine Loacker is professor of English and director of student assessment-as-learning at Alverno College. She was a major contributor to the development of Alverno's ability-based curriculum and student assessment process, which began in 1973, and she previously chaired Alverno's English department and the college's communication ability department. She edited *Self Assessment at Alverno College* (2000), was a contributing author to Mentkowski and Associates' *Learning That Lasts: Integrating Learning, Development, and Performance in College and Beyond* (2000), and coauthored "Problem Solving at Alverno College" (with K. O'Brien, D. Dathe, and M. Matlock) in *The Challenge of Problem-Based Learning* (1998).

Loacker consults with a wide range of colleges and universities on assessment in the United States and abroad. Her awards include a visiting fellowship from the Higher Education Research and Development Society of Australasia and a fellowship from the University of Dublin for directing seminars on student assessment. She received her B.A. from Alverno College, her M.A. from Marquette University, and her Ph.D. from the University of Chicago.

Marcia Mentkowski is professor of psychology and director of the educational research and evaluation department at Alverno College. She chairs the committee of administrators, faculty, and staff that fosters curriculum, program and institution-wide assessment, and inquiry on student learning outcomes and curricular validity. Two recent publications of hers—*Learning That Lasts: Integrating Learning, Development, and Performance in College and Beyond* (2000) and *Higher Education Assessment and National Goals for Education: Issues, Assumptions, and Principles* (1998)—received outstanding research publication awards from the American Educational Research Association division on educating professionals. She has facilitated the collaborative scholarship of Alverno faculty and staff teams, national professional associations, and foundation-funded consortia of institutions. She was AAHE (American Association for Higher Education) adviser to the Joint Committee on the Standards for Educational and Psychological Testing (American Educational Research Association, American Psychological Association, and National Council in Measurement in Education, 1999) and initiated the annual AAHE Research Forum (with Alexander Astin and Arthur Chickering, 1985), where she has led members in collaborative inquiry. Mentkowski was an invited visiting scholar at Harvard's Graduate School of Education and an invited speaker on assessment at a meeting of the American Psychological Association. She received the Kuhmerker Award from the Association for Moral Education and was named Distinguished Educator by the Encuentro Nacional de Educacion y Pensamiento in Puerto Rico. Mentkowski received her B.A. from Downer College of Lawrence University and her M.A. and Ph.D. from the University of Wisconsin, Madison.

Catherine A. Palomba recently retired from her position as director of academic assessment and institutional research at Ball State University. Previously, she was a research analyst at the Center for

Naval Analyses in Alexandria, Virginia, and was an associate professor of economics at West Virginia University, where she received two awards as an outstanding teacher. In 1998, the American Productivity and Quality Center recognized Ball State's assessment program as a "best practice" institution for assessing learning outcomes. Palomba has coauthored two books with Trudy Banta: *Assessment Essentials: Planning, Implementing, and Improving Assessment in Higher Education* (1999) and *Assessing Student Competence in Accredited Disciplines: Pioneering Approaches to Assessment in Higher Education* (2001). She earned a bachelor's degree from the Baruch School of the City College of New York, a master's degree from the University of Minnesota, Minneapolis, and a Ph.D. from Iowa State University—all in economics.

Marvin W. Peterson is professor of higher education and former director of the University of Michigan's Center for the Study of Higher and Postsecondary Education. He also serves as director of the Student Assessment Research Program of the National Center for Postsecondary Improvement at Stanford University. Previously, he was a faculty member at the Harvard Graduate School of Business Administration and a researcher at the University of Michigan's Institute for Social Research, and he was program director of the National Center for Research to Improve Teaching and Learning. He is past president of the Association for the Study of Higher Education (ASHE), the Association of Institutional Research (AIR), and the Society for College and University Planning (SCUP). He has served as editor for Jossey-Bass's monograph series *New Directions in Institutional Research,* and he has been a visiting faculty member and consultant both in the United States and abroad. His recent books include the *ASHE Reader on Planning and Institutional Research* (1999) and *Planning and Management for a Changing Environment* (with D. Dill and L. Mets, 1997), which reflect his interests in organizational behavior, change and transformation, and planning and institutional research. He has received recognition for his contributions to higher education from AIR and SCUP. Peterson received his baccalaureate degree in engineering and mathematics from Trinity College in Hartford, Connecticut, his M.B.A. from Harvard Graduate School of Business Administration, and his Ph.D. in higher education and organizational psychology from the University of Michigan.

Gary R. Pike is assistant vice chancellor for student affairs and is also director of student life studies at the University of Missouri, Columbia. He is also an adjunct assistant professor and member of the doctoral faculty in the Department of Educational Leadership and Policy Analysis. Before coming to Missouri, he was associate director of the Center for Assessment Research and Development at the University of Tennessee, Knoxville. He is the founding editor of the "Assessment Measures" column for the bimonthly periodical *Assessment Update,* which has been published by Jossey-Bass since 1989. Pike has published twenty-five articles and eight book chapters on student learning and assessment, and he is the only three-time winner of the Best Paper Award, presented by the Association for Institutional Research. He has also received an award for outstanding assessment research from the American College Personnel Association (ACPA), in 1998, and was named a senior scholar by ACPA in 2000. Pike received his bachelor's and master's degrees from Southwest Missouri State University and his doctorate in communication is from The Ohio State University.

Daisy Pama Rodriguez earned her B.A. in speech communication at San Francisco State University and her master's degree in college student personnel at New York University. She has worked at Weber State University in Ogden, Utah, in the Department of Student Activities, as the coordinator for student programs, and was a resident director there in the Division of Housing. Currently, Rodriguez is a Ph.D. student at Indiana University Bloomington, studying higher education administration. Her research interests include Asian Pacific American racial and ethnic identity development, student leadership programming and development, and issues related to social justice and diversity. In 2000, she received a Robert H. Wade Fellowship at Indiana University.

Mark D. Shermis is presently associate dean for research and grants in the College of Education at Florida International University (FIU) and is a professor in FIU's Department of Educational Psychology and Special Education. He received his B.A. at the University of Kansas and earned his master's and doctoral degrees from the University of Michigan. Shermis has played a leading role in bringing computerized adaptive testing to the World Wide Web, and for five years he has been involved in research with Ellis Page of Duke University on automated essay scoring. His most recent work has resulted in a book with Jill Burstein, *Automated Essay Scoring: A Cross-Disciplinary Approach* (forthcoming). Shermis's first book, *Using Microcomputers in Social Science Research* (with Paul Stemmer, Carl Berger, and Ernie Anderson, 1991) was one of the first successful texts on the topic. Other publications appear in such journals as *Educational and Psychological Measurement, Psychological Test Bulletin, Journal of Educational Computing Research,* and *Journal of Psychoeducational Assessment.* Prior to coming to FIU, Shermis was director of the Testing Center and associate professor of psychology at Indiana University-Purdue University Indianapolis.

Derek S. Vaughan is a doctoral student at the University of Michigan's Center for the Study of Higher and Postsecondary Education and is currently employed as a graduate research assistant with the National Center for Postsecondary Improvement—Project 5 at the university. Before enrolling at Michigan, he worked as a student affairs professional at Northwestern University, University of Wisconsin-Eau Claire, and Miami University. He has coauthored an article (forthcoming) with Marvin Peterson for the journal *Planning for Higher Education.* Vaughan received his B.B.A. and B.S. from Ohio University and earned his M.S. and M.B.A. from Miami University.

Steven L. Wise is a senior assessment specialist at the Center for Assessment and Research Studies at James Madison University, where he is professor of psychology. He received his B.A. and M.A. in psychology from the University of Maryland, Baltimore County, and his Ph.D. in educational measurement and statistics from the University of Illinois, Urbana-Champaign.

Barbara D. Wright received a B.A. in German and music from Trinity College (in Washington, D.C.), an M.A. in German and art history from Middlebury College, and a Ph.D. in German from the University of California, Berkeley. She served for over twenty years as a professor in the Department of Modern and Classical Languages at the University of Connecticut, until her retirement in Spring 2001. While at the University of Connecticut, Wright directed the women's studies program, chaired the German Section, and served on numerous committees, including two task forces on general education. From 1988 to 1990, Wright led a Fund for the Improvement of Postsecondary Education project to assess general education at the University of Connecticut, followed by a stint, from 1990 to 1992, as director of the American Association for Higher Education's Assessment Forum. Shortly after returning to the Storrs campus, Wright and coauthor Anna K. Kuhn published "Playing for Stakes: German-Language Drama in Social Context" (1992). Wright's publications cover a broad range—from Baroque tragedy, women in German Expressionism, and foreign language pedagogy, to the impact of technology on women's work and assessment of student learning. Wright continues to speak and consult frequently on assessment.

Building a
Scholarship
of Assessment

Part One

History and Current Status of Assessment

In Chapter One, Peter Ewell, dean of the outcomes assessment movement in higher education, provides a comprehensive overview of this movement, from its beginnings in 1985 to the present. He examines the intellectual roots of assessment in such research traditions as those associated with the impact of college on student learning, program evaluation, and "scientific management." He suggests two directions for action designed to transform assessment from a movement into a culture and four kinds of scholarship that could move the field forward over the next several decades.

Marvin Peterson and Derek Vaughan have been involved in a three-phase study of the current status of assessment conducted as a component of the research agenda of the National Center for Postsecondary Improvement. The focus of their presentation in Chapter Two is the organizational and administrative patterns of support for assessment that promote the use of assessment information in making decisions aimed at improving institutional effectiveness. Although the national studies confirm the overall impression that extensive use of assessment as a vehicle for guiding improvement is under way in only a small number of institutions, those studies do suggest some characteristics of successful programs and three conceptual models of institutional support for assessment that can improve its use in the future.

Chapter One

An Emerging Scholarship: A Brief History of Assessment

Peter T. Ewell

This chapter offers a brief historical and analytical review of the assessment movement, from approximately 1985 to the present. It first examines some major events and forces influencing assessment's evolution as a "scholarship," including demands for curricular and pedagogical reform, shifting patterns of accountability, and changes in instructional delivery. It also examines significant scholarly themes and issues that have arisen in assessment's short history in such realms as epistemology, methodology, politics, and the use of information. The chapter concludes that assessment scholarship has become rich, robust, and strong. Whether it can or should continue as a distinct conversation outside the mainstream of higher education is more debatable.

Forerunners

The intellectual roots of assessment as a scholarship extend back well before its emergence as a recognizable movement. Some of its most visible forebears relate to undergraduate learning and the student experience in college. Others, such as program evaluation and "scientific management," helped direct its conscious orientation toward action and improvement. Methods and techniques drawn from these established traditions decisively influenced the language and methods of early assessment practitioners and continue to do so today.

Student Learning in College

This research tradition examines collegiate learning as a particular application of educational and developmental psychology. As such, its primary objective is discipline-based hypothesis testing and theory building, though its authors have often drawn implications for practice. Some of this work dates back to the 1930s and 1940s (for example, Learned and Wood, 1938), and much of it focused on single colleges enrolling eighteen- to twenty-one-year-old students in traditional residential environments. General maturation and attitudinal development were thus as much of interest as cognitive gain (Chickering, 1969). By the end of the 1960s there was a large enough body of work in this area for Feldman and Newcomb (1969) to synthesize its findings, which was updated some two decades later by Pascarella and Terenzini (1991). On the verge of assessment's emergence in the late 1970s, a trio of volumes was especially influential: Astin's *Four Critical Years* (1977) established the metaphor "value-added" and promoted the use of longitudinal studies to examine net effects, Bowen's *Investment in Learning* (1977) helped establish a public policy context for assessment by emphasizing the societal returns on investment associated with higher education, and Pace's *Measuring the Outcomes of College* (1979) emphasized the role of college environments and actual student behaviors. The contributions of this research tradition to assessment were both conceptual and methodological. Among the most prominent were basic taxonomies of outcomes, models of student growth and development, and tools for research like cognitive examinations, longitudinal and cross-sectional surveys, and quasi-experimental designs.

Retention and Student Behavior

Closely related to research on college student learning, a distinct literature on retention emerged in the late 1960s and 1970s and had some very specific impacts on assessment practice. First, it quickly organized itself around a powerful theoretical model—Tinto's notion of academic and social integration (1975), which proved equally useful in guiding applied research on student learning (for example, Terenzini, Pascarella, and Lorang, 1982). Second, the phenomenon of student attrition constituted an ideal proving ground for new methodologies involving longitudinal study designs, specially configured surveys, and multivariate analytical techniques, later adopted by many assessment practitioners. Third and perhaps decisively, retention scholarship was action research: though theoretically grounded and methodologically sophisticated, its object was always informed intervention (for example, Lenning, Beal, and Sauer, 1980). Together, these features yielded an excellent model of applied scholarship that, consciously or unconsciously, many assessment practitioners worked to emulate.

Evaluation and "Scientific Management"

The 1960s and 1970s also saw the rise of program evaluation as an action research tradition. Occasioned by the many large-scale federal programs launched at that time, program evaluation first relied largely on quantitative methods. It was also related to a wider movement toward "scientific management" that quickly found applications in higher education in the form of strategic planning, program review, and budgeting. The kind of "systems thinking" embedded in this tradition demanded explicit attention to student outcomes (for example, Enthoven, 1970) in order to provide a needed "output variable" for cost-benefit studies and investigations of social return on investment. This tradition also yielded one of the most extensive taxonomies of collegiate outcomes ever produced (Lenning, Lee, Micek, and Service, 1977) and stimulated a range of surveys designed to provide campuses with information about how students used and perceived their programs. Literature drawn from program evaluation further provided assessment with a ready-made set of models and vocabularies (for example, Light, Singer, and Willett, 1990). Somewhat later, program evaluation began to embrace more qualitative methods (for example, Guba and Lincoln, 1981). These more "authentic" approaches, which emphasized holistic examination of organizational situations and often employed open-ended interviewing and participant observation, also provided an early language for assessment for those skeptical of overly empirical methodologies.

Mastery Learning

The mastery and competency-based learning movement began in elementary and secondary education, but quickly found postsecondary applications in adult and professional education by the mid-1960s. Because mastery-based designs for learning are based entirely on agreed-upon outcomes, assessing and certifying individual student achievement was always paramount. A related development was the assessment of prior learning. Corporate assessment centers, meanwhile, were developing ways to examine and certify complex higher-order abilities by observing group and individual performance of authentic tasks (Thornton and Byham, 1982). Collectively, these traditions provided the conceptual foundation for "alternative" institutions like Empire State, Evergreen State, Regents College, Antioch College, and the School for New Learning at DePaul, as well as, and by far the most influential, Alverno College (Alverno College Faculty, 1979). They also yielded a cadre of early assessment practitioners, skilled in evaluating student portfolios and other authentic evidence of student attainment. Two contributions were especially important for the early assessment movement: first, mastery methods posed an effective alternative to the prominent (and politically popular) "testing and measurement" paradigm; second, they could boast a track record that proved that assessment in higher education was not just a popular theory; it could actually be done.

◆ ◆ ◆

These four practice traditions and their associated literatures are quite different, and only a few educators in the early 1980s were reading them all. More significantly, their values and methodological traditions are frequently contradictory, revealing conceptual tensions that have fueled assessment discussions ever since. One is a clash of guiding metaphor between quantitative "scientific" investigation and qualitative "developmental" observation. Another addresses how assessment is positioned in the teaching-learning process: the "evaluation" and "measurement" traditions consciously divorce the process of investigating student attainment from the act of instruction in the name of objectivity; "mastery" traditions, in contrast, consider the two inseparable. A final distinction concerns the predominant object of assessment—whether its principal purpose is to examine *overall* program/institutional effectiveness or to certify what a *particular* student knows and can do. As any examination of early assessment citations will show, all four traditions helped shape language and practice in the early 1980s. What is surprising in retrospect is that such disparate scholarly traditions could be related at all and that they continue to inform such a lively scholarship.

Birth of a Movement

Although no one has officially dated the birth of the assessment movement in higher education, it is probably safe to propose that date as the First National Conference on Assessment in Higher Education, held in Columbia, South Carolina, in the fall of 1985. Cosponsored by the National Institute of Education (NIE) and the American Association for Higher Education (AAHE), the origins of this conference vividly illustrate the conflicting political and intellectual traditions that have been with the field ever since. The proximate stimulus for the conference was a report entitled *Involvement in Learning* (Study Group on the Conditions of Excellence in American Higher Education, 1984). Three main recommendations, strongly informed by research in the student learning tradition, formed its centerpiece. In brief, to promote higher levels of student achievement, it was recommended that high expectations be established for students, that students be involved in active learning environments, and that students be provided with prompt and useful feedback. But the report also observed that colleges and universities could "learn" from feedback on their own performance and that appropriate research tools were now available for them to do so.

This observation might have been overlooked were it not consistent with other voices. One set of voices came from within the academy and focused on curriculum reform, especially in general education. Symbolized by other prominent reports, like *Integrity in the College Curriculum* (American Association of Colleges, 1985) and *To Reclaim a Legacy* (Bennett, 1984), their central argument was that what was needed were coherent curricular experiences that could be shaped by ongoing monitoring of student learning and development. From the outset in these discussions, the assessment of learning was presented as a form of scholarship. Faculties ought to be willing to engage in assessment as an integral part of their everyday work. A concomitant enlightened, but unexamined, assumption was that the tools of social science and educational measurement, deployed appropriately, could be adapted in all disciplines to further this process of ongoing inquiry and improvement.

A second set of voices arose simultaneously outside the academy, consisting largely of state-based calls for greater accountability. In part, these calls were a byproduct of the far more visible attention then being paid to K–12 education, symbolized by the U.S. Department of Education's report *A Nation at Risk* (1983). In part, they stemmed from a renewed activism by governors and legislatures, based on their growing recognition that postsecondary education was a powerful engine for economic and workforce development. Both themes were apparent in yet another national report—revealingly titled *Time for Results* (National Governors' Association, 1986). As it was being issued, Colorado and South Carolina adopted assessment mandates requiring public colleges and universities to examine learning outcomes and report what they found. (A few other states, such as Tennessee and Florida, for varying reasons, had been doing assessment for several years, using common standardized tests.) By 1987, when the first stocktaking of this growing policy trend occurred (Boyer, Ewell, Finney, and Mingle, 1987), about a dozen states had similar mandates. By 1989, this number had grown to more than half (Ewell, Finney, and Lenth, 1990).

Given this history, the motives of those attending the first national assessment conference were understandably mixed. Many were there under the banner of *Involvement in Learning* (Study Group on the Conditions of Excellence in American Higher Education, 1984), seeking reasonable and valid ways to gather information to improve curriculum and pedagogy. At least as many (and probably more) were there in response to a brand new mandate. Clear to all were the facts that they had few available tools, they had only a spotty literature of practice, and they had virtually no common intellectual foundation on which to build. Filling these yawning gaps in the period of 1985–1988 was a first and urgent task for the scholarship of assessment. In beginning this task, practitioners faced three major challenges—of definitions, instruments, and implementation.

Definitions

One immediate problem was that the term *assessment* meant different things to different people. Initially, at least three meanings and their associated traditions of use had therefore to be sorted out. The most established definition had its roots in the mastery-learning tradition, where assessment referred to the processes used to determine an individual's mastery of complex abilities, generally through observed performance (for example, Alverno College Faculty, 1979). Adherents of this tradition emphasized development over time and continuous feedback on individual performance, symbolized by the etymological roots of the word *assessment* in the Latin *ad + sedere,* "to sit beside" (Loacker, Cromwell, and O'Brien, 1986). A far different meaning emerged from K–12 practice, where the term described large-scale testing programs like the federally funded National Assessment of Educational Progress (NAEP) and a growing array of state-based K–12 examination programs. The primary objective of such "large-scale assessment" was not to examine individual learning but rather to benchmark school and district performance in the name of accountability. Its central tools were standardized examinations founded on well-established psychometric principles, designed to produce summary performance statistics quickly and efficiently. Yet a third tradition of use defined assessment as a special kind of program evaluation, whose purpose was to gather evidence to improve curricula and pedagogy. Like large-scale assessment, this tradition focused on determining aggregate, not individual, performance, employing a range of methods, including examinations, portfolios and student work samples, surveys of student and alumni experiences, and direct observations of student and faculty behaviors. An emphasis on improvement, moreover, meant that assessment was as much about *using* the resulting information as it was about psychometric standards.

All three definitions raised explicitly the dichotomy of purpose apparent from the outset: accountability versus improvement. Other differences addressed methods and units of analysis—essentially whether quantitative or qualitative methods would predominate and whether attention would be directed largely toward aggregate or individual performance. Clarifying such distinctions in the form of taxonomies helped sharpen initial discussions about the meaning of assessment (Terenzini, 1989). They also helped further a terminological consensus that was centered on the use of multiple methods for program improvement (American Association for Higher Education, 1992).

Instruments

A second challenge faced by early assessment practitioners was the task of quickly identifying credible and useful ways of gathering evidence of student learning. Virtually all the available instruments were designed for something else. Ranging from admissions tests like the ACT Assessment and the Graduate Record Examinations, through professional registry and licensure examinations, to examinations designed to award equivalent credit, none of the available testing alternatives was really appropriate for program evaluation. Their content only approximated the domain of any given institution's curriculum, and the results they produced usually provided insufficient detail to support improvement. But this did not prevent large numbers of institutions—especially those facing state mandates—from deploying them. One exception was the ACT College Outcomes Measures Project (COMP) examination (Forrest and Steele, 1978). In many ways a harbinger, this examination was designed specifically to evaluate general education outcomes and support group-level inferences about student learning. It also constructed general education outcomes in novel ways, emphasizing the application of knowledge in real-world situations and (in its long form) requiring authentic demonstrations of performance.

In the period of 1986–1989, the major testing organizations quickly filled the instrument gap with a range of new purpose-built group-level examinations aimed at program evaluation—all based on existing prototypes. Among the most prominent were the ACT Collegiate Assessment of Academic Proficiency (CAAP), the Educational Testing Service (ETS) Academic Profile, and a range of ETS Major Field Achievement Tests (MFAT). Student surveys provided another readily available set of data-gathering tools, especially when they contained items on self-reported gain. While many institutions designed and administered their own surveys, published instruments were readily available, including the Cooperative Institutional Research Program (CIRP) Freshman and follow-up surveys, the College Student Experiences Questionnaire (CSEQ), and a range of questionnaires produced by organizations like ACT and the National Center for Higher Education Management Systems (NCHEMS).

The principal appeal of off-the-shelf tests and surveys in this period was their ready availability—a property enhanced when the first comprehensive catalogs of available instruments appeared (Smith, Bradley, and Draper, 1994). Faced with a mandate demanding immediate results, most institutions felt they had little choice but to use such instruments, at least in the short term. But there were also growing doubts about the wisdom of this approach (Heffernan, Hutchings, and Marchese, 1988), stimulating work on more authentic, faculty-made assessment approaches in the coming years.

Implementation

A third challenge faced by early assessment practitioners was the lack of institutional experience about how to carry out such an initiative. One question here concerned cost, and as a result, some of the first "how to" publications addressed financial issues (Ewell and Jones, 1986). Others considered the organizational questions involved in establishing an assessment program (Ewell, 1988). But absent any real exemplars, the guidance provided by such publications was at best rudimentary. Enormous early reliance was therefore placed on the lessons that could be learned from the few documented cases available. Three such early adopters had considerable influence. The first was Alverno, whose "abilities-based" curriculum, designed around performance assessments of every student, was both inspiring and daunting (Alverno College Faculty, 1979). A second early adopter was Northeast Missouri (now Truman) State University, which since 1973 had employed a range of nationally normed examinations to help establish the "integrity" of its degrees (McClain, 1984). A third was the University of Tennessee, Knoxville, which, under the stimulus of Tennessee's performance funding scheme, became the first major public university to develop a comprehensive multimethod system of program assessment (Banta, 1985). These three cases were very different and provided a wide range of potential models. They were also unusually well documented, yielding some of the first concrete examples of assessment scholarship.

In the late 1980s a second wave of documented cases emerged, including (among others) James Madison University, Kean College, Kings College, Ball State University, Miami-Dade Community College, and Sinclair Community College—many of which were responding to new state mandates. To a field hungry for concrete information, these examples were extremely welcome. More subtly, they helped define a "standard" approach to implementing a campus-level program, which was widely imitated.

◆ ◆ ◆

This founding period thus generated some enduring lines of assessment scholarship. One line of work addressed concept development and building a coherent language. The purpose here was largely to stake out the territory—though much of this early literature was frankly hortatory, intended to persuade institutions to get started. A second line of work concerned tools and techniques, and though all "forerunner" literatures were referenced here, strong reservations about standardized testing quickly emerged and persisted. A third strand comprised case studies of implementation, supplemented by a growing body of work addressing practical matters like organizational structures and faculty involvement. Finally, accountability remained a distinct topic for comment and investigation, looking primarily at state policy but shifting later to accreditation.

Into the Mainstream

By 1990, predictions that "assessment would quickly go away" seemed illusory. Most states had assessment mandates, though these varied in both substance and the vigor with which they were enforced. Accrediting bodies, meanwhile, had grown in influence, in many cases replacing states as the primary external stimulus for institutional interest in assessment (Ewell, 1993). Reflecting this shift, more and more private institutions established assessment programs. These external stimuli were largely responsible for a steady upward trend in the number of institutions reporting involvement with assessment. For example, in 1987 some 55 percent of institutions claimed that they had established an assessment program on the American Council of Education's (ACE) annual *Campus Trends* survey. By 1993, this proportion had risen to 98 percent (though the survey also suggested that most such efforts were only just getting started). Clearly, at least for administrators, assessment was now mainstream. But entering the mainstream meant more than just widespread reported use. It also implied consolidation of assessment's position as a distinct and recognizable scholarship of practice.

An Emerging Modal Type

As institutions scrambled to "implement assessment," it was probably inevitable that they would evolve similar approaches. And despite repeated admonitions to ground assessment in each institution's distinctive mission and student clientele, they approached the task of implementation in very similar ways. As a first step, most formed committees to plan and oversee the work. Following widespread recommendations about the importance of faculty involvement, most comprised faculty drawn from multiple disciplines. But partly because the press to implement was so great, assessment committees rarely became a permanent feature of governance or of academic administration.

The clear first task of these committees, moreover, was to develop an assessment plan. Often, such a product was explicitly required by an accreditor or state authority. Equally often, it was recommended by a consultant or by the burgeoning "how to" literature of practice (for example, Nichols, 1989). The resulting plans thus often had a somewhat formulaic quality. Most included an initial statement of principles, stated learning goals for general education and for each constituent discipline, a charge to departments to find or develop a suitable assessment method (frequently accompanied by a list of methods to be considered), and a schedule for data collection and reporting. Implementing such plans, in turn, often involved the use of specially funded "pilot" efforts by volunteer departments. Keeping track of implementation and reporting, moreover, often demanded the use of a tabular or matrix format (Banta, 1996), and this, too, became a widespread feature of the "standard" approach. Methods, meanwhile, were healthily varied, including available standardized examinations, faculty-made tests, surveys and focus groups, and (increasingly, as the decade progressed) portfolios and work samples.

A Literature of Practice

In assessment's early days, the products of its scholarship comprised a fugitive literature of working papers, loosely organized readings in *New Directions* sourcebooks, and conference presentations. But by the early 1990s, the foundations of a recognizable published literature could be discerned. Some of these works were by established scholars, who summarized findings and provided methodological advice (Astin, 1991; Pace, 1990). Others tried to document assessment approaches in terms that practitioner audiences could readily understand (Erwin, 1991; Ewell, 1991a). Still others continued the process of documenting institutional cases—of which there were now many—in standard or summary form (Banta and Associates, 1993).

The establishment of the movement's own journal, *Assessment Update,* in 1989, was also an important milestone in this period—providing relevant commentary on methods, emerging policies, and institutional practices. As its editorial board envisioned, its contents were short, practical, and topical, providing the field with a single place to turn for ideas and examples. *Assessment Update*'s existence also provided an important alternative to established educational research journals for faculty-practitioners who wanted to publish. This supplemented the already-established role of *Change* magazine, which provided an early venue for assessment authors and continued to print assessment-related essays regularly (DeZure, 2000). Through its Assessment Forum, moreover, AAHE issued a range of publications, building first upon conference presentations and continuing in a set of resource guides (American Association for Higher Education, 1997). In strong contrast to fifteen years previously, assessment practitioners in 2000 thus had a significant body of literature to guide their efforts, which included systematic guides to method and implementation (for example, Palomba and Banta, 1999), well-documented examples of campus practice (for example, Banta, Lund, Black, and Oblander, 1996), and comprehensive treatises integrating assessment with the broader transformation of teaching and learning (for example, Mentkowski and Associates, 2000).

Scholarly Gatherings and Support

Initiated on a regular annual cycle in 1987, the AAHE Assessment Forum was by 1989 *the* conference for practitioners, providing a regular gathering place for scholarly presentation and exchange. Sessions developed for the Forum required formal documentation and often ended up as publications. The Forum also maintained professional networks, promoted idea sharing, and provided needed moral support and encouragement. The latter was especially important in assessment's early years because there were few practitioners and they were isolated on individual campuses. Although the Forum remained the field's premier conference, other gatherings quickly emerged. Some, like the Assessment Institute in Indianapolis (which actually began at the University of Tennessee, Knoxville), concentrated largely on orienting new practitioners. Others arose at the state level, including (among others) the South Carolina Higher Education Assessment Network (SCHEA), the Washington Assessment Group (WAG), and the Virginia Assessment Group (VAG), and often were directly supported by state higher education agencies. Some of these state-level groups published regular newsletters updating members on state policy initiatives and allowing campuses to showcase their programs. Funding support for assessment scholarship also became more accessible, primarily through the federal Fund for the Improvement of Postsecondary Education (Cook, 1989). In addition to directly supporting assessment activities, FIPSE's need for formal reports and evaluations helped stimulate the field's growing inventory of published work.

A "Semi-Profession"

Although assessment remained largely a part-time activity, entering the mainstream also meant a rise in the number of permanent positions with assessment as a principal assignment. Position titles like "assessment coordinator," with formal job descriptions, are now commonplace, usually located in academic affairs offices or merged with institutional research. The creation of such positions was in large measure a result of external pressure to put recognizable campus programs in place. Certainly, such roles helped build badly needed local capacity and infrastructure. But in many cases they also created real tensions about the ownership and benefits of the assessment process.

Early conversations, meanwhile, considered the advisability of creating a national professional organization for assessment similar to the Council for Adult and Experiential Learning (CAEL). A strong consensus emerged to maintain assessment as an "amateur" activity—undertaken by faculty themselves for the purpose of improving their own practice. Avoiding excessive professionalization was important because it promoted later linkages with the scholarship of teaching. But large and growing numbers of individuals on college and university campuses, often without conscious choice, have nevertheless adopted careers identified primarily with assessment as a distinguishable field.

◆ ◆ ◆

For assessment as a whole, one clear result of entering the mainstream is an established community of practice that in some ways resembles an academic discipline. Among its earmarks are an identifiable and growing body of scholarship, a well-recognized conference circuit, and a number of "sub-disciplines," each with its own literature and leading personalities. Certainly, this is a significant achievement—far beyond what numerous early observers expected. But these very attributes have also decisively shaped, and in some ways limited, assessment's impact on instruction and campus culture. Most campus assessment activities, for example, continue to be implemented as *additions* to the curriculum, designed for purposes of program evaluation rather than being integral to teaching and learning. The fact that implementation so often centers on "doing assessment" rather than on improving practice through clear linkages to budget and pedagogy, moreover, can easily isolate the process from the everyday life of both faculty and administrators. Those doing assessment have evolved a remarkably varied and sophisticated set of tools and approaches and an effective semiprofessional infrastructure to support what they do. But few faculty as yet practice assessment as a part of their everyday work. Although firmly established in the mainstream by the year 2000, assessment as a movement is still striving for the cultural shift its original proponents had hoped for.

Episodes and Debates

Throughout its brief history, assessment has addressed a varied set of intellectual issues that have actively stimulated debate. Meanwhile, the movement went through several telling episodes that forced reaction and rethinking. Each episode prompted deeper understanding, though none has been entirely resolved. As a result, past events continue to influence the course of this evolving scholarship.

The "Ineffability" Debate

Perhaps the most basic debate that arises as faculty face assessment is the extent to which educational outcomes can be specified and measured at all. Indeed, a frequent early counterargument was that *any* attempt to look at outcomes directly was both demeaning and doomed to failure. Related critiques noted that assessment's principal vocabulary appeared confined to education and the social sciences—not always the most respected disciplines on any college campus. More pointedly, both the rhetoric and the implied methods advanced by the assessment movement have frequently been characterized as "positivist" and excessively mechanistic. Dissecting this classic complex of faculty reservations about assessment reveals some quite different underlying issues. Some are legitimately methodological, including appropriate reservations about the ability of off-the-shelf instruments and forced-choice methods to fully reflect collegiate learning, or fears about "teaching to the test." Some are profoundly philosophical, based on a recognition that deep learning is always holistic, reflective, and socially constructed. Still others are predominantly political, derived from faculty fears about loss of autonomy and creeping management control, as well as concerns about external intrusion into the curriculum.

What makes things complicated is that all three issues are often bound up in a single sense of discomfort (for example, Peters, 1994). But the resulting debate about "ineffability" has proven helpful in deepening assessment scholarship. At one level, it forced practitioners to sharpen the philosophical grounding of the movement—rooting it in the tenets of scholarship and the process of teaching and learning. It also reemphasized that the evidence used by assessment must always rest upon a peer-based community of judgment (Mentkowski and others, 1991; American Association for Higher Education, 1992). Finally, the debate forced explicit recognition of the fact that evidence is consistently constrained by the context in which it is generated (Mentkowski and Rogers, 1988) and by the uses to which it is put (Messick, 1988). Epistemological issues of this kind thus remain at the heart of the movement and remain healthily and vigorously contested (Ewell, 1989; Harris and Sansom, 2001). But protests based solely on principle or politics have steadily diminished.

The "Value-Added" Debate

The question of whether assessment's primary focus should be placed on documenting absolute levels of student attainment or on institutional contributions to developing student abilities arose early (Ewell, 1984). Reasons for centering attention on "talent development" were compelling. First, this approach was normatively appealing and had the admirable property of leveling the playing field among different kinds of institutions. Assessing institutional quality in this way thus made more sense than using traditional markers like resources and reputation (Astin, 1985). Ascertaining "net effects" also made good sense from a research point of view, recognizing that incoming student ability is the largest predictor of any outcome (Pascarella, 1987; Pascarella and Terenzini, 1991). Finally, some institutions were already practicing "value-added" approaches and finding them useful in demonstrating effectiveness (McClain and Krueger, 1985).

But the classic approach to assessing learning gain—testing students on entry and then retesting them at exit—posed perplexing conceptual issues and formidable methodological problems. Conceptually, it was argued, a pretest was often simply silly because students had not yet been exposed to the subject on which they were being tested (Warren, 1984). The term *value-added*, moreover, suggested a mechanistic view of education, in which students were viewed as "products" and learning merely additive. Actually determining growth, meanwhile, entailed multiplicative sources of measurement error and sometimes led to real misinterpretations of underlying phenomena (Hanson, 1988; Baird, 1988; Banta and others, 1987). Although active discussion of this topic diminished in the 1990s, it helped propel assessment toward a useful synthesis. Most important, these discussions helped forge a growing consensus that paths of student development should not be seen as linear and additive but rather as organic and transformational. A methodological entailment of this growing consensus was longitudinal designs for assessment, capable of capturing large numbers of variables about both outcomes and experiences. Such longitudinal studies required an analytical model based on multivariate statistical control instead of simple "test-retest" approaches, and could be further enhanced by the use of qualitative methods like periodic interviews and focus groups. Finally, all agreed that for policy purposes, information about *both* levels of attainment and institutional contributions was needed.

The TQM Episode

In the early 1990s higher education institutions began experimenting with Total Quality Management (TQM), a set of ideas and techniques borrowed directly from business, to help improve their administrative operations (Seymour, 1991). Linking such notions with assessment was appealing because the two movements shared many attributes. Both began with a systemic approach to change and, indeed, viewed change itself as imperative. Both emphasized the need to listen carefully to those whom the system was trying to serve, although the notion of students as "customers" immediately grated. Finally, both held that concrete information about performance was a critical part of a continuous cycle of planning and improvement. Recognizing such parallels, AAHE incorporated a track on TQM—quickly relabeled Continuous Quality Improvement

(CQI)—into its Assessment Forum and issued a number of publications linking assessment and CQI (for example, American Association for Higher Education, 1994a).

But explicit attempts to fuse assessment and Total Quality were not successful, and after its initial flurry of activity, Total Quality has not fared well on campuses. Partly, this was a matter of language. Whereas assessment could ultimately adopt the discourse of scholarship, Total Quality never shed its corporate flavor—especially in the eyes of skeptical faculty. Partly, it was because the quality movement in business and industry itself had peaked. Yet much was synthesized by assessment—perhaps unconsciously—from this encounter. It reinforced "systems consciousness" and cemented the need to collect information about both outcomes and processes. Sometimes bitter "customer" discussions helped underline the need to listen carefully to student voices and to shift assessment's perspective from faculty "teaching" to student learning. Total Quality thus proved useful to assessment largely as a metaphor. At the same time, it taught object lessons about the risks of both alien language and the appearance of fad.

The National Assessment Episode

In 1990, the National Education Goals Panel established the nation's first objectives for collegiate learning. More specifically, it called for the development of valid and reliable assessments to track progress in critical thinking, communication, and problem solving (National Education Goals Panel, 1991). This action mirrored simultaneous and growing state interest in collegiate assessment, as a majority of the states had adopted assessment mandates for public colleges and universities by the mid-1990s. The Goals also signaled the beginning of a significant, though short-lived, period of aggressiveness by the U.S. Department of Education within the realm of postsecondary accountability, marked by such initiatives as the Student Right-to-Know Act and the State Postsecondary Review Entities (SPREs). Like the latter, the proposed national assessment never happened, though a major design effort to create it helped stimulate useful thinking about how a large-scale, authentic assessment of collegiate learning might actually be deployed (National Center for Education Statistics, 1994). Similar calls for a "NAEP for College" have periodically arisen, stimulated by both accountability demands and international comparisons (National Center for Public Policy and Higher Education, 2000).

To be sure, such episodes have had but little impact on the day-to-day practice of assessment on most college campuses. But together with their state-level counterparts, they provide a constant reminder that accountability was part of assessment's birthright and is intimately entwined with its future. Continuing scholarship aimed at developing appropriate and timely responses to periodic accountability demands as they arise will therefore always be needed.

◆ ◆ ◆

Each of these issues illustrates how assessment discourse has grown in sophistication and has built a particular set of shared understandings. All remain centers of active debate. But few are now posed in the black-and-white terms in which they first arose, and each has helped stimulate improvements in methods and approach.

Into the Future

Social and educational movements, whatever their object, have one of two typical fates. Unsuccessful movements vanish after only a few years, with little left behind. Successful ones disappear equally as "movements" because their core values become part of the dominant culture and their practices are fully institutionalized. So far, the assessment movement has experienced neither. On the one hand, levels of activity are unprecedented. The vast majority of institutions continue to report engagement with assessment, conference attendance is burgeoning, publications abound, and a growing body of practitioners see assessment as their primary professional practice. On the other hand, at most institutions—and above all, for most individual faculty—assessment has not become a "culture of use" (López, 1997). The resulting paradox raises two questions, both highly relevant to the movement's future. First, what is it that has sustained assessment for so long, and what will continue to do so? Second, what has prevented assessment from fulfilling its original promise, and how might it ultimately achieve these ends? Answers to both these questions, admittedly, are speculative and uncertain. But, as the answers eventually play out, they will decisively affect the scholarship of assessment.

Why Didn't Assessment Go Away?

In assessment's first decade, the question *When will it go away?* was frequently posed. This was largely because the movement was diagnosed by many as a typical "management fad"—like Total Quality or Management by Objectives (MBO)—that would quickly run its course (Birnbaum, 2000). Yet assessment has shown remarkable staying power and has undoubtedly attained a measure of permanence, at least in the form of a visible infrastructure. Several factors appear responsible for this phenomenon. Probably the most important is that external stakeholders will not let the matter drop. State interest is now stronger than ever, fueled by demand-driven needs to improve "learning productivity" and by burgeoning state efforts to implement standards-based reform in K–12 education (Ewell, 1997b). Accreditation agencies, meanwhile, have grown increasingly vigorous in their demands that institutions examine learning outcomes, though they are also allowing institutions more flexibility in how they proceed (Eaton, 2001). Market forces and the media are not only more powerful, they are also far more performance-conscious and data-hungry than they were two decades ago. Assessment thus has become an unavoidable condition of doing business: institutions can no more abandon assessment than they can do without a development office.

The last twenty years have also seen a revolution in undergraduate instruction. In part, this results from technology, and in part, it reflects the impact of multiple other movements, including writing across the curriculum, learning communities, problem-based learning, and service learning. Together, these forces are fundamentally altering the shape and content of undergraduate study. Such changes are sustaining assessment in at least two ways. Most immediately, new instructional approaches are forced to demonstrate their relative effectiveness precisely because they are new. Assessment activities therefore are frequently undertaken as an integral part of their implementation. More subtly, the very nature of these new approaches shifts the focus of attention from teaching to learning. In some cases, direct determination of mastery is integral to curricular design (O'Banion, 1997). In others, common rubrics for judging performance are required to ensure coherence in the absence of a more visible curricular structure (Walvoord and Anderson, 1998). Assessment has thus been sustained in part because it has become a necessary condition for undertaking meaningful undergraduate reform—just as the authors of *Involvement in Learning* (Study Group on the Conditions of Excellence in American Higher Education, 1984) foresaw.

Why Broad but Not Deep?

As important as assessment's longevity, though, is the fact that it has survived in a peculiar form. Most campuses are indeed "doing something" in assessment. But the kinds of fundamental transformations in instruction that might have resulted from examining systemic evidence of student learning have mostly not happened. Instead, for the majority of institutions, assessment remains an add-on, done principally at the behest of the administration and sustained as a superstructure outside the traditional array of academic activities and rewards. Reasons for this widespread condition, ironically, mirror those that have sustained assessment for almost two decades. First, widespread and visible external demands generally set the tone for initial engagement. Most campuses still do assessment because somebody tells them to. Regardless of how the telling is done (and external bodies have been more sensitive and flexible than is usually acknowledged), responses risk being both reactive and mechanistic.

Moreover, like other efforts to accomplish meaningful undergraduate reform, assessment must usually be implemented across the grain of deeply embedded organizational structures. Rewards for engaging in it remain scant for both institutions and individuals. So, like similar activities not rooted in disciplines or departments such as first-year experience programs or general education, assessment is frequently sustained as a *separate* activity, ensconced in an "office" and nurtured through special-purpose funding. Similarly, as Peterson and Vaughan report in Chapter Two, assessment results are rarely central to institutional planning and decision making, even when undertaken outside the glare of public scrutiny. Partly, this is because of continuing faculty fears about negative consequences. Ironically, it stems equally from faculty expectations of no consequences at all—that considerable effort will be expended gathering information that will never be used. Much of the appeal of the kinds of activities that *have* been adopted on a widespread basis, like classroom assessment, is that the benefits of feedback are both immediate and apparent (Angelo and Cross, 1993). At the institutional and program levels, the benefits of assessment have been far less immediately visible.

As this last observation suggests, two fundamental changes will be needed to transform assessment from a movement into a culture. One is at the level of teaching and learning and requires shifting assessment's conceptual paradigm from an evaluative stance that emphasizes checking up on results to an emphasis on assuming active and collective responsibility for fostering student attainment. Forces that might aid this conceptual transformation include the growing salience of ability-based credentials, which are fast becoming a way of life in many occupations and professions (Adelman, 2000). Multi-institutional attendance patterns are meanwhile fueling demands to reposition articulation and transfer from course-based "seat time" to performance-based attainment. Perhaps most important, reform efforts like writing across the curriculum and problem-based learning, together with technology, are forcing faculty to think far more concretely and collectively about learning outcomes and how to certify them.

A second needed transformation is at the level of academic administration and requires evolving a largely top-down, management-oriented use of information in planning and decision making toward a culture that more fully embodies the principles of a learning organization. Forces that might help this transformation are far less easy to identify but include growing competition from nonuniversity providers and insistent demands to create modes of instruction that are both efficient and effective.

Such developments, if they occur, will influence the scholarship of assessment profoundly. In its literature, there will likely be growing sophistication in discussions of methodology, capitalizing on emerging knowledge about how to forge consensual judgments about authentic performance (for example, Walvoord and Anderson,

1998; Mentkowski and Associates, 2000) and about using technology to deliver assessments based on complex, interactive problems. There will be new demands for work on organizational transformation, in which assessment is addressed but is fused with other systemic changes aimed at changing the environment for teaching and learning (for example, Gardiner, 1994; O'Banion, 1997; Harvey and Knight, 1996). At a different level, assessment will gradually become an integral part of each faculty member's reflective practice, documented through the scholarship of teaching (Shulman, 1993; Hutchings, 1996). And faculty will increasingly collaborate in this work, reflecting their growing assumption of collective responsibility for learning.

Such developments are consistent with the tradition of robust, participatory, and practice-oriented scholarship already established by the assessment movement. If they emerge, they will constitute significant contributions to both theory and practice. More important, because assessment's principal tenets will at last be embodied in the work of higher education on a day-to-day basis, its life as a "movement" may finally be over.

Chapter Two

Promoting Academic Improvement

Organizational and Administrative Dynamics That Support Student Assessment

Marvin W. Peterson and Derek S. Vaughan

Scholars and assessment professionals have argued that student assessment should not be an end in itself but should be used for educational and institutional improvement (Banta and Associates, 1993; Ewell, 1997a). To do that, institutions have invested a great deal of faculty and administrative effort in designing, promoting, supporting, and implementing student assessment. Although there is an extensive body of descriptive information on institutional approaches to student assessment (Banta and Associates, 1993; Banta, Lund, Black, and Oblander, 1996) and an array of case studies and small sample surveys, there is little systematic evidence on the organizational and administrative patterns and strategies institutions have adopted to support student assessment, on how they have responded to external demands, or on how they use student assessment information for academic decisions and educational and institutional improvement (Peterson, Einarson, Trice, and Nichols, 1997).

This chapter addresses that void in three ways. First, it focuses on the organizational and administrative patterns that institutions have adopted to assess, promote, support, and use student assessment. Second, it draws on a national research effort that provides a comprehensive profile of what those institutional patterns are.

And third, it examines how those organizational and administrative patterns are related to the use of student assessment information for making educational decisions that promote institutional improvements in order to inform institutional leaders (Peterson, Einarson, Augustine, and Vaughan, 1999a).

A Research-Based Model: A Three-Phase Research Project

To address how institutions promote and support the use of student assessment for educational improvement, the National Center for Postsecondary Improvement (NCPI) supported a three-phase project. Phase I consisted of an intensive review of the research literature (Peterson, Einarson, Trice, and Nichols, 1997) and the development of a conceptual framework. Phase II involved a national survey that inventoried and analyzed institutional patterns of all two- and four-year colleges and universities (Peterson, Einarson, Augustine, and Vaughan, 1999a). And Phase III involved developing case studies of seven diverse institutions actively engaged in student assessment.

The intent of this chapter is to draw on the results of all three phases to inform our understanding of how institutions promote and support student assessment. Readers interested in the actual research results can access these at the NCPI Web site (http://www.umich.edu/~ncpi/52/52.html).

Organizational and Administrative Support for Student Assessment: A Framework

Based on the literature review, seven distinct domains of organizational and administrative support for student assessment emerged. These domains were used to create the conceptual framework of organizational and administrative support for student assessment (see Figure 2.1) that guided the construction of the national survey instrument and the organization of our case studies and serve as the basis for our discussion in the remaining sections. Briefly, the seven domains are:

- The primary *external influences* on student assessment, which are the federal government, the state government, and regional

Figure 2.1. Conceptual Framework of Organizational and Administrative Support for Student Assessment

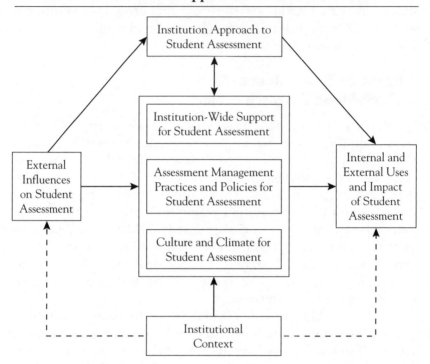

accreditation associations. Several federal reports and regulations have promoted assessment (Peterson, Einarson, Trice, and Nichols, 1997), but few studies have been done to show their influence on institutional assessment efforts. In 1997, forty-six states had reported some type of student assessment activity (Cole, Nettles, and Sharp, 1997). Although accreditation associations have received less attention (Peterson, Einarson, Trice, and Nichols, 1997), they appear to have a significant influence on the assessment efforts of institutions (Banta, 1993; Ewell, 1993).

• *Institutional context* includes institutional type, (Steele, Malone, and Lutz, 1997), control—public or private—and size, which have been cited as factors that contribute to differences in the approaches to and forms of support for student assessment.

- *Institutional approaches to student assessment,* which can be described by the type or content of assessment, the breadth of students assessed, the methods of assessment, and the number and types of reports about and studies of student performance that are conducted (Peterson and Augustine, 2000).

- *Institution-wide support for student assessment,* which encompasses the mission emphasis on student assessment, internal and external purposes for conducting student assessment, the type of administratively supported activities, incentives, or governance arrangements highlighting assessment, the existence of a planning group for, or an institutional policy on, student assessment, and administrative and faculty leadership for student assessment.

- *Assessment management policies and practices,* which are the mechanisms through which institutions support student assessment efforts and increase the likelihood of using the information collected (Ewell, 1993; Peterson, Einarson, Augustine, and Vaughan, 1999a) in areas such as resource allocation, computerized student assessment information systems, reports on assessment purposes and activities, breadth of distribution of information, student participation, faculty and administrative professional development involving student affairs staff, faculty evaluation and awards, and academic planning and review processes.

- *Institutional culture and climate for student assessment,* which are often mentioned in the student assessment literature (Banta and Associates, 1993). *Culture* refers to the deeply embedded values and beliefs collectively held by the members of an institution that can have a positive or negative impact on the assessment effort (Banta, Lund, Black, and Oblander, 1996); *climate* refers to the "current patterns or important dimensions of organizational life, together with members' perceptions and attitudes toward them" (Peterson, 1988, p. 31). The concept of climate includes constituent's perceptions of their institution's assessment approach, its institution-wide support efforts, its assessment policies and practices, and its uses of student assessment (Peterson, Einarson, Trice, and Nichols, 1997).

- *The uses and impact of student assessment.* If it is to be a means to educational and institutional improvement (Banta and Associates, 1993; Peterson, Einarson, Trice, and Nichols, 1997), student assessment information must be used for educational decision

making, and its internal and external impact on an institution must
be understood.

Survey and Case Studies

The national survey instrument was based on the conceptual framework developed from the literature review and was designed to be a
comprehensive inventory of each institution's organizational and
administrative patterns. In 1998, all 2,524 institutions (excluding specialized and proprietary) of postsecondary education were surveyed;
55 percent (1,393) responded. Descriptive patterns were analyzed
by institutional type and control, and regression analyses on relationships among key variables were conducted. (For a detailed discussion, see Peterson, Einarson, Augustine, and Vaughan, 1999a.)

The case studies were conducted at institutions identified in
the national survey for their extensive involvement with assessment.
A major research university, two public comprehensive universities,
a selective private university, a liberal arts college, and two community colleges were included. The case studies were designed to
examine the internal dynamics of institutional support for student
assessment.

Organizing for Student Assessment:
An Incomplete Revolution

Drawing on data from the national Inventory of Institutional Support for Student Assessment and using the framework, it is possible to profile the student assessment movement by describing how
institutions approach assessment, the institution-wide patterns they
use to promote it, the assessment management policies and practices they have in place to support it, and how they use student
assessment information. Before examining these institutional patterns, there is an important caveat about institutional context.

The Role of Institutional Context

Institutions of differing types (associate of arts, liberal arts, comprehensive, and research/doctoral), control (public or private),
and size will vary in how they approach, promote, support, and use
student assessment. However, an examination of those variations

in the national inventory revealed differences that were either small or obvious. For example, public institutions were more influenced by state assessment patterns, large institutions were more likely to collect postcollege outcomes information, associate of arts institutions collected more entry-level skills data, and so forth. It is beyond the scope of this chapter to examine those variations. Four monographs examine the patterns in each of four primary types of institutions—associate of arts and baccalaureate (Peterson, Augustine, Einarson, and Vaughan, 1999a and 1999b) and comprehensive and doctoral/research (Peterson, Einarson, Augustine, and Vaughan, 1999b and 1999c).

Institutional Approaches to Student Assessment

Institutional approaches to student assessment dimensions were examined in three primary areas: the type or content of assessment data collected, the methods used, and the types of analyses conducted.

Table 2.1 identifies the percentages of institutions that reported collecting various types of student assessment data for all or many of their undergraduate students. Clearly, institutions most often collect data on objective, easily obtained indicators like student progress (96 percent), academic plans (88 percent), or satisfaction (74 percent) rather than measures of student cognitive or affective development. Most are interested in assessing basic skills (78 percent) but give far less attention to learning outcomes. However, emphasis on assessing students' competence in general education and in their major is extensive; it is reported in over 50 percent of the institutions. It is also interesting to note the extensive attention being given to postcollege outcomes. Professional outcomes (63 percent), further education (61 percent), and satisfaction after graduation (57 percent) are all assessed more often than are the four types of cognitive outcomes or affective development. The minimal interest in former students' civic and social roles (23 percent) is both the lowest of all types and perplexing in light of current attention to civic learning and engagement.

Institutions reported substantial use of tests and other instruments to collect assessment data related to student satisfaction (96 percent), basic readiness skills (94 percent), and alumni satisfaction (91 percent)—and they tended to rely on institution-ally developed instruments rather than on commercially available or nationally normed ones.

Despite the extensive critique of quantitative or objective tests and the interest in alternative methods of assessment, nontraditional or student-centered methods were almost never used on an institution-wide basis for undergraduates, and when they were, it was only by a small number of academic units in any institution. Furthermore, very few institutions reported collecting any assessment data at two different points in time to assess change.

Relatively few institutions reported conducting studies of the relationship between various institutional experiences and student performance, and almost 40 percent reported doing no such studies. The most common studies were management-oriented, examining the relationship of admissions policies (42 percent) and financial aid policies (30 percent) with student performance. Relatively few institutions examined relationships of educational experiences (such as course patterns, advising, extracurricular activities, teaching methods, and academic resources) and student performance. And, by far, the least amount of attention was given to the relationship of student and faculty interaction with student performance—one of the variables known to have the greatest impact.

Similarly, reports based on student assessment data that were prepared were primarily profiles of student outcomes at broad levels of aggregation—institution-wide (69 percent) or by academic program (65 percent), with less attention given to examining special student populations (46 percent) and course-level performance (36 percent).

In sum, the picture is one of institutions being extensively engaged in objective, easily quantifiable, and more academic management-oriented assessment of current students, giving considerable attention to postcollege assessment but substantially less attention to cognitive development and affective learning issues. Methods are primarily instrument-driven but with some exemplary use of nontraditional and student-centered methods. Reporting results at broad levels of aggregation and paying limited attention to studying the relationship between student experiences and their performance offer extensive opportunities to improve the analytic use of student assessment data.

Table 2.1. Type and Extent of Student Assessment Data Collected for All or Many Students

Dimension and Type	Percent of Institutions
Plans, Placement and Progress:	
Academic Plans or Intention	80
Basic Skills	88
Progress	96
Cognitive Assessment:	
Higher-Order Thinking	34
General Education	54
Competence in Major	53
Professional Skills	34
Affective Assessment:	
Affective Development	35
Involvement and Engagement	55
Satisfaction	74
Postcollege Assessment:	
Professional Outcomes	63
Further Education	61
Satisfaction	57
Civic and Social Roles	23

Institution-wide Support

This study suggests that whereas excellence in undergraduate education is often stressed in an institution's mission (82 percent), a focus on student outcomes (52 percent) is less often mentioned and student assessment as an institutional priority (19 percent) is usually not included.

Considering an institution's purposes for engaging in student assessment, an external purpose—preparing for accreditation (69 percent)—was clearly the highest, followed by two internal purposes—improving student achievement (59 percent) and improving academic programs (55 percent). Meeting state requirements was rated lower, even by public institutions. Improving instruction (35 percent) and allocating internal resources (21 percent) were the lowest-rated purposes for engaging in student assessment, despite the apparent link of each to program improvement. This previews a theme that emerges later—the reluctance to use budgets to promote student assessment or to use student assessment for faculty evaluation and reward.

Although most institutions had introduced two or three institution-wide administrative and governance activities to support student assessment, the most frequently reported were faculty governance committees on assessment (58 percent) and workshops for administrators (56 percent). Highly visible institution-wide events (such as campus symposia and retreats) are occasionally used (41 percent), as is the inclusion of student representation on assessment groups (33 percent). The least used activities are incentives for academic units (27 percent), the participation of administrators in student assessment (6 percent), and the establishment of board of trustees committees on assessment (13 percent). About half of all institutions reported a plan or policy requiring student assessment by all academic units, while 70 percent have an institution-wide group responsible for overseeing student assessment.

Although structural arrangements, as noted, usually provide for faculty involvement in student assessment on an institution-wide basis, administrators were clearly seen as the most supportive group on most campuses, with academic administrators at 72 percent, chief executive officers at 59 percent, and student affairs administrators at 53 percent. While individual faculty often played key roles in assessment initiatives or led key committees or planning groups, faculty governance, at 24 percent, was not seen as very supportive.

While student assessment has seldom risen to a mission priority in most institutions, it may benefit from the strong emphasis on excellence in undergraduate education usually espoused and the moderately high levels of support for both externally oriented purposes (accreditation) and internally oriented purposes (improving student achievement and academic programs). Institution-wide activities promoting student assessment, the presence of plans, policies, and campus groups to guide it, and strong administrative leadership are also dominant patterns of organizational and administrative support.

Assessment Management Policies and Practices

Institutions were asked to indicate whether they had certain policies or practices that supported student assessment in nine specific areas of activity. The resulting pattern was quite mixed.

On the whole, institutions reported an extensive set of practices designed to provide access to student assessment information and to distribute assessment reports widely. Practices in developing computer-based information system capabilities to support collection and processing of student assessment data were substantially lower. And institutions rarely budgeted funds to support student assessment efforts or allocated funds to units, based on student performance indicators.

Many institutions had policies designed to assure the use of student performance indicators in academic planning and review and to encourage student involvement in assessment activities. However, they made substantially less use of policies that assessed professional development opportunities related to student assessment for faculty, academic administrators, and student affairs staff. And they almost never adopted policies designed to link participation in student assessment activities or student performance to faculty evaluation and rewards.

So the pattern of management policies and practices designed to support student assessment is mixed. Practices promoting access to, and preparing reports on, student assessment, as well as policies to use it in academic program review, are common. However, there is ample opportunity to strengthen computer-based student tracking systems and professional development opportunities for faculty and administrators on most campuses. The very limited policies and practices in areas related to budgeting and resource allocation and in faculty evaluation suggest the need to examine the controversial nature of linking student assessment to these two critical academic management areas.

Uses and Impacts of Student Assessment

Institutions' reports on their use of student assessment in educational decision making and the resulting impact provided the most surprising and disappointing results of the national inventory.

Using student assessment data for decisions was rated on a four-point scale, ranging from "student assessment data not used" (1) to "student assessment data very influential" (4). Five of ten educationally related decisions ranked in the 2.4—2.6 range ("data used but not influential" to "data somewhat influential"). These are decisions that address designing or reorganizing programs and majors, modifying student assessment policies and practices, modifying general education, modifying teaching methods, and modifying academic support services. Student assessment data were not regarded as influential in making educational decisions related to revising undergraduate mission and goals, reorganizing student affairs units, allocating resources to academic units, or modifying out-of-class learning or distance education. For faculty decisions related to promotion, tenure, and rewards, student assessment data apparently are not used.

The impact of assessment data was examined in fifteen areas related to student impact (4), faculty impact (4), and external impact (7). It was rated on a four-point scale, from "not monitored" (1) to "positive impact" (4). In twelve of the fifteen impact areas, 80–90 percent of the respondents indicated that the area was either "not monitored" or was "monitored but student assessment had no known impact." In the four student impact areas (satisfaction, retention/graduation, grades, and external or postcollege achievement), at none of the institutions did more than 20 percent of the respondents indicate that the area was monitored or that student assessment had a positive impact. Of the four faculty impact areas (campus discussion, satisfaction, interest in teaching, teaching methods), two areas were reported as having been affected positively by student assessment—campus academic discussion (33 percent) and teaching methods (38 percent). Finally, of the seven external impact areas (applications, state funding, accreditation, private fundraising, grants, communication, reputation), only one area was reported as having been affected positively by student assessment—accreditation (42 percent), and that is to be expected, since it is required.

Thus, while student assessment information is being used for educational decisions related to academic issues, it seems to have been only moderately influential in certain decision areas and is usually not used in decisions about faculty. In terms of the impact of student assessment data, the very limited evidence of positive impact is disappointing, given the various pronouncements about its value in institutional improvement. However, this pattern of limited use in education decisions and the failure to monitor many impact areas suggests where to focus attention in developing an institution's student assessment processes.

An Overview: Incomplete Institutionalization

Inasmuch as institutions report limited use of student assessment data for decision making and even more limited impact, one might conclude that assessment has not been a very useful effort. However, there is another perspective. The institutional profile just depicted is one of incomplete development or institutionalization of a student assessment process. The profile suggests extensive involvement in assessing students (over 95 percent report using two or more types of assessment), a substantial array of institution-wide patterns promoting it, a mixed pattern of assessment management policies and practices to support it, limited use in decision making, and either no monitoring of impact or impact that is very limited. Thus, the contribution of student assessment to institutional and academic improvement may not be known until greater attention is given to more fully developing a comprehensive pattern of organizational and administrative support.

Organizing Student Assessment for Institutional Improvement

While a profile of institutional patterns is useful, a careful analysis of the survey and case study results of the national study suggests other important insights for organizing student assessment that addresses institutional improvement.

The Role of External Influence and the Primacy of Internal Purposes

Clearly, student assessment has been a major focus of state governments and accrediting associations in recent years. The argument about whether assessment is or should be driven by demands for external accountability or by institutional concerns for improvement has been a major topic of discussion (Aper, 1993; Ewell, 1997a). Data from our study have shed some light on this debate.

In the previous discussion it was noted that preparing for institutional accreditation was the highest-rated institutional purpose for engaging in student assessment, followed by moderately high ratings for two internal purposes—improving student achievement and improving academic programs. Among public institutions, the rating for meeting state requirements was similar to that for the two internal improvement purposes. This suggests that institutions see both as important.

To test this internal versus external influence issue further, two sets of regression analyses were conducted. In the first set, institutional use of cognitive, affective, and postcollege assessment constituted three dependent variables (Peterson and Augustine, 2000). These were each regressed on dimensions (or variables) from three domains: (1) state governance authority, state assessment policies, accrediting region, and conduct for state-required or accreditation purposes from the external domain, (2) institutional type, and (3) institutional mission emphasis, administrative and governance activities, faculty and administrative support, and conduct for internal institutional purposes from the institution-wide support domain.

In each of the three regressions with the extent of use of cognitive, affective, and postcollege assessment activity, having internal improvement purposes for conducting assessment was the dominant predictor, usually followed by one of the other three institution-wide support dimensions. Accreditation had a minor influence but usually reflected the length of time the accreditation agency had been engaged in student assessment. The state variables and external purpose variables had no influence on the amount or extent of student assessment.

In a second set of regressions, variables from all domains except culture (external, approach, institutional type, institution-wide support, and assessment management policies and practices) were regressed on two dependent variables representing the use of student assessment information in educational decisions and faculty decisions (Peterson and Augustine, 2000). These results are discussed in the next section. The key finding is that none of the external domain dimensions had any significant influence on the extent to which student assessment was used in academic decision making.

These results clearly suggest that while both internal institutional and external factors may influence institutions to initiate assessment activities, the external factors have little influence on the extent to which institutions do differing types of student assessment and have no influence on institutions' use of student assessment in decision making. Internally oriented purposes for conducting student assessment and internal institutional dynamics are far more influential. Our case studies reinforce this finding. While all seven institutions acknowledged the role of accreditation in their initial decisions to begin doing student assessment, none found that it influenced how they were organized to support, promote, or use it. The five public institutions all experienced differing state policies and acknowledged that these had some initial influence, but all had engaged proactively to shape the state requirements to serve their own purposes and then developed their own support and use patterns. External accountability may play an initiating role but has little impact on how student assessment is organized, promoted, supported, or used.

Organizational Strategies That Promote the Use of Student Assessment

Scholars and proponents of student assessment have emphasized the importance of planning for and developing an organizational strategy to promote and support student assessment (Banta, Lund, Black, and Oblander, 1996; Ewell, 1997a) and have suggested many ways to approach that task (Banta, Lund, Black, and Oblander, 1996; Ewell, 1988). However, the literature suggests no theory of assessment and little in the way of systematic or conceptual models for organizing to support student assessment (Peterson, Einarson, Trice, and Nichols, 1997). Using the framework and the data from the national inventory, four regression models (one for each institutional type) were run, using an index of the use of student assessment data in education decision making as the dependent variable. (A faculty decision-making index and impact variables could not be used as dependent variables because of the lack of variance previously noted on these variables.) All dimensions (or variables) from the five domains (external influences on, institutional context, approach to, institution-wide support for, and assessment management policies and practices for student assessment) were used as independent predictor variables in this analysis.

The results suggested that several dimensions from four of the domains (except external influences) were significant predictors of the use of student assessment data in all four of the institutional-type regression models (Peterson and Augustine, 2000). The models themselves accounted for a substantial portion of the variance (R^2 ranged from .41 to .60 for the four models). This suggests the need for a comprehensive approach to student assessment that pays attention to the development of organizational structures, activities, policies, and practices in all four institutional domains to enhance the use of assessment data in decisions that serve institutional improvement. However, a pattern analysis of the dimensions that are significant predictors suggests three implicit but somewhat different strategies or conceptual models for organizing to promote and support student assessment (Peterson and Vaughan, 2000) that incorporate all of the dimensions that contributed to increased use of student assessment data.

An *institutional assessment strategy* views assessment as an integral component in developing external relationships and internal mission and purpose. It is critical to develop an institutional relationship with, and a proactive stance toward, state and accrediting agencies that meet their requirements yet are responsive to internal purposes for assessment. By incorporating student assessment into its mission, an institution is increasing the importance of assessment as a means of educational and institutional improvement. Student assessment should also be incorporated in the purpose statements of individual units across campus. Having a well-developed and coordinated plan for student assessment is also useful. Organizationally, it is important to have some institution-wide group to guide assessment efforts, broad patterns of participation, resource allocation that supports student assessment, and a program to periodically evaluate the process. Thus, promoting student assessment through a clearly defined strategy, which incorporates it into the more formal organizational and administrative framework, can become an important determinant of whether the resulting information will be used in making academic decisions.

A *rational information and analysis strategy* reflects the extent to which institutions collect, study, and disseminate information on student performance and how they organize for it. The greater the extent to which institutions collect a wide variety of student assessment information and do studies of or research on factors that improve student performance, the more likely they are to use the data to make academic decisions. To support this, they need to develop computer-based student tracking and assessment systems. Furthermore, institutions need to increase access to this information for constituents across the campus and to provide reports externally as well as internally. In doing so, they increase the likelihood of the information being used in the academic decision-making process. This information-based model incorporates an integrated pattern of data collection and management, analysis, reporting, and distribution of results, leading to increased availability for use in decision making.

The *human resource or developmental strategy,* as its name indicates, suggests that institutions can emphasize enhancing faculty, student, and staff capacity to contribute to the student assessment process. This includes structuring opportunities for involvement, providing incentives to participate in professional development and training opportunities to improve knowledge and skills, and rewarding involvement in student assessment activities. These types of policies and practices are designed to engage members of the faculty, staff, and student body, and they should enhance a sense of ownership and ultimately promote the use of assessment information in decision making.

These models and strategies are not mutually exclusive. All contain elements that seem to contribute to the use of student assessment. In our institutional case studies, the three institutions that made most active use of student assessment for institutional decision making and academic improvement initiatives had all three models or strategies as part of their comprehensive approaches to organizing for and supporting assessment.

Integrating Student Assessment with Academic Improvement and Management Approaches

While the national inventory focused primarily on the organizational patterns for student assessment, our case studies highlighted an important lesson in organizing for student assessment. Much of the literature, like the inventory, assumes that student assessment can be organized and administered separately and that the data can then be made available for state and accrediting reports, academic decision-making needs, and institutional improvement efforts.

In the three case study institutions that used student assessment information most extensively, assessment was not a separate activity or process but was closely integrated with a broader approach to academic management, teaching, and curriculum improvement efforts. For example, at a large public research university, student assessment efforts were largely decentralized to its various schools and colleges. Yet most of these academic units were closely allied with the institution's highly respected Unit for Curricular and Instructional Innovation, which assisted units with developing new educational initiatives and built student assessment into that process. In the academic management arena, academic unit-level student assessment was integrated into the university's centrally coordinated program review process. This process was responsive to the state's mandated program review process, which incorporated a student outcomes requirement that allowed units the flexibility to link with requirements of their professional accreditation organizations.

In a selective private university, extensive institution-wide student assessment efforts were a central part of the approach to academic management of the institution. A periodic strategic planning process relied on student assessment data and reports as one of its major resources. An institution-wide evaluation group, which examined issues on an annual basis to identify academic priorities for the next year, drew heavily on student assessment information. An ongoing academic review process (each unit was reviewed every five years) had guidelines that emphasized the use of student assessment information in each unit's self-study. Academic units were provided with information from the central student assessment effort but also developed, gathered, and analyzed data relevant to their own needs and purposes. A centrally staffed institutional research office oversaw a comprehensive collection of student data, analyzed it, and saw that it got into the different academic management arenas.

Finally, a comprehensive public university made the collection of assessment data of all types a cornerstone of its institution-wide continuous-quality improvement process, a related strategic planning process, and an annual review of data on unit performance in the annual budget and resource allocation process. An administrative office was charged with building an extensive institutional database, including various student assessment measures, and with designing key quality indicators for all academic managers and committees.

All three institutions also had institutional activities and programs that provided opportunities for faculty development, training, and instructional improvement centered around student assessment. The other four institutions had fewer well-developed institutional patterns for promoting and supporting student assessment and used the data less for decision making. However, they were attempting to integrate student assessment into their internal management and improvement efforts and to deemphasize its use primarily for meeting state or accreditation requirements.

The Need for Multifaceted Leadership

While the national survey data have highlighted the predominant pattern of administrative support for student assessment on most campuses, and other studies have suggested the need for both faculty and administrative support, our case studies have suggested the need not only for a broad base of support for student assessment but also multifaceted leadership for four different types of leadership as necessary for the development of a strong institutional pattern for student assessment.

- The need for *externally oriented leadership* was exemplified by some of our institutional executive officers. One of them convinced state leaders of this need with regard to his institution's continuous-quality approach and avoided a more restrictive set of state-mandated measures. Another convinced state agency staff to deemphasize institution-wide indicators and focus more on school and college measures. Others found ways to use state or accreditation requirements to help sell student assessment on their campuses. Still others developed strong relationships with national professional associations and experts to build campus assessment capacity.

• *Strategic leadership* focuses on a comprehensive view of the institution's overall approach to student assessment, how to build the organizational patterns to promote and support it, and how to use it. This was exemplified by two presidents who were aware of the various organizational domains of student assessment and how to integrate this with an academic management philosophy. More often, this is a role played by the chief academic officer, who is aware of both the institution's approach to academic management and its strategy for promoting educational improvement or change, and is knowledgeable about student assessment. In one institution, it was a role played, largely behind the scenes, by a long-term institutional research officer with an extensive interest in student assessment.

• *Process leadership* is performed by a person or group familiar with how to engage faculty and administrators in training and development in the many aspects of student assessment, how to help units organize assessment activities, and how to link individuals involved in student assessment with those involved in broader academic management or educational improvement efforts at the institution. One person in the provosts' office at our large public research university comes to mind. She was able to engage representatives from diverse schools and colleges in learning about, organizing for, and using student assessment for educational change and improvement initiatives.

• *Technical leadership* is a need that is often overlooked (or is assumed to be already met). This role requires knowledge about the design and use of various types of assessment measures, doing research and analysis that link institutional experiences to student performance, and developing and managing computer-based student data systems. In most of our case studies, different individuals played one or more of these roles.

Clearly, these four facets of leadership for student assessment will seldom be found in one individual or even in one group. However, in our three most highly developed institutions, all four are present.

Creating a Comprehensive Institutional Culture

As this chapter and the research on which it is based suggest, after a decade and a half, the student assessment revolution at the institutional level is far from complete. Institutional approaches to student assessment are extensive but place less focus on student learning outcomes. Institution-wide support programs are extensive, assessment management policies and practices are unevenly developed, use of student assessment information for academic decision making is limited, and monitoring of impacts is spotty or nonexistent. Whether student assessment makes a difference at the institutional level is still an unanswered question.

However, institutions are coming to grips with the conflict over external and internal (accountability versus improvement) purposes and learning how to address the former while giving weight to the latter. There is evidence that our organizational and administrative patterns do influence the use of student assessment data in academic decisions. The role of student assessment data for faculty decisions and for resource allocation is apparently still controversial or, at least, not widely promoted or done. Three strategies of organizing for student assessment and four facets of leadership for student assessment seem to be emerging. The value of integrating student assessment with an institution's primary academic management and its educational improvement process or functions is being recognized.

While creating a campus culture for student assessment is often suggested, it is still a difficult concept to comprehend or measure. Without belaboring many of the conflicting definitions of culture, the following characteristics of an institution with a comprehensive culture for student assessment are suggested:

- The institution's organizational and administrative pattern for student assessment is fully developed. It has a well-formulated approach to student assessment, an institution-wide strategy to support it, a well-developed set of policies and practices to promote it, and it uses student information for educational decisions and monitors its impacts.

- The purposes for undertaking student assessment are clearly understood by all campus constituencies.
- Institutional, information-based, and human resource strategies for student assessment are evident.
- Student assessment is well integrated with the institution's academic management approach and its educational improvement efforts.
- All forms of leadership for student assessment (external, strategic, process, and technical) are present and visible.

Within this comprehensive or holistic pattern, a commitment to student learning as the central purpose of education and to the importance of demonstrating student performance and using that knowledge for the improvement of the institution are key values. Three of the seven institutions we visited fit this profile of institutions that have a comprehensive culture for student assessment. But all three have enjoyed over a decade of stable leadership consisting of all four of the key facets—with leaders who have valued student assessment or the measuring of academic performance and have persisted in developing the institutional patterns to promote, support, and use student assessment.

Part Two

Theoretical Foundations of Assessment

In Chapter Three, Peter Gray explores two sets of philosophical assumptions that he believes clash as faculty members approach assessment and all too often inhibit their adoption of the concept. He sees objectivist and utilitarian assumptions underlying one side of the debate and subjectivist and intuitionist assumptions fueling the opposition. Gray defines assessment as a form of inquiry, with learning as hypotheses, educational practice as context, evaluation as data collection, and decision making as direction for improvement. He urges that scholars undertake metaevaluations of this process.

In Chapter Four, Dary Erwin and Steven Wise discuss five areas of scholarship that provide theoretical frameworks for outcomes assessment: psychology and education, analytical methods, public policy and organizational behavior, technology, and combinations of these approaches. They decry the types of indicators currently employed in national ranking systems and state accountability mandates because they have so little to do with student learning. These authors call for a more sophisticated response to the development of indicators—a response based on one or more of the areas of scholarship they describe.

Marcia Mentkowski and Georgine Loacker are true pioneers in assessment, having provided leadership for three decades for the "assessment as learning" approach that has earned Alverno College worldwide recognition. In Chapter Five, they describe some features of and findings from scholarly work in assessment conducted by national associations and consortia of institutions. They also suggest some steps to follow in carrying out collaborative assessment scholarship.

George Kuh, Robert Gonyea, and Daisy Rodriguez broaden the concept of assessment to encompass student development both in and outside the classroom. In Chapter Six, they trace the origins of the assessment of student development in college and describe a number of examples of scholarly assessment in this arena. They also furnish a bridge to Part Three by considering some of the specific tools and methods that are being used by scholars in this arena.

Chapter Three

The Roots of Assessment
Tensions, Solutions, and Research Directions
Peter J. Gray

The gap between writing a plan and putting it into action epitomizes the fundamental issue faced when any innovation is introduced: how to change beliefs and behaviors so that a new way of doing things becomes part of a culture. This is a dilemma faced by regional and disciplinary accreditation agencies, state higher education agencies, higher education administrators, and faculty when they consider adopting student learning outcomes assessment. Any scholarship of assessment must investigate why this gap exists and suggest how it might be bridged.

There are two sets of philosophical assumptions at the heart of the tension over assessment that result in a gap between planning and doing. These assumptions influence the way people think about concepts related to assessment, for example, student learning, instruction, evaluation, and the use of assessment information. One tradition includes objectivist and utilitarian assumptions associated with the scientific movement in education that began in the early part of the twentieth century (Merwin, 1969; Ewell, 1989); the second includes subjectivist and intuitionist assumptions related to the professional authority that formed the foundation of accreditation when it was first devised in the 1920s and then was advanced by the North Central Association of Schools and Colleges (House, 1978; Stufflebeam, 2001).

People tend to argue from these positions to justify the adoption of assessment or to counter such justifications. Therefore, setting these two sets of assumptions in opposition brings into sharp contrast the fundamental issues that inhibit the adoption of assessment, thereby causing a gap between planning and doing.

A scholarship of assessment must first describe the relevant phenomena associated with it. Second, it must create a model or theory of assessment that is based on the perceived reality and that incorporates concepts and insights from related fields. Third, it must be guided by some fundamental questions that test the appropriateness and utility of the constructed model or theory.

This chapter begins with a discussion of two perspectives that are important sources of the tension that exists around the adoption of assessment. This discussion will help explicate the key characteristics of assessment. Then, a process of assessment is described that synthesizes features from both perspectives and draws lessons from the literature in such related fields as educational evaluation and planned change. Finally, some ideas are presented that might guide future research on assessment.

Two Perspectives

As Marchese (1987) notes "assessment is not something just invented: a rich variety of approaches to knowing about student learning has evolved, through decades of research and campus experience" (p. 4). One approach to knowing about student learning is embodied in a positivist or scientific view of education. This began with the work of Tyler, who suggested that educational outcomes should be described in terms of student behaviors, "which should then serve as the objectives for teaching and as a basis for testing" (Merwin, 1969, p. 12).

Higher education has over the years adopted a variety of rational, positivist, scientific, and objectivist program evaluation models "visible in wave after wave of imported business techniques such as MBO, PPBS, zero-based budgeting, strategic planning, and, most recently, 'institutional effectiveness'" (Ewell, 1989, p. 9). In the past, student learning outcomes assessment, primarily in the form of objective tests, has provided the "persistently missing 'outcomes' information" for these systems (p. 10).

Another perspective relies on a subjectivist and intuitionist ethic that values the tacit knowledge of professional authorities. Here, knowledge and authority are based on expertise gained through experience. As initially conceived, accreditation was conducted by a professional elite comprised of credible authorities, including higher education faculty and administrators. They relied on tacit or implicit knowledge to render judgments about sister programs and institutions. In addition, the self-study was and is an important part of the accreditation process. This provides an opportunity for perspectives of local experts or authorities to be incorporated into the decision-making process. This ethic thus has the potential for being pluralist and democratic, even though it is essentially elitist.

The differences between these two perspectives may be illustrated by describing the ways the major elements of assessment are viewed. These elements include student learning, educational practice and experiences, evaluation, and decision making. In describing these elements, the sources of tension regarding the adoption of assessment will be considered.

Student Learning

When educational outcomes are discussed in relation to objectivist and utilitarian assumptions, they are described as knowable in advance, specifiable, measurable, and related to behaviors that can be directly observed. This close relationship to behaviors has led to outcomes being called behavioral objectives. Educational outcomes may be narrowly focused on general education types of knowledge and skills, for example, mathematics, oral and written communication, and technological literacy, or they may be focused on discipline-specific facts, terms, concepts, and processes. And they may be more broadly focused on higher-order cognitive knowledge and skills, as well as affective outcomes. However, given the assumptions underlying this ethic, in the end, educational outcomes are to be described in terms of student behaviors, "which should then serve as the objectives for teaching and as a basis for testing" (Merwin, 1969, p. 12).

The description of student learning based on a subjectivist and intuitionist ethic is much less explicit, since tacit knowledge is valued. Some descriptions may be quite conceptually clear, specific, concrete, and even behavioral (actions or movements). However, many of them will be more vague, general, abstract, and nonbehavioral (states of being) (Gray, 1975). There is no assumption that learning will ultimately be defined in terms of behaviors. Instead, there is a focus on the whole range of knowledge, skills, and values of an educated person. Individual faculty members, educational administrators, staff, students, and others may have a say in the description of anticipated, intended, or desired outcomes, as is appropriate, since they are responsible for teaching and learning and therefore may be considered authorities. In addition, the relationship of student learning to teaching and testing is much less precisely defined and offers a wider range of choices.

Educational Practices and Experiences

Educational practice that is based on a view of student learning as specifiable, measurable, and related to behaviors that can be directly observed tends to take the form of skills training, rote memorization, or programmed instruction, where behaviors themselves become the focus of learning. However, there are many other important learning outcomes that can be closely related to observable behaviors. This is especially true in introductory courses or other educational experiences where information about the terms and facts, concepts and theories, methods and materials, and tools and technologies of a subject area is taught. In addition, students may be expected to be able to use or apply this knowledge for purposes of analysis, synthesis, and evaluation. They may also be expected to come to appreciate and even adopt the beliefs and values of a discipline or subject area. And there may be potential learning related to students' feelings of competence and self-worth, social/team work abilities, and career or professional development. Ideally, instruction not only is organized around these types of learning but also includes opportunities for students to learn how to demonstrate learning in observable ways. A presumed benefit of the explicit view of learning is that it can guide educational practice. Clarity about outcomes is seen as a powerful means of ensuring that learning occurs, because it can help faculty and students decide how they should use their time and energy.

Designing and implementing educational practices and experiences related to a subjectivist and intuitionist ethic is much less prescriptive than that just described. The relationship between learning and educational practice is dynamic. It may be only after considerable practical experience that the goals of teaching and learning can be articulated and subsequently used to guide practice. In fact, some people who adhere to this ethic might claim that knowing in advance what learning should occur is antithetical to education.

As Cohen and March (1991) state, assuming "goals come first and action comes later is frequently radically wrong. Human choice behavior is at least as much a process for discovering goals as for acting on them" (p. 414). This suggests constructivist assumptions that see knowledge as "one or more human constructions, uncertifiable, and constantly problematic and changing" (Stufflebeam, 2001, p. 7). Such assumptions may also be part of the subjectivist and intuitionist ethic.

Evaluation

According to scientific models, the purpose of evaluation is to provide explicit information through objective tests and measures guided by precisely specified, if not behavioral, objectives. Information may be quantitative or qualitative, but it must provide observable evidence of learning. In this approach, the relationship of learning and evidence is tightly coupled. In fact, the outcomes of education (learning) and the behaviors to be used as evidence of learning are often the same. Norm-referenced or criterion-referenced standardized tests, performance measures, and other forms of objective testing are the desired methods of evaluation. Statistical reliability and validity are often the criteria used to determine the quality of evaluation methods and results. While formative information is valued, summative information is often preferred. And experimental and quasi-experimental designs may be chosen to provide information about a course, program, or institution's impact.

Based on their rhetoric, it would appear that many legislators, members of the general public, and people in higher education equate assessment with standardized testing. They seem to believe that such testing is "capable of providing meaningful answers about learning" (Ewell, 1989, p. 7). As a result, "'rising junior' exams and other similar testing mechanisms are often the first thing called for when people contemplate assessment" (p. 7). Institutional report cards, program rankings, or other comparative rubrics may be a desirable result of the evaluation process, according to an objectivist and utilitarian ethic.

Consistent with the subjectivist and intuitionist ethic, the evaluation of learning relies on professional judgment because of its presumed complexity, sophistication, or time frame. Some learning may be complex, in that the whole is greater than the sum of its parts. Some learning is very sophisticated or advanced. And some learning may take a long time to occur. In these cases, expert judgment is called for, based on "mature and practiced understanding" (Dreyfus and Dreyfus, 1986, p. 30).

Such judgment is based on information gathered by evaluation methods as varied as the learning they are intended to document. In addition to objective tests and measures, other means of collecting qualitative and quantitative information may be used as deemed relevant and appropriate by the instructor and professional authority. This may include the collection of artifacts related to student work, content analysis of diaries and logs, interviews of key informants, questionnaires and surveys, and photographs and videotapes of performances. In fact, an advantage of this approach is that those evaluation methods embedded in courses and curricula are valued most. The key criteria for determining the quality of evaluation methods is that they are authentic and consistent with the learning to be documented and that they conform to prevailing norms set by professional authorities within a given field.

Use

This brings us to the presumed utility of assessment information from the rational, positivist, objectivist, empiricist, and scientific perspectives. Consistent with the underlying assumptions of these perspectives, the primary idea of *use* is for decision making, that is, instrumental use (Weiss, 1998). For example, an instrumental use of information may be to judge the merit or worth of individual student learning in order to assign a grade and thereby differentiate among students. Another instrumental use of evaluation information is to hold programs and institutions accountable for their effectiveness in fostering student learning. Such information also may be used to determine the differential allocation of resources, for example, faculty salary lines, operating budgets, or facilities.

This managerial function is exemplified by "such statewide efforts as Tennessee's 'performance funding' experiment—intended to provide an empirical foundation for rewarding effective performance and for gathering sound statewide management information" (Ewell, 1989, p. 9). The idea that "there is a direct parallel between production in social services and in manufacturing" (House, 1978, p. 7) is evident in many such state-mandated accountability requirements and public discussions of the improvement of higher education. However, the relationship between such information gathered through objectivist methods and necessary improvements is tenuous at best, since the range of outcomes is often restricted and there is little or no contextual information about why particular results were obtained. In addition, using this information to hold courses, programs, or institutions accountable for learning can result in "invidious comparisons and thereby produce unhealthy competition and much political unrest and acrimony" (Stufflebeam, 2001, p. 20).

From the subjectivist and intuitionist perspective, decisions related to learning and decisions about the merit or worth of courses, programs, or institutions are based on professional authority and expertise gained through experience. The incorporation of pluralist and constructivist assumptions further opens up the range of decision makers and decisions. The professional authority perspective assumes intuitionist ethics (what is good and right are individual feelings or apprehensions) rather than utilitarian ethics (the greatest good for the greatest number). Because of the perceived dynamic nature of teaching and learning, the evaluation of learning and subsequent decisions rely on "higher-level decision-making strategies and hierarchies predicated upon rules, intuitions, and multiple perspectives" (Altschuld, 1999, p. 483).

While specifically related to program and institutional accreditation, in the form of reflective journals, self-study may be a way for students to make judgments about their own learning and the impact of educational experiences. The program or institutional self-study acknowledges local expertise and is the organizing vehicle for accreditation reviews. The burden is on the local faculty, administrators, students, and staff to present a clear, articulate, fair, and accurate picture. In fact, to a great extent, the accreditation review is a process of verifying or refuting the claims of self-study, based on the prior and immediate experiences of an expert review panel. In doing so, summative judgments of quality and formative suggestions for improvement naturally occur.

Because of the open nature of the subjectivist, intuitionist, pluralist, and constructivist ethics, it may be difficult to reach consensus on learning, practice, evaluation, or the use of information. However, unexamined or perfunctory consensus may hide some important strengths and weaknesses. In either case, power struggles can occur within a course, program, or institution or between those doing a self-study and the review panel, because of a lack of clarity or differing views.

Of course, the most dramatic power struggles can occur when completely different ideologies come into conflict. The gap between developing an assessment plan and putting the plan into action may be a result of such struggles. The development of a plan is very much a rational, positivist approach to assessment that has clear scientific management overtones. Individuals within a department (such as the chair or a senior faculty member) or within the institution's administration (such as the provost's office or the office of institutional research) typically are charged with developing the plan. When a team, task force, or committee is formed to create the plan, most members will share the managerial perspective. Therefore, the resulting plan will likely have fairly precise statements about how learning should be described or even what it should be. Learning may be tied directly to specific course offerings or instructional activities, perhaps even in the form of a rationalist scheme such as a matrix. Evaluation methods will tend to be objective tests and measures. And while the plan may stress formative decisions related to improvement, there may be an undercurrent of summative decisions about quality and the allocation of resources.

When an attempt is made to implement such plans, there may be a lack of commitment on the part of most faculty, staff, and administrators, since they were not involved in the plan's development. This is typical when an innovation is introduced. There may be conflicts over the assumptions embodied in the plan, especially from those subscribing to subjectivist, intuitionist, pluralist, and constructivist ethics. The fact of assessment, and even more so the mere hint of summative judgments, may raise issues of autonomy and academic freedom. When faced with an innovation, one of the first things people want to know is how it is going to affect them. In particular, regarding assessment, they want to know what decisions will be made, who will make them, and on what criteria these decisions will be based. All of these issues contribute to the gap between having a plan and putting it into action.

Proposed Process of Assessment

By synthesizing features from both objectivist and subjectivist perspectives, or at least allowing them to coexist without impinging on each other, it may be possible to create a process that ameliorates the major impediments to implementing assessment just described. In addition, there are lessons that can be drawn from the literature in related fields to help facilitate the implementation of assessment.

Assessment has many of the perceived disadvantages typical of education innovations, such as little relative advantage over existing ideas, low compatibility with current values and past experiences, high perceived complexity, a perceived monolithic nature, and low visibility of results (Rogers, 1968). Therefore, its adoption needs the type of leadership that offers "people pathways and permissions to do things they want to do but feel unable to do for themselves. That sort of energy evokes energies within people that far exceed the powers of coercion" (Palmer, 1993, p. 9). Such leadership taps into people's intrinsic motivation for competence, success, quality, and continuous improvement. (See Curry [1992] in Gray, 1997, regarding specific roles that leaders can play to facilitate such change as the implementation of assessment.)

The implementation of an innovation like assessment also demands a well-thought-out series of activities that move it from innovation to institutionalization. The process of planned change and the concepts of the adoption of innovation should guide these activities (Gray, 1997; Hall, Loucks, Rutherford, and Newlove,

1975). Helping people progress from awareness to integration takes careful planning. It is not a linear process but rather a recursive one. And people may be at different levels or stages in relation to different elements of an innovation, such as the description of student learning versus evaluation methods. Of course, it is likely that different people in a unit or across an institution will have different assumptions about assessment, given their particular perspective. Therefore, administrative leadership and institutional support for assessment must extend across many cycles of use and over an extended period of time, rather than consisting mainly of a single experience or a short-term series of events (Gray, 1997).

Building faculty ownership is the key to successful implementation, since assessment is about teaching and learning, for which faculty are primarily responsible. Therefore, assessment must start where faculty are, acknowledging their existing ideas, current values, and past experiences (Rogers, 1968). This will help to dispel the view of assessment as complex and monolithic in nature, and, at least for individual faculty, it will enhance the visibility of results.

Assessment for Improvement and Accountability

The first thing to do is to be clear about what assessment is and understand its purpose. For example, the term *assessment* is often used synonymously with testing and measurement. It has also been defined as a process, "the systematic collection, review and use of information about educational programs undertaken for the purpose of improving student learning and development" (Palomba and Banta, 1999). For the purposes of this discussion, student learning outcomes assessment is described as a form of systematic inquiry with the following elements: learning as hypotheses, educational practices and experiences as context, evaluation as information gathering, and decision making as direction for improvement.

The purpose of assessment can be seen as improvement *or* accountability. As a means of improvement alone, it is like faculty development: it is entirely up to the individual or group responsible for certain learning and educational practices and experiences. Accountability alone is akin to outcomes assessment or performance testing and is closely related to the scientific movement in education. Making improvement the focus of accountability presents some interesting possibilities but also raises some important questions, such as Who decides what improvements are needed? Who has access to the information related to improvement? and Who sets the criteria and standards for judging success? This is the same dilemma faced when considering faculty development as an element of performance review, for example, for promotion and tenure or for merit pay decisions.

Stufflebeam (2001) describes a decision/accountability-oriented approach to evaluation that has as its purpose "to provide a knowledge and value base for making and being accountable for decisions" (p. 56). He goes on to say that this approach's "most important purpose is not to prove but to improve" (p. 56). This approach is classified as a type of improvement/accountability evaluation.

The advantages of defining assessment for improvement and accountability can be described using the decision/accountability-oriented approach to evaluation as a model. Foremost among the advantages is that it can incorporate both objectivist and subjectivist perspectives. This approach's philosophical underpinnings include an objectivist orientation to finding best answers to context-limited questions while also subscribing to the principles of a well-functioning democratic society and including stakeholders from the bottom up. It also legitimizes the use of many different information-gathering methods as is appropriate to answering questions posed by a variety of constituents. In effect, stakeholders at all levels are viewed as authorities whose subjectivist and intuitionist perspectives are not only valid but also necessary.

Assessment based on a decision/accountability-oriented approach can involve the full range of stakeholders by encouraging faculty members to consider learning from a student's perspective, engaging students in the evaluation of learning, and supporting the effective use of evaluation findings by faculty and students. In beginning with faculty members and their individual responsibilities, this approach is comprehensive in attending to context, input, process, and outcome, all of which are familiar to faculty. Context includes the setting of instruction, whether face-to-face or online, as well as facilities, class size, and instructional resources. Inputs include the prior knowledge and experience of students, faculty preparation, and the expectations about teaching and learning that faculty and students bring.

In defining the elements of assessment, it is important to identify faculty members as being primarily responsible for setting the context for student learning through the design and implementation of educational practices and experiences. In addition, they are the primary developers and implementers of evaluation methods and the primary users of the resulting information. An excellent vehicle around which faculty can organize assessment for improvement is a learning-centered syllabus (Grunert, 1997). And a syllabus is a document with which all faculty members are familiar.

All manner of learning should be valued. Learning can be defined in terms of discipline–specific knowledge and skills, and attitudes, and it involves terms and facts, concepts and theories, methods and materials, tools and technologies, and perspectives and values. General education and liberal studies outcomes include basic skills in oral and written communication, mathematics, scientific and technological literacy, study skills, awareness of contemporary issues, appreciation of different social and cultural perspectives and experiences, and the like. Professional and career development, as well as personal growth and development, may be outcomes of an academic program, student affairs programming, or an experiential learning center program. Professional development may involve teamwork, leadership, and positive self-esteem and self-confidence. Career development may involve self-awareness and career exploration in addition to résumé writing and job interviewing abilities. Personal growth and development includes knowledge, skills, and values related to such areas as emotional/physical health and well-being, responsibility for one's actions, responsible and respectful behavior toward others, and honesty and integrity in relation to one's own values.

Some statements of learning may be quite conceptually clear, specific, concrete, and even behavioral (involving actions or movements). But many of them will be more vague, general, abstract, and nonbehavioral (involving states of being) (Gray, 1975). This is the case because they cover the range of knowledge, skills, and values of an educated person. Individual faculty members, educational administrators, staff, students, and others may have a say in the description of anticipated, intended, or desired learning, as is appropriate.

The process includes faculty and student activity around learning. On the faculty side, this includes teaching practices such as lectures and other in-class and out-of-class interaction, instructional materials and assignments, and structured practical experiences. On the student side, this means attending class and engaging in such activities as note taking, taking part in discussions, completing assignments, and participating in other experiences that promote learning.

There is no presumption of a need for the prior specification of learning or of a strict causal relationship between educational practices and experiences and learning. In fact, as Lindblom (1959) suggests, it may be much less a matter of rationally "choosing the means that best satisfied goals that were previously clarified and ranked" (p. 80) and more like a process of "successive limited comparisons" or "disjointed incrementalism" (p. 81), where impulse, intuition, faith, and tradition might play important roles. In this view of decision making, "means and ends are not distinct" and therefore "means and ends analysis is often inappropriate or limited" (p. 81). However, at some point there needs to be a description of both learning, which may be intuitive and based on multiple perspectives, including those of faculty members, students, and others, and the types and quality of educational practices and experiences in which faculty and students engage. Providing the information for these descriptions is the function of evaluation.

Since it does not specify the methods of evaluation, assessment based on a decision/accountability-oriented approach can balance the use of quantitative and qualitative methods embedded in a course or other educational experience. Preferred evaluation methods are those that are authentic, in that they fit naturally with the purpose and structure of a course. They should be an integral part of the teaching and learning process. They may be quantitative or qualitative. They may be observations, interviews, surveys, checklists, essays, or multiple-choice exams. They may involve the critique of student work such as performances or tangible products. Any evaluation method that a faculty member has devised for a given teaching/learning experience may be acceptable. The difference is that instead of only being used to grade students, the method also provides information to guide the improvement of both teaching and learning.

As a form of systematic inquiry for improvement and accountability, assessment must be guided by questions. These may be typical improvement and accountability questions such as those suggested by Stufflebeam (2001), including what learning is being addressed, what alternative educational practices and experiences are available and what their comparative advantages are, what kind of plan or syllabus should guide teaching and learning, what facilities, materials, and equipment are needed, what roles faculty, students, and others should carry out, whether the course is working and whether it should be revised, how the course can be improved, what the outcomes are, whether the course is reaching all of the students, whether the faculty and students effectively discharge their responsibilities, whether the course is worth the required investment, and whether the course is meeting the minimum accreditation requirements. These questions embody the kinds of decisions to be made as a result of seeing assessment as systematic inquiry.

Finally, assessment based on a decision/accountability-oriented approach emphasizes that assessment must be grounded in the democratic principles of a free society, which respects academic freedom and faculty autonomy. Therefore, decisions about using and sharing evaluation information are left to individual faculty members or groups of faculty. However, a fundamental expectation is that information about improvements will be shared. For example, a summary of improvements in courses and other learning experiences and a description of how they came about could be submitted as part of an annual review process at all levels. This could be similar to an annotated list of publications, a description of research, or a summary of campus and professional service activities. Samples of syllabi, evaluations, and changes made in instructional content, materials, and organization could be included for illustrative purposes. It is important to remember that the form and content of the information should be determined locally by faculty within programs and departments.

Using this approach as a model, assessment can aid decision making at all levels regarding improvement because, while it begins with faculty members and their individual responsibilities for teaching and learning, it can be used for departments, programs, schools and colleges, and whole institutions. For example, the learning-centered syllabus (Grunert, 1997) can serve as a prototype for descriptions of learning, educational practice, and evaluation at the classroom level, and, it can serve in modified form, where these elements are described more generally, at other levels. In this way, it can provide a rationale and framework of information for helping faculty be accountable for their decisions and actions.

In addition to faculty-level assessment, there can be program- and department-level assessment that is internal to an institution. In this case, department chairs, program directors, and deans would be responsible for summarizing individual faculty-led improvements and any efforts aimed at improving courses taught by many instructors or teaching assistants, sequences of courses, programs of study, and so forth. Using a format similar to that of the course-related learning-centered syllabus, they would summarize learning as hypotheses, educational practices and experiences as context, evaluation as information gathering, and decision making as direction for improvement.

External accreditation agencies may specify learning, instruction, and evaluation methods related to a discipline or program of study. In such cases, these specifications become part of the context of assessment that can be incorporated into department and individual faculty members' plans.

In addition, there is institutional accreditation by a regional accrediting body. Rather than seeing accountability and improvement as being "in fundamental opposition, one 'wrong' and the other 'right'" (Ewell, 1989, p. 5), the direction of accreditation agencies should become one of holding institutions accountable for a process of continuous improvement. The regional accreditation standards that focus on the assessment of student learning outcomes should require institutions and their academic and student affairs units to provide evidence that individuals and groups of faculty and staff have engaged in assessment for the purpose of improvement. Such groups may include faculty in academic departments, programs, schools, or colleges, as well as staff members responsible for nonacademic student programs.

The self-study process should involve the gathering of information from across campus to provide evidence of improvement, including samples of syllabi and program descriptions, evaluation materials and methods, and changes made in instructional content, materials, and organization that improve teaching and learning as a result of the consideration of evaluation findings. The external review panel would review these materials based on "mature and practiced understanding" (Dreyfus and Dreyfus, 1986, p. 30).

Having assessment as part of a context larger than an individual faculty or staff member's responsibility can key it to professional standards. This can offset the disadvantages of close collaboration of stakeholders that may be an impediment to improvement if the situation is politically charged, as it can be on many college campuses. By conducting metaevaluations of assessment activities by external groups both on and off campus, it may be possible to "counteract opportunities for bias and to ensure a proper balance of the formative and summative aspects" that are inherent in the decision/accountability-oriented evaluation approach (Stufflebeam, 2001, p. 58).

Research on Assessment

Assessment is defined in this chapter as a form of systematic inquiry with the following elements: learning as hypotheses, educational practices and experiences as context, evaluation as information gathering, and decision making as direction for improvement. Conducting metaevaluations of actual assessments based on this definition—in other words, doing research on assessment—can help identify the qualities and characteristics that make assessment meaningful, manageable, and sustainable (Program Assessment Consultation Team, 1999).

Such assessment scholarship can benefit from the literature on the scholarship of teaching. In fact, the improvement of educational programs, courses, and experiences can be an example of the scholarship of teaching if it is based on assessment as a form of systematic inquiry. This form of scholarly teaching involves classroom assessment and evidence gathering, being knowledgeable about current ideas about teaching and learning, and inviting peer review and collaboration. It can help create more informed and thoughtful—that is, more scholarly—instructors (Hutchings and Shulman, 1999). In addition, focusing on practical questions about teaching and learning can help engage faculty in assessment, since "it is extremely difficult to argue as a responsible academic that it is wrong to gather information about a phenomenon, or that it is inappropriate to use the results for collective betterment" (Ewell, 1989, p. 11), especially if that phenomenon is teaching and learning, for which faculty members are primarily responsible.

In addition, engaging faculty in research on assessment puts the power over assessment into their hands, individually and in groups. For example, they decide what questions are meaningful for their courses. Such questions can be rephrased to address course sequences, students' programs of study, and all-campus programs, such as a general education curriculum. Research on assessment questions should identify the qualities, characteristics, or circumstances that inhibit or facilitate the use of assessment information.

Weiss (1998) describes several uses of assessment information, in addition to the instrumental use intended for immediate decision making. For example, there is *conceptual use,* which enhances people's "understanding of what the program is and does" (p. 24). This understanding may not be used immediately, but eventually people may "use their new conceptual understandings in instrumental ways" (p. 24) to make decisions about future assessments. Another "kind of use is to mobilize support" (p. 24), whereby information can become "an instrument of persuasion" (p. 24). A fourth "kind of use is influence on other institutions and events— beyond the program being studied" (p. 24). These uses may suggest types of research on assessment.

Accreditation was initially based on a set of assumptions that treated education and teaching as a craft rather than as a set of explicit, externalized techniques. It was assumed that education and teaching used naturalistic methodologies, were directed more at nontechnical audiences like teachers or the general public, used ordinary language and everyday categories of events, were based more on informal than formal logic, defined use in terms of the observer's interests, blended theory and practice together, and had as their goal improving the understanding of the particular individuals (House, 1978). Investigating these assumptions and reaffirming their efficacy through the scholarship of assessment can provide the foundation for successfully closing the gap between expectations for assessment and assessment practice.

Chapter Four

A Scholar-Practitioner Model for Assessment

T. Dary Erwin and Steven L. Wise

To even the casual observer, it is inescapable that public policy in higher education is directing assessment practice toward a "high stakes" usage environment. That is, assessment results are increasingly "counting" toward institutional funding, state appropriations for higher education, governance, and reputation. In this high stakes environment, the quality and credibility of learning outcome data are becoming more sophisticated and complex. This chapter suggests several areas within the assessment process where great potential exists for improving our assessment practices. In turn, these areas also serve as a framework whereby a multitude of new scholarship and research opportunities exists.

The Need for a Sophisticated Response

Burke, Modarresi, and Serban (1999) observed that three-fourths of the states "had some form of performance reporting." That is, some funding is awarded based on the institution's performance or some list of indicators. Most institutions, however, refused to contribute to the formation and definition of these indicators, perhaps thinking that the calls for accountability were a fad that would soon go away. Instead, as people in evaluation well know, accountability demands have not gone away, and overseers outside higher education often have chosen poorly conceived indicators. For example, such indicators have included the percentage of alumni contributing to the institution or the percentage of enrollees ultimately graduating.

Recently, *Measuring Up 2001: State by State Report* (National Center for Public Policy and Higher Education, 2000) gave each state an "incomplete" grade on available learning indicators. One need look no further than *U.S. News & World Report* to find rankings that are largely based not on outcomes but on perceptions of institutional quality and reputation provided by college presidents or admissions directors, measures of institutional resources, and characteristics of incoming students. While certainly important to any system, these rankings have little to do with student learning, which is traditionally assessed by using achievement and developmental measures.

Higher education has only to look at K–12 for a reminder of what can happen if poorly conceived and constructed tests are implemented. Some states utilize narrowly focused tests that lack the sophistication of the National Assessment of Educational Progress (NAEP) at the federal level (Miller, 2001).

Burke, Modarresi, and Serban (1999) clearly state the challenge to design useful learning indicators: "Will educators take the lead in helping to develop the necessary approaches, or will they leave the action to outsiders and have to take what they get as a result?" (p. 23). We can only hope that those of us in the business of documenting student learning will respond in thoughtful, credible, and substantial ways.

This chapter describes five areas for needed scholarship. Each area identifies possible lines of scholarly inquiry and several questions that assessment practitioners need to be able to address.

Psychological and Educational Foundations

Assessment is about measuring student abilities and all the complexities that human behavior brings to the process. Measuring attributes of people is different from many other evaluation efforts, and certain theories and conceptual approaches are helpful to understand. Although there are numerous ways to categorize the psychology of educational assessment, four subareas are critical: cognitive development, psychosocial development, student motivation, and educational environments.

Cognitive Development

Although many assessment instruments focus on subject matter knowledge, many educators claim that the development of thinking skills is a central, implicit goal of college. In his model of meta-cognition, Schraw (1998) describes the goal of education as moving people from domain-specific cognition, which has limited transferability, to more conceptual levels, where people develop mental models and personal theories of thinking. Smith and Pourchat (1998) and Manktelow (1999) outline a variety of other approaches to adult learning cognition.

Assessment scholars are working on at least three applications of cognitive development. First, generic critical thinking and problem-solving skills across the curriculum are mentioned in nearly every discussion of general education. The National Education Goals (Corrallo, 1991) gave a public policy blessing to critical thinking and problem solving. Other established lines of scholarship lie in philosophy (see Chaffee, 1998; Facione, 1990; Kuhn, 1999) and psychology (see Stanovich and West, 1999, 2000).

Second, construction of assessment instruments must take into account both subject matter knowledge and cognitive levels. In many ways, education has not moved beyond Bloom's Taxonomy of Cognitive Skills (1956) in the test specification process. Embretson (1998, 1999) and Willson (1991), for example, construct distractors (wrong answers in a selective response format) according to a cognitive scheme. They recognize that incorrect answers may provide information regarding students' erroneous thinking; hence, wrong answers may provide as much useful assessment information as correct answers.

Third, several disciplines need better thinking paradigms to describe their unique approaches to instruction. For instance, Parsons (1987) utilized cognitive developmental theory in formulating stages of esthetic development. Several major disciplines have knowledge bases with short shelf lives, and identifying fleeting knowledge as the basis for assessment may cause instruments to quickly become outdated. Moreover, scholars in some major disciplines and areas of general education cannot agree upon a canon of common knowledge. In both situations, thinking strategies often become the desired focus of assessment. However, new cognitive models and conceptual approaches to assessing student learning are needed.

Psychosocial Development

While recognizing that cognitive development is important, Astin (1987) has reminded us of the importance of affective aspects of development during college. Although traditionally a purview of student affairs, increased attention is being focused on this area of college student outcomes. No doubt most of us would list concepts such as maturity, personal growth, interpersonal relationship skills, independence, identity and self-concept, and curiosity as important attributes that presumably are affected positively by the college experience.

In the past, comparisons were made between off-campus and on-campus students. Now, the advent of technologically delivered instruction necessitates comparisons with traditionally delivered on-campus instruction. The value of psychosocial outcomes may emerge as a key difference between these two types of instruction. The landmark review of scholarship in this area was conducted by Pascarella and Terenzini (1991).

Student Motivation

When no personal consequences are associated with test performance, many students are not motivated and consequently give less than full effort to the test (Wolf and Smith, 1995). If students are not motivated to do their best, their test performances are likely to be affected adversely, and the test giver is unlikely to ascertain the true proficiency levels of the students.

Although some solutions to the motivation problem have been proposed, the effectiveness of such solutions remains unclear. For example, some researchers have suggested that alternative forms of assessment, such as authentic assessment, self-assessment, or peer assessment, may have the benefit of being more intrinsically motivating to students. However, there is little empirical research to support this assertion. In fact, evidence exists (Wolf, Smith, and Birnbaum, 1995) that assessment methods requiring more effort from students (such as writing essays) are more adversely affected by low student motivation than methods requiring less effort (such as multiple-choice items). Because assessment methods that appear to be more intrinsically motivating (such as authentic assessment) also require more effort from students, it is unclear whether the use of such methods would alleviate or exacerbate the motivation problem.

Student motivation is a serious threat to validity in a number of testing contexts. Wainer (1993) expressed concern that the lack of consequences for students could influence their test performance on statewide testing systems, as well as equating procedures and international comparisons of students. Wolf and Smith (1995) suggested that this problem extends to norming studies on the NAEP. In higher education assessment, the challenge to motivate our students to give their best effort when there are few or no personal consequences is probably the most vexing assessment problem we face. Hence, identifying assessment methods that effectively motivate students is an area that deserves serious attention from assessment scholars.

Educational Environments

The fourth area to which scholarship must be addressed pertains to research on the effectiveness of educational interventions or environmental impact. Opportunities for research exist in environmental or ecological psychology; however, for this chapter, a broader conceptualization of educational environments will be described. Currently, the primary focus in outcome scholarship is on the identification, the clarification, and, particularly, the measurement of learning and development. Much work remains to be done, as is illustrated throughout this chapter. Nevertheless, questions about what works are still relevant. What produces change or improvements in outcomes? What aspects of the educational environment can be encouraged or changed? What educational environments or combination of subenvironments interacts to produce optimal learning and developmental outcomes?

In the past, instructional methods were relatively constant (for example, lecture-based) and evaluation of learning was variable (for example, instructor classroom tests). Now, instructional methods are varied with technology and other new delivery methods, and common assessment methods will become more frequent. How does assessment relate to these newly evolving models of providing education?

From the viewpoint of scholarship, instructional approaches may be conceived as one of several subenvironmental influences on college outcomes. Micek and Arney's categorization of subenvironments (1974) is still a useful place to start. These subenvironments may be organizational (for example, multiple institutions for a single student, or asynchronous versus bisynchronous), physical (for example, location of the learner, location of services, such as living-learning centers, and location of educational providers), social (for example, clubs and organizations, or one's roommate), fiscal (for example, type of financial aid package), or instructional (for example, learning styles or degree of engagement).

While assessment practitioners now focus primarily on measuring outcomes, future directions call for identifying which combination and interactions of these subenvironments will produce optimal learning and development.

Analytical Methods

We see three broad, overlapping areas of inquiry that are particularly relevant to the scholarship of assessment: qualitative methods, measurement, and statistics.

Qualitative Methods

Assessment has been and perhaps will continue to be constrained by the mandates of public policy that have favored, if not required, tests and other objective, quantitative performance indicators. And, certainly, educators have a responsibility to ensure the quality and validity of these measures, as will be discussed in the next section. Qualitative studies, nevertheless, also play a key role because assessment is a process and not just a collection of numbers for analysis.

Creswell (1997) outlined five "traditions" or areas of qualitative methodology: biography, phenomenology, grounded theory, ethnography, and case study. For explanations and discussions of these traditions, the reader is referred to Denzin (1989), Moustakas

(1994), Strauss and Corbin (1990), Hammersley and Atkinson (1995), and Stake (1995). For our purposes, how can qualitative inquiries help educators in the assessment process?

First, qualitative studies may provide our best way of gaining an understanding of which educational interventions work best. In quantitative studies, the researcher is testing hypotheses such as whether one intervention works better than another. Sometimes educators do not even know what to compare. Qualitative studies are ideal for discovery, particularly when we do not know enough to formulate a hypothesis. A second area of contribution for qualitative information may be in communicating results. The case study and biography are helpful ways to illustrate and explain outcome results when numbers simply do not portray the meaning of the collegiate experience.

Qualitative studies usually deal with unknown causes, variables, and an absence of explanatory theories (Silverman, 2000). Qualitative inquires are very useful for describing these unknowns in natural settings. The scholarship of discovering true outcomes, educational interventions, and audience needs will probably come from qualitative approaches. Unfortunately, confusion exists as to what encompasses a qualitative study; qualitative is not what is left over after quantitative research is done. Assessment practitioners should view qualitative approaches as a valuable set of research methods that complement more quantitative methods.

Measurement

From one perspective, the current assessment boom exists because of the invalidity of existing measures of quality. Input measures such as levels of student achievement at entry and outputs such as graduation and retention rates, as well as performance indicators of operational efficiency, are not strong indicators of student learning and development. Ewell (National Center for Public Policy and Higher Education, 2000) discusses the inadequacy of existing learning-based tests, arguing that they should reflect our best knowledge of instrument design. How to demonstrate validity of locally developed assessments is a central issue and a fruitful line of scholarship (Mentkowski and Associates, 2000). How can assessment methods that were originally intended to provide direction for improvement be adapted for use in demonstrating account-ability? How can we build more credible assessment instruments that minimize measurement errors and capture the intended learning?

The contexts of K–12 education and organizational behavior encompass a long history of measurement. Although many principles in these settings are applicable to the college context, particular attention in scholarship should be directed toward new formats for test questions, use of standard setting procedures (how high to set passing marks), the design of scoring rubrics for constructed response assessment formats, and ways to analyze more complex thinking processes. Many areas of measurement are relevant to the scholarship of assessment, but we will focus on three in particular: constructed response item formats (how to evaluate student products, processes, or performances), item response theory models for complex thinking processes, and structural equation modeling.

Constructed Response

Compared with selected response formats such as those used in multiple-choice tests, student-constructed responses have the potential to provide a richer array of information to assessment practitioners. Unfortunately, many assessment projects based on constructed responses fail because little planning is done regarding how the resulting data are to be analyzed. For instance, although much positive rhetoric has been devoted to the use of portfolios, the question remains: What does one do with these student products in hand? In addition to the problem of how to structure the types of products within the portfolio, faculty should consider what they hope to discover and what learning they expect before they assign portfolio construction to students. Then, how will the portfolios be evaluated? A rigorously constructed rating scale is a key to summarizing the extent of learning. Past research (Cohen, Swerdlik, and Phillips, 1996; Goldstein and Hersen, 1984; and Silva, 1993) has shown the value and shortcomings of behavioral rating scales, and much more work needs to be done to obtain useful portfolio ratings. Generalizability theory (Brennan, 1983) also offers a measurement model that can be useful in identifying the most reliable ways to collect and rate student-constructed responses.

Item Response Theory

Item response theory (IRT) describes a family of models that represent what happens when a student encounters a test item. Although the most basic models specify that the probability that the student will pass the item is simply a function of student proficiency and characteristics of the item (such as level of difficulty), more recent models represent a marriage of cognitive psychology and measurement. Such models are particularly promising for higher education assessment.

An example of such a model is the generalized graded unfolding model (Roberts, 2000; Roberts, Donoghue, and Laughlin, 2000), which would be useful for cognitive development approaches with stages or levels of greater complexity. For example, certain test responses might group together within a given level of cognitive complexity but would be inversely related to other groupings of test items characteristic of a higher level of cognitive complexity. This unfolding model gives us a technique to analyze levels of thinking, as opposed to the more traditional approach of including discrete items about subject matter knowledge. As educators employ more complex cognitive processing models in their disciplines, assessment professionals should utilize appropriate techniques to assist them in constructing or analyzing student responses.

Structural Equation Modeling

Another useful analytical procedure is structural equation modeling (SEM) (Hoyle, 1995; Kaplan, 2000). SEM is both a measurement model for estimating reliability and validity and an advanced statistical framework for testing models of relationships among many variables or outcomes.

Consider the model in Figure 4.1. Readers will choose particular subsets of these measures according to their institutional or organizational needs, but SEM is a technique to analyze the presumed causal relationships among campus subenvironments, the many college outcomes, and postgraduation behaviors. Although

Figure 4.1. A Possible Structural Equation Model for Studying Causal Relationships Among Background Characteristics, Outcomes, and Postbaccalaureate Behaviors

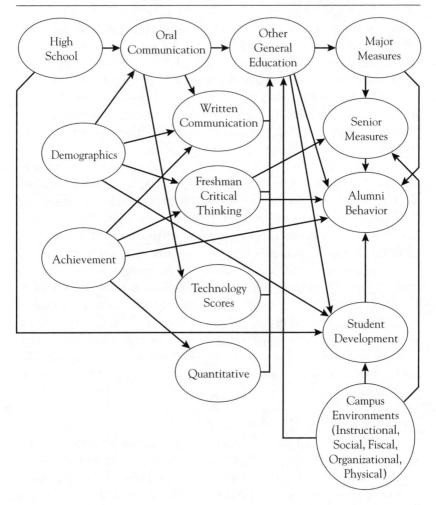

there are many dimensions or factors, SEM allows us to study their complex relationships simultaneously. Thus, SEM helps us understand the complex relationships among the multiple variables that are important to assessment.

Statistics

Like measurement, the field of statistics offers much in handling data. The challenge to assessment researchers, however, is not the development of new statistical methods; rather, it is to understand the types of data summaries that convey institutional quality most effectively, and to identify methods for clearly communicating statistics to relevant constituencies.

Two branches of statistics—descriptive and inferential—are particularly helpful to assessment professionals. In descriptive statistics, educators reduce a large amount of data to more easily managed indices, such as averages. In inferential statistics, educators may have only a small sample and may need to generalize to a larger group, such as graduating seniors. In both cases, the procedures and interpretations are vital if the intended audience is to believe and use the findings. Certainly, these issues overlap with political and communication perspectives, but the framing of the data is also critical.

"Visualization is critical to data analysis" (Cleveland, 1993, p. 1). Assessment's challenge is to present complicated information to lay audiences effectively. Scholarship needs lie in areas of data encoding and graphing strategies. Wainer's work (1996, 1997) illustrates how NAEP data can be presented in a variety of visual formats. Assessment personnel should identify an array of displays that will appeal to our various audiences, such as campus administrators, government officials, and the lay public.

More research is needed to analyze the perspectives of the various audiences that assimilate assessment information. How can technical information be presented to lay audiences? How can information about complex student outcomes such as thinking strategies be presented in understandable ways? How can competing audience goals be reconciled (for example, having assessment applications fit both improvement and accountability purposes)?

A related line of scholarship focuses on the organizational culture in higher education institutions and how organizational communication can be facilitated (Griffin, 1999). Through an understanding of the various organizational cultures, practitioners can gain a better understanding of the obstacles to assessment use and the ways in which these obstacles can be overcome.

Public Policy/Organizational Behavior

In many ways, the public policy aspects of assessment receive more attention than the implementation strategies of practice. Ewell helps practitioners understand where mandates come from and why. States, the federal government, accrediting bodies, business and industry, the public, and even higher education have put forth economic, political, and social reasons for a deluge of policies pertaining to educational accountability. Accountability is popular now, and "experts" abound. Assumptions are made in each issuance of policy, yet we don't know if these policies will accomplish desirable accountability or improvement goals.

Knowledge of the ways in which higher education is governed and organized is also useful. Do financial incentives such as performance funding and budgeting result in improved practice? How should certification of knowledge and skills be coordinated in centralized ways to ensure credibility while promoting innovation? How can incentives be structured to reward quality over quantity (for example, head counts)? Instead of having acts imposed upon us in higher education, how can we shape the formation of public policy to benefit consumers and educators? How will alternative educational providers, such as corporate universities, mesh with traditional instructional delivery systems? All of these questions beg for systematic inquiry.

Technology

Assessment personnel use technology in the delivery of assessment methods (for example, computer-based testing), in the maintenance of assessment information, and in a variety of calculations. Although much attention is given to the use of technology for instructional delivery, far less is devoted to the use of technology for assessment instruments. Multimedia formats, quicker feedback, and decision rules for test item presentation (such as computerized adaptive testing) offer new possibilities. In Chapter Eight, Shermis and Daniels offer one exciting line of scholarship: electronic reading of constructed responses from students (see also Foltz, Kintsch, and Landauer, 1998).

In addition, the prevailing model of computerized student information systems will change on college campuses. The old models were built primarily to handle finance and registration functions. As Ewell discusses in the initial chapter of this volume, the retention literature showing that good information is vital to this process has expanded. But good student information, wide-ranging in scope, is not usually available to the educator for advising purposes. How can our student information systems grow in concept and function and not just in data elements? How can higher education make these computer information systems more useful as decision support systems?

To what extent do advisers currently utilize assessment information from general education, the major, and student development to assist in promoting students' progress and growth? Integrated databases have the potential to make assessment information widely available to faculty and staff who will use this information in advising and educating students. How should these information systems be structured, maintained, and supplied with relevant information about quality?

Integrating the Parts

The scholarship areas previously described are neither discrete nor all-inclusive, and solutions to many problems in the field of assessment will require attention in two or more of these areas. For example, a connection between artificial intelligence and measurement is emerging as innovative assessment methods are developed that are matched with how students learn. Furthermore, these new assessment methods inform us concerning how we may use computers in assessments more effectively. And as we address the problems associated with student motivation, we can enhance the effectiveness of our new assessment methods. Thus, different research areas are linked, and the most creative and effective researchers will understand the relationships among the areas and how advances in one area will have implications for other areas.

Conclusion

In the 1980s, when assessment practice was dominated by "happy amateurs," as Ewell claimed, practitioners came from faculty and administrative ranks and varied backgrounds. In some cases, these backgrounds supported the advancement of assessment practice, but sometimes they did not. Since that time, assessment mandates for institutions have proliferated, the consequences of assessment have increased, and the complexity of practice has grown for campuses, educational associations, and higher education as a whole. While attendance at assessment conferences such as that sponsored by the American Association for Higher Education has remained steady, the presentation topics are inexorably evolving from the question *Why are we doing this?* to *How do we do this better?* Best practices in assessment are often "broad but not deep," to use Ewell's language. For instance, how many times have we seen students' self-perceptions of their own learning posited as surrogate outcomes, only to watch their lack of credibility with outside audiences imply our weak commitment to calls for data about quality?

Admittedly, the various areas identified in this chapter are disjointed at first glance. What do cognitive development, psychosocial development, student motivation, qualitative methods, measurement, constructed response, item response theory, statistics, structural equation modeling, public policy, and technology have in common? The answer is, they are all aspects of the *practice* of assessment. Assessment is an emerging profession, and like any profession, it draws upon multiple disciplines. Established lines of scholarship, the primary focus of this book, remain ill-defined and devoid of assessment-specific research applications at this point. Nevertheless, the need and opportunity exist for developing lines of scholarship that lead to better evidence of accountability and better student learning and development. Research questions are ubiquitous; it is time for scholarship to mature. Higher education is beyond the question of whether assessment *should* exist and is now asking how it can incorporate better methodology and yield greater benefits for students and society.

Higher education faculty have taken pride in the instructional rigor of their disciplines. Educators should expect no less sophistication in how we document our work with students. Some knowledge can be applied now, but there are many gaps to fill in creating our field's scholarship. The new scholarship of assessment requires our attention; it is now time to advance our field with systematic and thoughtful study.

Chapter Five

Enacting a Collaborative Scholarship of Assessment

Marcia Mentkowski and Georgine Loacker

The approach to a scholarship of assessment in this chapter considers issues that emerge when educators across a range of disciplines and institutions are engaged in the renewal of undergraduate education. Curriculum and institutional transformation can be influenced positively when assessment is learning-centered and student learning outcomes are primary measures of individual student and educational system outcomes. Scholarship can play a role in sustaining efforts of transformation when it connects learning, teaching, and assessment; calls for joint responsibility for inquiry; and integrates theory, research, and practice.

In this chapter we trace what has been learned about assessment from several collaborative inquiry processes and products that meet scholarly criteria. We discuss issues that assessment scholars have experienced in association-sponsored activities and funded consortia of institutions. We close with implications for an effective collaborative scholarship of assessment.

Definitions and Criteria

We view a scholarship of assessment as part of a broader discussion educators are having about the scholarship of teaching and learning. Just as Hutchings and Shulman (1999) distinguish between scholarly teaching and the scholarship of teaching, we distinguish between scholarly assessment and the scholarship of assessment.

Scholarly assessment means that each educator is using the best available knowledge and skills to create, validate, and continually improve instruments and assessment processes toward improving and demonstrating student learning. A key question for scholarly assessment is "How do we do assessment more effectively so that it meets its purposes and expectations?"

The *scholarship of assessment* means to actively pursue systematic inquiry on assessment as a member of a community of professionals. Extending scholarly assessment to include a scholarship of assessment suggests a gradually maturing field that challenges the meaning, methods, results, and consequences of assessment.

In our analysis of scholarly activities, we use these basic features of scholarly and professional work as criteria for scholarship:

- The activity requires a high level of discipline-related expertise.
- The activity breaks new ground, is innovative.
- The activity can be replicated or elaborated.
- The work and its results can be documented.
- The work and its results can be peer-reviewed.
- The activity has significance or impact (Diamond, 1995, p. 21).

Rationale for Collaborative Scholarship

Scholars of assessment are as closely tied to questions about the meaning of the undergraduate degree as they are to assessing student learning outcomes toward improving undergraduate learning. Three issues arise: (1) connecting learning, teaching, and assessment; (2) taking joint responsibility for inquiry; and (3) integrating theory, research, and practice.

Connecting Learning, Teaching, and Assessment

Topics for scholarship include what ought to be, can be, and is being learned. *Scholarly assessment* usually focuses on what is being learned. *Scholarship of assessment* extends that focus to the reflective core of the individual student as well as to the reflective core of a classroom, educational program, institution, or system of institutions. Here, faculty and staff need to balance *what students ought to learn* (in order to benefit both learner and society), *what is possible for students to achieve* (reasonable yet high expectations), and *what students are actually learning* (now and later, linked to teaching). Thus, assessment becomes new knowledge to each and all: student, faculty and staff member, department, institution, accrediting agency, and state policy board. Each needs to engage the deeply held values inherent in balancing what is, what ought to be, and what is possible. Discovering this balance often calls for scholarly activities where connection and engagement are the norm.

Other sources of intellectual challenge in a scholarship of assessment are the changing definitions of complex student learning outcomes and how students ought to be taught to learn them. These challenges inspire commitment to joint curriculum renewal. Yet connecting assessment results to strategies for continuous improvement calls for similar commitment to collaborative learning by educators. When assessment as a means to improvement connects with how faculty determine, define, and teach student learning outcomes across and within the disciplines, then administrators, faculty, and staff are more likely to value joint interpretation of assessment results. Does educators' collaborative work have the potential for *breaking new ground*—a criterion for scholarship?

Taking Joint Responsibility for Inquiry

At an early stage, the assessment "community of practice" focused attention on demonstrating learning outcomes and improving learning. In the American Association for Higher Education (AAHE), educators from across the fine arts, humanities, and sciences disciplines, as well as those from educational research, measurement, judgment, and evaluation, began to take joint responsibility for assessment. This new field has also required campus teams of administrators, faculty, and staff who are committed to the renewal of undergraduate learning. These various groups may view generating and using assessment data about student learning as (1) a means of communication across campus in the struggle for renewal, (2) a credibility and trust-building exercise that creates public dialogue with outside audiences asking for accountability, and (3) a scholarly activity that leads to new discoveries, connections, applications, and improved teaching and student learning.

When educators enact a collaborative scholarship of assessment, there is an opportunity to meet the scholarly criterion—*the activity breaks new ground, it is innovative.* When interdisciplinary conceptual frameworks are brought to the table and integrated by multidisciplinary teams, the possibility for creating educational theory is there. Even so, scholarly activity still *requires a high level of discipline-related expertise.* Each team member becomes responsible for articulating, negotiating, and pooling his/her diverse perspectives and expertise, sources of ideas and evidence, and contexts of practice to develop innovations through rigorous and deliberative inquiry (see Mentkowski and Associates, 2000).

For the scholarship of discovery to merge with the scholarship of integration and application (Boyer, 1990), scholarly products need to provide new insights, integrate multiple sources, and show benefits for teaching approaches that lead to student learning. Products also need to invite rigorous internal and external *peer review of both the work and its results,* another form of collaborative scholarship.

Integrating Theory, Research, and Practice

Another issue for the assessment community has been integrating theory, research, and practice, because a key advance in the movement was to conceptualize assessment as an integrating function. This has meant developing a shared understanding of the value and means of studying how learners are now learning—across a major program or entire curriculum—so that educators in quite different roles can share in determining the *ought* of undergraduate learning. Making complex student learning outcomes such as critical thinking explicit across general education means understanding learning and assessment as developmental yet cyclical processes. In this context, a scholarship of assessment has become more interdisciplinary and inclusive across levels of educational practice.

The usual strains of creating a multidisciplinary field have challenged the AAHE community from the start. AAHE leadership called meetings of heterogeneous assessment leaders from across various sectors and created a kind of pluralism that still maintained a clear focus for the movement and enabled the institutionalization of program, curriculum, or institution-wide assessment of some kind at many colleges and universities. Without this gradually increasing involvement across higher education, assessment might have languished as just another fad stemming from a single discipline. Other such developments survived by connecting with broader issues in higher education—for example, writing across the curriculum, educational research on learning styles and processes and cognitive development, systems approaches to higher education management, and new psychometric theories in measurement and evaluation. Individuals from disciplines that rely more on interpretive analyses and judgments than a measurement and systems theory approach often have made up more than half of the participants at AAHE assessment conferences. From the start, how each group might learn from the others has been a key issue, and many leaders in the assessment movement began early to conduct workshops and other activities for a broad range of educators who had responsibilities for assessing student learning. The ultimate success of the movement is dependent on the broad expertise across the disciplines that results from the learning/teaching/assessment connection and makes collaborative scholarship particularly appropriate.

Processes and Products of Collaborative Scholarship

Mastering collaborative scholarly processes as a community may involve conferencing and face-to-face interactive study, data collection, analysis, and interpretive synthesis that is followed by the authoring group's critique of its product, response to external peer review, and some form of publication. They may also result in a scholarly product. Here we assess several such products for ways they might meet scholarly criteria: research agendas, principles, and conceptual frameworks; publications from consortia of institutions where representatives have helped to conceptualize, study, and build a language for assessment; and documents from contributors to the revision of the standards for educational and psychological testing. These products may be an association's publications including articles, research agendas, and monographs; reports to funding agencies, or a consortium's conference proceedings published as a book or other document.

Some of these products may have such a limited audience that the product alone, even though it meets one scholarly criterion—*the work and its results can be documented,* ultimately fails to meet another criterion—*the activity has significance or impact.* Multiple campus authorship becomes critical in these cases because the product has the potential to influence broader program or institutional renewal and needs to meet the criterion—*the activity can be replicated or elaborated.*

The following analysis of processes and products illustrates (1) determining what to study, (2) creating conceptual frameworks, (3) elaborating (adapting rather than replicating) scholarly activity across consortia of institutions, and (4) contributing to learned societies. Our analysis is limited to products that, in our view, meet the Diamond (1995) criteria. It is also limited to products resulting from a collaborative process and synthesis of results that we formulated or otherwise participated in. Thus, we experienced the historical and social context of these works, which has influenced our analysis.

Determining What to Study

The necessary connection between learning and assessment has begun to require that scholarly assessment incorporate broader frameworks. Yet the meaning of what is, ought to be, and can be learned is continually changing. An analysis of eight research agendas from the American Association for Higher Education Research Forum (1987–1993) and from Mentkowski and Chickering (1987) shows members consistently articulating new meanings for assessment and its role as a grounding function in the academy, provided that its connection to student learning is made explicit. An analysis of annual research agendas created by 1,850 AAHE Research Forum contributors from approximately 609 institutions, associations, or agencies between 1985 and 1996 tracks this topic in higher education renewal:

> The discourse shifted back and forth—from teaching to learning to assessment; from general education to the major to institutional context to community. . . . We questioned how to become more

responsive and responsible for student outcomes. Assessment was a "topic" at first. It quickly became central to building public trust as we pondered the call for new evidence and using it to improve. We wondered how to connect assessment across levels: student, classroom, curriculum, state, national. Linking inputs, interventions, and learning outcomes meant connecting teachers with student needs, institutions with their missions, and public expectations with new standards [American Association for Higher Education Research Forum, 1996].

This issue has been central to results from collaborative inquiry that have sustained the assessment movement—for example, the report *Involvement in Learning* (Study Group on the Conditions of Excellence in American Higher Education, 1984). Leaders in the assessment community have been determined to reframe assessment as a means to learning for each member of the campus at every level of practice. "The conversation eventually returned to involvement in teaching and dimensions of the faculty role: teacher, learner, assessor, service provider, scholar. Ultimately it included a redefinition of scholarship and the creating of a 'knowing' community where faculty could recommit to the professoriate's value and ethical base and its moral compact with students, institutions, and society" (American Association for Higher Education Research Forum, 1996).

The struggles associated with collaborative inquiry are evident:

As we connected *topics* to broaden and deepen the range of issues, we engaged in more complex discussions. Presenters and participants showed an unusual impatience for talk about definitions and moved quickly to get beyond the hot topic and a set of buzz words to scout out the ambiguities and disconfirming evidence in areas that had high priority for improving educational quality. We often gravitated to the conflicts among purposes, perspectives, and even persons to probe new ways of thinking about a problem. . . .
New questions, recycled through earlier ones, prompted a more sophisticated level of understanding . . . Connections between theory, practice, and improvement became more explicit. New *insights* emerged over time . . . linking assessment to learning brought insight to how student development could walk hand

in hand with holding students to expectations, and clarified how standards could give meaning to degrees [American Association for Higher Education Research Forum, 1996].

Creating Conceptual Frameworks

In the late 1980s and early 1990s, the AAHE Assessment Forum regularly convened twelve assessment leaders from eleven institutions, associations, and agencies to explore a vision of education that linked assessment and improved student learning. From this broader effort came the publication of *Principles of Good Practice for Assessing Student Learning* (American Association for Higher Education, 1992). The principles were created to support campus assessment leaders. Their aim was to "synthesize important work already done and to invite further statements about the responsible and effective conduct of assessment" (p. 1). The principles were widely disseminated by AAHE and were used to frame scholarly contributions (Banta, Lund, Black, and Oblander, 1996). They connected assessment practice with other disciplines, notably the work on learning principles in learned societies, such as the American Psychological Association (Lambert and McCombs, 1998; Mentkowski, 1998). The tone of the principles is clearly based in educational values and vision.

Assessment leaders participating in the development of the principles were well aware of the deeper paradigm shifts that assessment practitioners were confronting in conducting scholarly assessment, and a parallel document—*Catching Theory Up with Practice* (Mentkowski, Astin, Ewell, and Moran, 1991)—more fully articulated these shifts and synthesized informal conversations held over a three-year period—some of them audiotaped, transcribed, and analyzed. K. Patricia Cross noted in the foreword of that publication that the conversation was not framed around how to assess but, rather, how to think about assessment. The authors' analysis confronted the lack of theoretical underpinnings to support and direct assessment practice. E. Thomas Moran noted, "I think one of the reasons why assessment has failed to have the impact on faculty cultures that we hoped it would is that we're not allowing other ways of knowing to surface in the assessment process. There's a hegemony of traditional psychometric theory; other ways of know-ing that are characteristic of other disciplines—for example, the humanities—are not seen as relevant or valid in generating assess-ment data" (p. 17). Moran also comments, "In traditional empiri-cism, instrumental or technical reasoning dominates over other forms of inquiry and judgment. Because empiricism downplays historical and social context, there's too little consideration of 'community' as a source of knowledge, values, or behavior. The instrumental logic of empiricism leads us to focus on the *means* by which we know something, rather than focusing on the substantive questions we are attempting to resolve" (p. 19).

As "how to do assessment" began to reflect broader conceptual frameworks and a wider range of methods and instruments, vari-ous higher education institutions that had been developing broad-based support for assessment on their own campuses were well positioned to contribute to theories of assessment that were con-nected to curriculum and program development. It remained to connect assessment to learning as part of each individual student's learning process—as a way to maximize learning for individuals, their personal development, and their ability to connect knowing and doing (Loacker, Cromwell, and O'Brien, 1986). Such efforts to connect learning, assessment, and curriculum became particu-larly relevant because these efforts closely related what ought to be learned with how and when students were actually learning.

Some in the field began to see the development of connections among learning, curriculum, and assessment primarily in terms of "institutional case studies" or "campus exemplars" and assumed that campus assessment models have their primary origins in extant learning theories, measurement theories, or higher educa-tion systems theories. In our view, the scholarship of assessment is also embedded in and connected to how students and faculty have conceptualized learning and developed curriculum on those cam-puses that have forged the connections effectively. Examples include Alverno College, Central Missouri State University, Clark College (Vancouver, Washington), Clayton State College and Uni-versity, James Madison University, Kings College, and Purdue University School of Pharmacy and Pharmacal Sciences.

Assessment leaders at these campuses have often been stymied because the meaning of assessment seems to become so embedded in institutional assessment systems theory that assessment becomes an end in itself. Institution-wide assessment has seemed to drift farther toward accountability purposes that push campuses to compete with each other for funding rather than toward linking assessment purposes more strongly to an institution's mission for undergraduate learning. Clearly, one philosophical framework within the liberal arts and student affairs promises individual growth and learner development of high-level intellectual skills that enable contribution to others and to society. This conceptual framework, grounded in what ought to be learned and assessed, seemed to some to have less weight in the debate. However, it had a salutary effect. It contributed to the early recognition that assessment cannot succeed without scholarship to connect learning, teaching, and assessment.

Elaborating Scholarly Activity Across Consortia of Institutions

Campuses that have emphasized these links in assessing what students are learning have joined together to form consortia to study renewal in learning-centered education. They have recognized that they can learn together from assessment programs with quite diverse goals, thus meeting the scholarly criterion—*the activity can be replicated or elaborated.*

For example, the Consortium for the Improvement of Teaching, Learning and Assessment (1992), funded by the W.K. Kellogg Foundation, included thirty-two representatives of eleven diverse institutions from five educational levels: secondary, community college, college, university, and graduate professional school. Through a collaborative process, institutional representatives published questions to guide development of an outcome-oriented, performance-based curriculum:

- How do we conceptualize outcomes?

- What complex, multidimensional abilities (outcomes) do we have in common, and what developmental levels and performance criteria define them?

- What are our assessment principles?

- What is good evidence?

- How do we create a community of learning?—a community of judgment?

- How do we validate performance assessment—in particular, expert judgment?

- How do we use information from assessment to improve teaching and learning?

- How do we communicate what we have learned so that we and others can use the information? [p. 6]

These questions speak to joint scholarship and illustrate that "the social structure of scholarship is organized around communication" (Fox, 1985, p. 255). As a result, the Consortium for the Improvement of Teaching, Learning and Assessment (1992) (1) conducted close analyses of their practice for what they had learned and studied goal achievement toward learning-centered education, (2) documented evidence for broad curriculum and institutional changes within and across institutions that sustain improvement, and (3) generated shared educational assumptions about learning, assessment, and curriculum. They used the products to create public dialogue at workshops and conferences.

In the Faculty Consortium for Assessment Design, sponsored by the Fund for the Improvement of Postsecondary Education, eighty-two educators in disciplines ranging from biology to writing to integrated arts at the twenty-four participating institutions collaborated to review principles of student assessment and design. The educators then developed, implemented, and evaluated more than sixty-five assessment instruments for use on their various campuses (Schulte and Loacker, 1994). The questions that shape assessment design probe the validity of the assessment process: "For each outcome, what are the indicators or broad criteria that I will look for in a student's performance to verify that he or she is demonstrating the expected outcome? . . . If someone other than I will assess, how will I train the assessors? . . . How will I build in the opportunity for students to assess their own performance? . . . How will I deal with grades for the assessment? How will this assessment connect with other courses in the curriculum?" (pp. 196–197).

An assumption underlying the Faculty Consortium for Assessment Design work was that learning that *does* accrue is easily lost—or "forgotten"—after most multiple-choice exams. Rather, learners maximize learning processes and outcomes when they have diverse opportunities to demonstrate what they have learned across a curriculum and to integrate it via capstone assessments. Learners do better when they are assisted to contrast and integrate their own interpretations of learning experiences and performances via self assessment and analyses of their own portfolios. These assumptions—particularly on the value of self assessment—needed further study and therefore spurred studies on our own campus.

Probing the essential connections between student assessment and deep and durable learning has led us and our colleagues to integrate four data sources: (1) formal research and theory, (2) reviews of literature and practice, (3) collaborative inquiry by educators from a hundred diverse institutions in ten consortia, and (4) learning by educating—that is, developing the understanding that emerges from the continually changing context of educators' experiences and their constantly modified practice. What did we learn from this diversity of viewpoints about the relationships between lasting learning and self assessment? Learning endures beyond the college experience, in part, when students have internalized the components of assessment processes through a multitude of assessment strategies and opportunities to evaluate their own work. Students who were able to self assess also connected their integrative assessment experiences to the faculty's rationale for self assessment. Formal longitudinal research showed that learning becomes deep and expansive because three transformative learning cycles integrate four domains of growth. One such cycle clarifies the critical role of self assessment: students' capacity for assessing their own role performance—using criteria and standards from diverse sources—connects one domain of growth (performance) with another (self-reflection) (Mentkowski and Associates, 2000). Exploring how self assessment contributes to learning in varied disciplines has also led to the discovery of a generic framework of developmental behaviors that can provide a starting place for study (Alverno College Faculty, 1979/1994; 2000). Would these findings hold up to further collaborative inquiry across campuses?

The Pew Charitable Trusts has supported the Student Learning Initiative (SLI) (2002), which is made up of seventy-one representatives of twenty-six institutions that have created a framework of principles and practices involved in making student learning a central focus. One characteristic of learning-centered institutions that developed the framework is that they are "coordinating teaching and assessment to improve student learning" (p. 3). The SLI Consortium learned that:

> No dimension of assessment practice is as widely shared among the members of this initiative as self assessment. Yet, from our sharing of experiences, we realize that we have only begun to tap the potential for learning through self assessment. Self assessments by students should move beyond assertions without evidence or detailed listings of behaviors without reflection. At its best, self assessment includes careful observations and analysis of one's performance and judgment of its quality or effectiveness. What we have discovered through our discourse is that self assessment, like any other higher order intellectual skill we may have identified as a learning outcome for our students, needs to be carefully taught in a developmental way [Student Learning Initiative, 2002, p. 17].

In this ground-breaking observation, self assessment is a student learning outcome that connects assessment, learning, and teaching.

Contributing to Learned Societies

The criterion for scholarship—*the activity has significance or impact*—is further illustrated in collaboration across professional associations. The connection between what ought to be learned and how to assess it has brought campus assessment leaders into the dialogue about revising the standards for educational and psychological testing. Early in the movement, assessment leaders had articulated the problems of using standardized testing as the primary mechanism for assessing student learning outcomes (Adelman, 1986). When the American Educational Research Association (AERA), the American Psychological Association (APA), and the National Council on Measurement in Education (NCME) standards for educational and psychological testing were being revised from 1994 to 1999 (American Educational Research Association, American Psychological Association, and National Council on Measurement in Education, 1999), the AAHE had an opportunity to influence this process. Some members saw this as an opportunity to modify the *Standards* to reflect the current theory, research, and practice in higher education assessment, and also to provide substantive arguments for an evolving psychometric theory for performance assessment and the need to emphasize consequential validity in validating assessment processes and instruments (see Messick, 1994; Rogers, 1994). Other members were not so sure of the benefits.

> Participants in the June 13, 1994, discussions debated how "assessment," as it has been diversely defined and articulated in higher education theory and practice, ought to be included in the *Standards*. Some participants suggested that the *Standards* remain specific to their original purposes and audiences and that higher education assessment theory and practice not be included.
> One concern is that experimentation and interdisciplinary dialogue may be lost. Efforts to professionalize assessment by a few disciplines could become exclusionary and so limit the range of potential practitioners or practices. Another concern is that the current *Standards* are designed primarily for psychological testing of individuals for clinical assessment, for educational testing used for selection to educational programs, or for credentialing. These purposes do not necessarily converge with the newer purposes of assessment that include individual student learning and development, demonstrating changes in complex student learning outcomes over time as a result of curriculum, judging program and institutional effectiveness in terms of student learning outcomes, and so on. The *Standards* may not be able to integrate all of the multiple frameworks involved: diverse value systems, epistemological paradigms, and role perspectives.
> Other participants suggested that the *Standards* do converge across purposes, even as emerging purposes and practices expand and challenge the *Standards*. Still others suggested that the *Standards* should be extended to include the concept of assessment (as distinct from testing) with appropriate definitions and distinctions among key terms, concepts, and applications [American Association for Higher Education, 1994b, p. 3].

Thirty-five AAHE members from the arts, humanities, and sciences disciplines at twenty-four institutions, associations, and agencies (some were also members of AERA, APA, or NCME) documented and synthesized their collaborative inquiry over a four-year period, including their individual written perspectives. Members interactively articulated the difficulties with standardized testing more precisely, engaged in public dialogue, interwove their own concerns with those of the *Standards* revision team through testimony, and provided an ongoing synthesis of their arguments for the revision team (American Association for Higher Education, 1994b; Joint Committee on the Standards for Educational and Psychological Testing, 1994). Some of what they concluded follows.

- New purposes for assessment need to be examined in the context of practice. Assessment is justified because it facilitates student learning, yet this purpose for assessment is not addressed in the *Standards*. Institutional improvement and learning are also new purposes. Each should be addressed.

- New purposes imply new uses. Because assessment serves multiple purposes, many new uses may be attended to in the *Standards,* such as individual student learning, program and institutional improvement, institutional planning, state and institutional policy setting, accreditation, program review, and performance funding. The *Standards* should not be so stringent that they discredit diverse and multiple uses for assessment, such as student learning outcomes assessment . . .

- The assessment of complex, multidimensional, integrated student learning outcomes—such as critical thinking, effective communication, and problem solving—implies new assessment theory and revised *Standards* that include student performance assessment within the context of the disciplines and professions (integrating assessment of knowledge, behavior, skills, attitudes, dispositions, and values) as well as links to performance indicators of institutional effectiveness . . .

- The validity and reliability of new purposes, uses, and forms of performance assessment and performance indicators call for an extended exploration of contextual and consequential validity. . . .

- Assessment should: be flexible in mode, avoid harm *and* promote learning, assess educational outcomes as advertised and that students have had an opportunity to learn, provide students opportunity to question assessments, and provide prompt and comprehensive feedback on performance . . . [American Association for Higher Education, 1994b, pp. 4–7].

Did this and other group feedback meet the scholarly criterion— *have significance or impact?* One example stands out. Many AAHE group members expected to see the term *fairness* defined diversely as lack of bias, equitable treatment in the testing process, and equality in outcomes of testing. Due in part to the AAHE group contributions, we believe, *fairness* is now also defined as opportunity to learn in the *Standards.* However, the group had also argued that individual feedback on student performance and opportunity to self assess in relation to explicit performance criteria are essential parts of opportunity to learn. Nevertheless, these elements are not included specifically in the meaning of fairness as an opportunity to learn; nor do the *Standards* emphasize the role of assessment that assists the individual to design his or her future learning—a role that establishes consequential validity. In the AAHE group's view, assessment ought to be a learning opportunity for students who seek to improve and for administrators, faculty, and staff who are improving curriculum and assessment systems. Recent studies of measuring learning opportunities underscore this point (Herman, Klein, and Abedi, 2000).

A continuing issue for the scholarship of assessment concerns how feedback and self assessment opportunities should be designed so that faculty and other assessment staff can use assessment results for instrument validation and program improvement. Such a new understanding of feedback and self assessment can strengthen educator performance and can contribute to effective assessment processes—a long-term goal of scholars of assessment. The 1999 *Standards,* however, do not include faculty-designed instruments among instruments that should meet the *Standards.* Consequently, the assessment community must set its own criteria.

Implications for a Collaborative Scholarship of Assessment

An effective joint scholarship of assessment involves:

- Creating opportunities for determining questions, processes, products, and uses that meet criteria for scholarship
- Shaping the role of professional associations, "exemplar" campuses, and consortia of institutions as active contributors of scholarly experiences and products rather than as passive case studies
- Mapping the sources of contributors' expertise and creating processes for rigorous deliberative inquiry
- Encouraging each member to provide, analyze, and integrate practices that meet disciplinary criteria for scholarship
- Integrating ways of knowing about assessment (for example, formal research, literature and practice review, collaborative inquiry, and learning about assessment by doing it), and developing methods from points of coherence within a diversity of disciplines and practices, as well as taking joint responsibility for results that articulate value conflicts and differences of interpretation
- Presenting and publishing joint results that engage public dialogue and can be studied for impact
- Encouraging scholars of learning, teaching, and assessment to conceptualize educational theories of assessment that consolidate psychometric and learning theories
- Integrating the value frameworks of other disciplines with those inherent in the professional role of assessment practitioner and developing criteria for the role of assessment designer and assessor as part of the professoriate, as well as studying how the faculty role and criteria for performance intersect with those of practicing professionals in educational research, evaluation, and measurement
- Studying the impact of joint scholarship on student learning outcomes, assessment processes, and infrastructures for assessing student learning that is deep, durable, expansive, purposeful, and responsible

Acknowledgments

The authors acknowledge the 2,082 individuals from approximately 705 institutions, associations, and agencies who have co-led and participated in creating the scholarly products cited in this chapter. Individual contributors are named in the original documents. In particular, we thank American Association for Higher Education (AAHE) Research Forum supporters Lou Albert, Barbara Cambridge, Russ Edgerton, Margaret A. Miller, Yolanda Moses, Kathleen Curry Santora, and Research Forum organizers of long standing: Arthur Chickering, K. Patricia Cross, Catherine Marienau, Judith Reisetter Hart, and Sharon Rubin. We also thank AAHE assessment directors from 1985 to 2002: Ted Marchese, Pat Hutchings, Barbara Wright, Karl Schilling, Tom Angelo, Barbara Cambridge, Catherine Wehlburg, Linda Suskie, and Peggy Maki.

Chapter Six

The Scholarly Assessment of Student Development

George D. Kuh, Robert M. Gonyea,
and Daisy P. Rodriguez

Developing human potential is a core function of higher education. Although thousands of studies have focused on various aspects of college student learning and development, much of this research has not been used in any systematic way to improve institutional policies and practices or the assessment methods and tools used to collect the data. It's now time to do so, particularly since colleges and universities are being pressed from many quarters to document what students gain from attending college. A scholarly approach to assessing student development differs from traditional research studies of the impact of college on students in two important ways. First, scholarly assessment projects are designed to produce high-quality information that can be used for various purposes, such as guiding policy and decision making, improving practice, and demonstrating effectiveness to external authorities. Second, the process of instrument development, data collection, and reporting of results is iterative, mediated by reflection and continuous improvement. These ideas are consistent with Boyer's (1990) useful knowledge and the scholarship of application and also the contributions on scholarly practice (Carpenter, 2001), the scholar-practitioner model (Schroeder and Pike, 2001), and communities of practice (Blimling, 2001).

This chapter examines the current state of the art of the scholarship of student development assessment. First, we define student development and briefly summarize the origins of various approaches to assessing it. Our focus is on tools and methods used to assess aspects of undergraduate student development that are influenced by experiences inside or outside the classroom, rather than on tests or other devices designed to measure content acquisition at the individual major or specific classroom levels. Then we draw on examples from the field to illustrate how scholarly approaches to assessing student development are helping to modify educational practice and improve assessment instruments and processes. Finally, we share some observations about the state of the art of the scholarship of assessing student development.

Student Development Defined

Student development is both a process and a holistic set of desired outcomes (Banta and Associates, 1993; Evans, Forney, and Guido-DiBrito, 1998; Kuh and Stage, 1992; Rodgers, 1989). As a process, student development is the unfolding of human potential toward increasingly complicated and refined levels of functioning. As a set of outcomes, student development encompasses a host of desirable skills, knowledge, competencies, beliefs, and attitudes students are supposed to cultivate during college. These include (a) complex cognitive skills such as reflection and critical thinking, (b) an ability to apply knowledge to practical problems encountered in one's vocation, family, or other areas of life, (c) an understanding and appreciation of human differences, (d) practical competencies such as decision making, conflict resolution, and teamwork, and (e) a coherent integrated sense of identity, self-esteem, confidence, integrity, aesthetic sensibilities, spirituality, and civic responsibility (American College Personnel Association, 1994; Kuh and Stage, 1992). More than a few instruments and protocols have been developed to assess this broad range of human abilities, skills, and competencies, and we mention some of these tools in this chapter. For a more complete review of many of these instruments and protocols, see Borden and Zak Owens (2001), Upcraft and Schuh (1996), Evans, Forney, and Guido-DiBrito (1998), and Palomba and Banta (1999).

Assessing Student Development: 1930s to the Present

Student development assessment dates back to at least the 1930s with studies of both currently enrolled students (for example, Jones, 1938; McConnell, 1934; Pressy, 1946) and alumni (Havemann and West, 1952; Newcomb, 1943). Through much of the 1960s, the focus was on measuring attitudes, interests, and other aspects of personality functioning of traditional-age college students, such as authoritarianism and motivation for learning. The Omnibus Personality Inventory (OPI), the California Psychological Inventory, and the Minnesota Multiphasic Personality Inventory were used frequently enough during the 1950s and 1960s to warrant the development of national norms. The OPI was particularly popular, becoming the instrument of choice for multiple institutional studies of student development (Chickering, 1969; Clark and others, 1972). Then, as now, pencil-and-paper questionnaires tended to dominate assessment efforts, though some definitive work was done with individual interviews of alumni (for example, Newcomb, 1943; White, 1952) and enrolled students (Heath, 1968).

Interest in measuring the impact of college on students came of age in the 1960s, stimulated in large part by the publication of such classics as *Changing Values in College* (Jacob, 1957), *The American College* (Sanford, 1962), *The Impact of College on Students* (Feldman and Newcomb, 1969), *Education and Identity* (Chickering, 1969), *No Time for Youth* (Katz and Korn, 1968), and *Growing Up in College* (Heath, 1968). This work, coupled with the emergence of the national college student research program of the University of California, Los Angeles (UCLA) (Astin, 1977; 1993), prompted the much-needed formulation of developmental theories in the 1960s and 1970s that described the complex, holistic processes by which students grow, change, and develop during the college years. The emergence of student development theory, in turn, shaped the next generation of assessment tools and processes. In fact, the conceptual underpinnings of many student development assessment tools are rooted in one or more of four categories: psychosocial theories, cognitive-structural theories, person-environment interaction theories, and typology models (Kuh and Stage, 1992; Rodgers, 1989; Widick, Knefelkamp, and Parker, 1980).

Psychosocial theories describe how individuals resolve challenges and personal growth issues at different stages or periods during the life cycle with the development of identity being central. Chickering's (1969) theory is the best known, holding that every student must master seven "vectors of development": developing confidence, managing emotions, developing autonomy, establishing identity, developing freeing interpersonal relationships, developing purpose, and developing integrity. The Student Developmental Task and Lifestyle Inventory (Prince, Miller, and Winston, 1974; Winston, 1990) measures three of Chickering's vectors: establishing and clarifying purpose, developing mature interpersonal relationships, and developing autonomy. Albert Hood, from the University of Iowa, and several of his doctoral students, developed a collection of instruments known as the Iowa Student Development Inventories, which, taken together, assess all but one of Chickering's seven vectors: developing integrity (Hood, 1986). Instruments have also been developed specifically to measure the psychosocial development of Blacks and Latinos, including Sue's Minority Identity Development model (Sue and Sue, 1990) and Cross's Model of Psychological Nigrescence (Cross, Strauss, and Fhagen-Smith, 1999).

Cognitive structural theories describe the processes by which people move from fairly simplistic, dualistic ("right or wrong") judgments and reasoning abilities to more complicated, reflective understandings and constructions of reality. Among the prominent theorists in this family are Perry (1970), King and Kitchener (1994), Baxter Magolda (1992), Kohlberg (1981), Gilligan (1982), and Fowler (1981). Originally, development was assessed via standardized interview protocols, but, more recently, pencil-and-paper instruments have been developed to make measuring certain aspects of cognitive-structural development more feasible. In addition, certain of the theories and instruments have been adapted for use with Black and Latino students (see Atkinson, Morten, and Sue, 1993; Banks, 1993; Shaw, 2000).

Person-environment interaction theories hold that individual performance is optimized when one's needs and abilities are congruent with the demands of the environment (Strange and Banning, 2001). Although these models do not describe developmental processes or outcomes, they do help explain why some students find certain institutional environments compatible and others unappealing. This, in turn, contributes to student-institution fit and satisfaction, which directly and indirectly affect various aspects of student development (Pascarella and Terenzini, 1991) as well as student satisfaction and retention (Astin, 1977, 1993; Bean, 1986; Bean and Bradley, 1986; Pascarella and Terenzini, 1991; Tinto, 1993). Examples include Holland's theory of vocational choice (1973, 1985, 1994), Stern's need/press theory (1970), and Moos's social ecological approach (Moos, 1979; Moos and Brownstein, 1977; Moos and Insel, 1974), using such tools as the University Residence Environment Scale (Moos and Gerst, 1976) and the Classroom Environment Scale (Moos and Trickett, 1976) to describe the characteristics of different environments.

Typology models sort individuals into categories according to their similarities and differences related to how they manage and cope with common developmental tasks inherent in the collegiate setting. Inventories using this approach have been developed by Myers-Briggs (Myers and Myers, 1995) and Kolb (Ballou, Bowers, Boyatzis, and Kolb, 1999; Boyatzis and Kolb, 1991). As with the person-environment models, typologies do not claim to describe development per se, but, rather, they explain individual preferences that can help predict performance under various circumstances. For example, after analyzing patterns of student self-reported behavior, Kuh, Hu, and Vesper (2000) discovered eight dominant groups of undergraduates, some of whom were very engaged in educationally purposeful activities.

Another perspective that is increasingly being used to assess student development is to look at process indicators that represent the extent to which students engage in the activities that predict desired learning and personal development outcomes. Process indicators include such activities as studying, reading, writing, interacting with peers from diverse backgrounds, discussing ideas from classes and readings with faculty members, and so forth (Kuh, 2001a). The college student development research shows that these types of activities are precursors to high levels of student learning and personal development (Banta and Associates, 1993; Ewell and Jones, 1996). Among the better-known process indicators are the seven "good educational practices," such as setting high expectations and providing prompt feedback (Chickering and Gamson, 1987), as well as other features of student-centered learning environments, which include focusing resources on first-year students and creating a learner-centered culture (Education Commission of the States, 1995). This approach to assessing the student and institutional behaviors associated with student development is very appealing because it provides information that can be used immediately to improve undergraduate education. The conceptual underpinnings for this approach are consistent with Astin's "theory of involvement" (1984), Pace's concept of "quality of effort" (1982), and the "involving colleges" framework described by Kuh and others (1991). Instruments that assess student engagement include the College Student Experiences Questionnaire (Pace and Kuh, 1998), The College Student Report (Kuh, 1999), and UCLA's College Student Survey.

This brief review shows that a variety of theoretical and empirical models exist to guide the scholarly assessment of undergraduate student growth and development as well as the conditions that optimize progress toward desired outcomes. Theory development is not complete, certainly—especially with regard to historically underrepresented groups such as racial and ethnic minority students and older students. For a more thorough treatment of the student development theories that undergird these and related assessment tools, see Evans, Forney, and Guido-DiBrito (1998) and Rodgers (1989).

The Current Status of the Scholarly Assessment of Student Development

In this section we describe some approaches to assessing student development that meet the emerging criteria for a scholarly approach and that illustrate the range of activities currently being used. The results of such assessments can be used in at least three ways: to validate/confirm the need to undertake and continue certain initiatives, to provide a rationale for policy and programmatic interventions, and to focus conversations about policy, programs, and practices (including assessment) that need attention.

To get a sense of the current state of the art of the scholarship of student development assessment, we sought information from several dozen colleagues at different types of colleges and universities who are assessing various dimensions of student development.

We posed three questions to these key informants:

1. What aspects of student development are being assessed and how?
2. How are student development assessment results being used to improve policy and practice?
3. How are student development assessment results being used to improve the assessment process itself?

Table 6.1 summarizes examples of assessment efforts at sixteen different institutions. A few of the examples are based on student development theory. Most of the illustrations are substantively and methodologically consistent with the current literature on college outcomes, and the majority provides evidence of student learning in response to requests from such external authorities as accreditation or state agencies. In almost every case, the data are intended to be used to improve some aspect of undergraduate education, though the degree to which policies and practices are being changed in response to the data is less clear. In some instances, different people and offices are assessing various aspects of student development. Some of these efforts are coordinated, whereas others are independent of one another. To illustrate the various approaches to the scholarly assessment of student development, we elaborate on several of the examples listed in Table 6.1.

From Inquiry to Assessment: Examples of Research with Assessment Implications

Two of the examples in Table 6.1 are products of projects that began as scholarly inquiries driven by intellectual interests of researchers. For several decades, University of Maryland, College Park, professor William Sedlacek has studied such areas as admissions, retention, student aid, noncognitive skill development, racial and cultural identity, and institutional impact on diversity. His eclectic set of data collection tools includes closed-ended questionnaires, short-answer instruments, interview techniques, and portfolio assessment. Sedlacek's data are being used for assessment and institutional improvement purposes. For example, his Noncognitive Questionnaire assesses the abilities of persons with nontraditional

Table 6.1. Selected Examples of the Scholarly Assessment of Student Development

School	Student Development Theory Applied or Domains Assessed	Assessment Instrument or Inquiry Process	Reflection, Learning, and Improvement of the Assessment Process	Use of Results in Policy and Practice
Alverno College	Ability-Based Education. Learning within eight abilities: communication, analysis, problem solving, valuing, social interaction, global perspectives, effective citizenship, and aesthetic response.	The process is called "student assessment-as-learning," whereby the individual is judged while practicing performance-based criteria. Along with faculty and staff, the assessment process involves off-campus professionals.	The campus has developed a strong assessment culture among faculty, staff, and students.	The assessment center keeps a video portfolio of each student, and students can view their own assessment records as part of the formative assessment process.
Appalachian State University (ASU)	Student use/attitudes and the campus environment with regard to alcohol and drugs, retention, and campus environment issues.	Core Alcohol and Drug Survey (Core Institute, 1994). Locally developed Freshman Lifestyle Surveys. Telephone surveys.	ASU has learned that smaller, targeted assessments are often more effective than broad, sweeping efforts.	Increased enforcement of marijuana use. Hired a part-time psychiatrist to do periodic med-checks. Banned credit card solicitors from campus.

(continued)

School	Student Development Theory Applied or Domains Assessed	Assessment Instrument or Inquiry Process	Reflection, Learning, and Improvement of the Assessment Process	Use of Results in Policy and Practice
James Madison University (JMU)	Moral development, identity development, leadership skills, and a wide array of student development outcomes.	Locally developed instruments, rubrics, and processes assess students on Erwin's Scale of Intellectual Development (1991), the Erwin Identity Scale (Erwin and Delworth, 1980), and other developmental schemes.	JMU has created a "culture of assessment" on the campus. Student affairs professionals are provided with expert support and guidance by the Center for Assessment to develop instruments to assess their programs.	Program development must include an assessment plan.
Longwood College	Students' activity patterns and satisfaction. Monitoring intellectual, personal, and social development. Student use/attitudes and the campus environment with regard to alcohol and drugs.	Cooperative Institutional Research Program (CIRP) (Higher Education Research Institute, 1966). College Student Experiences Questionnaire (CSEQ) (Pace and Kuh, 1998). National Survey of Student	As a result of the assessment process, Longwood has identified three clusters of student development goals: intellectual development, personal development, and social development.	Refined cocurricular programs to meet student needs, interests, and aspirations. Results confirmed welcomed progress in cocurricular activities for seniors and in civic virtue. Implemented the On-Campus

Institution	Focus	Instruments	Assessment Action	Use of Results
		Engagement (NSSE) (Kuh, 1999). Core Alcohol and Drug Survey (Core Institute, 1994). Harvard School of Public Health College Alcohol Study (Wechsler, 1999).		Talking About Alcohol program, changed enforcement policies, and created alcohol-free residence halls.
Lynn University	First-year student adjustment and success factors.	Assessment is conducted through participation in the Freshman Seminar. Students complete the College Student Inventory (Strail, 1988), write journals and reflection papers, and work on projects.	Set goal to develop a comprehensive network of information: quantitative and qualitative.	Student mentors use the information to guide students toward specific campus resources.
North Carolina State University	Critical thinking and student efforts toward educationally purposeful activities.	California Critical Thinking Skills Test (Facione, 1992), CSEQ (Pace & Kuh, 1998).	Discontinued use of a locally developed critical thinking instrument.	Funds earmarked to promote assessment by faculty members.

(continued)

Table 6.1. Selected Examples of the Scholarly Assessment of Student Development, *continued*

School	Student Development Theory Applied or Domains Assessed	Assessment Instrument or Inquiry Process	Reflection, Learning, and Improvement of the Assessment Process	Use of Results in Policy and Practice
Old Dominion University	To identify at-risk first-year students.	Old Dominion University Freshman Survey (Pickering, Calliott, and McAuliffe, 1992).	Survey data were factor-analyzed, and factors were found to be better predictors of at risk students than traditional methods.	A one-credit orientation course and additional advising were initiated to assist students identified as being at risk.
Pennsylvania State University (PSU)	Student issues, expectations, usage, and satisfaction on specific topics such as academic integrity, class attendance, sexual assault, and undergraduate student government (see www.sa.psu.edu/ sara/pulse.shtml).	Locally developed telephone surveys using a customized computer software program are conducted by trained student surveyors.	PSU has pioneered in making assessment accessible to students, faculty, and staff, not only by making results easy to view and understand, but also by allowing assessment topics to be initiated by any member of the campus community.	Results are posted on the Web and sent via a listserv to interested students, faculty, and staff.

Institution				
Truman State University (TSU)	Learning within each academic discipline. Student effort toward educational processes and resources.	Locally developed portfolio program. CSEQ (Pace and Kuh, 1998).	TSU recognized that they lacked formative assessment opportunities for students and worked with the CSEQ Research Program to create a Student Advising Report.	Based on positive results, the faculty senate made the portfolio program mandatory for all disciplines. Advising meetings with first-year students in Residential College Program include a discussion of individual responses to the CSEQ.
University of Maryland, College Park	Student satisfaction and retention issues for new students and transfer students. Sedlacek-Brooks Model (1976).	Sedlacek's tools: Situational Attitude Scale (Sedlacek and Brooks, 1967), questionnaires, short answer instruments, interview techniques, portfolio assessment. Noncognitive assessment is also conducted.	Putting theory into practice through the use of locally developed instruments.	Identified "pain points." Held a daylong retention summit of deans and student life professionals. Developed a transition course for transfer students.

(continued)

Table 6.1. Selected Examples of the Scholarly Assessment of Student Development, *continued*

School	Student Development Theory Applied or Domains Assessed	Assessment Instrument or Inquiry Process	Reflection, Learning, and Improvement of the Assessment Process	Use of Results in Policy and Practice
University of Missouri, Columbia	Student learning and personal development. Student use/attitudes and the campus environment with regard to alcohol and drugs. Reflective judgment (higher order critical and reflective thinking).	Collegiate Assessment of Academic Proficiency (CAAP) (American College Testing Program, 2000), CSEQ (Pace and Kuh, 1998), NSSE (Kuh, 1999), Core Alcohol and Drug Survey (Core Institute, 1994), and Wood's (1983) Reflective Judgment instrument.	Wood developed paper/pencil instrument to make assessment more economical than interview protocol.	Discovered need for and expansion of Freshman Interest Group Program. Developed "Dry 2000" program in Greek system. Results used to improve instruction in the psychology program.
University of South Carolina, Sumter	Communication skills, service to campus and community, critical thinking, leadership, and moral, physical, and social develop-ment.	Student Development Transcripts (SDT).	Expanded data collection for the SDT to include reason for participating and demographic analyses of student activities.	Academic advisers were given read-only access to SDTs via the computer network for more holistic advising conversations. Student affairs staff members

				were able to provide a more balanced plan of developmental activities for students.
University of Southern Indiana (USI)	Factors affecting developmental growth in distance learning. New student growth, perceptions, and transition.	Learning Support Needs (LSN) questionnaire (C. Harrington, personal communication, February 23, 2001), reflective photography and journaling.	Developed the LSN questionnaire as a response to a need to understand how to make distance learning as effective as traditional campus-based learning.	Results spurred a change in approach to the first-year transition. That is, students are encouraged to develop writing skills by maintaining (not distancing) contact with home. USI also learned about the pattern of adjustment for the first semester, and developed programs to target students around the fifth week where students need more engagement.

(continued)

Table 6.1. Selected Examples of the Scholarly Assessment of Student Development, *continued*

School	Student Development Theory Applied or Domains Assessed	Assessment Instrument or Inquiry Process	Reflection, Learning, and Improvement of the Assessment Process	Use of Results in Policy and Practice
Wake Forest University	Learning with and about computers and information technology, as well as faculty-student interaction.	Launched an Institutional Strategic Plan in 1995 entitled "Plan for the class of 2000" including IBM laptop computers provided to all entering freshmen and faculty , a new first-year seminar course, and fellowships for 150 students to perform joint research with faculty members. Assessment plan uses the CSEQ (Pace and Kuh, 1998), CIRP (Higher Education Research Institute, 1966), freshman essays, Higher Education Data Sharing (HEDS) Consortium	Evaluation committee of faculty, administrators, and students charged with setting goals, conducting assessments, and reflecting on the assessment process.	Faculty established a Computer-Enhanced Learning Initiative to develop effective uses of computers in instruction. Renewed commitment to reduce the student-faculty ratio, to the personalization of the professor-student relationship, and to small institutional size. Recommended establishment of a standing committee on teaching.

| Western Governors University (WGU) | Collegiate-level reasoning and problem solving, as well as intellectual skills that underpin practical competencies. | Alumni/ae Survey, HEDS Senior Survey, HERI Faculty Survey, and locally developed faculty and student computer surveys. Reflective Judgment model (King and Kitchener, 1994). Fischer's (1980) Dynamic Skill theory. | WGU strives to develop a culture of evidence. Individual assessment data are aggregated to assess entire degree programs. Efforts piloted to assess general education competencies. Assessment is moved from student self-reports of learning outcomes to a measurement-based system to meet accreditation requirements. | Implemented Web-based tutorials and problem-solving coaches. Revised statement of collegiate reasoning and problem-solving competencies to be more developmentally appropriate. |

(continued)

Table 6.1. Selected Examples of the Scholarly Assessment of Student Development, *continued*

School	*Student Development Theory Applied or Domains Assessed*	*Assessment Instrument or Inquiry Process*	*Reflection, Learning, and Improvement of the Assessment Process*	*Use of Results in Policy and Practice*
Winthrop University	Student personal growth and development.	Learning and Study Strategies Inventory (LASSI) (Weinstein, Palmer, and Schulte, 1987).	Conducted follow-up studies to determine the effectiveness of LASSI scales in predicting freshman-year grade point average.	Students were given explicit feedback on their attitudes and approaches toward academic work. Faculty were given information to aid their advising. Administrators used results for recruitment and retention.

experiences and has been used by the University of Maryland's medical school to defend its decision to forego standardized tests and grades in the admissions process in lieu of other measures. The Gates Millennium Scholars program employs Sedlacek's noncognitive assessment procedure in identifying students of color who will receive scholarships. Other institutions using Sedlacek's noncognitive system for various purposes include North Carolina State University, Oregon State University, The Ohio State University, John Fisher College, Prairie View A&M, and Louisiana State University.

Philip Wood, from the University of Missouri, Columbia, developed a pencil-and-paper instrument to assess the higher-order critical and reflective thinking described in William Perry's (1970) theory of intellectual and ethical development. Wood wanted to develop a tool that would accurately measure the intellectual functioning consistent with King and Kitchener's (1994) reflective judgment (RJ) model but that would also be easier and more economical to administer than the RJ interview protocol. He was also interested in improving instruction in his psychology department. The results of his research revealed different views and assumptions about teaching and students. For example, faculty members were typically surprised to discover that first-year students exhibited a relatively low capacity for reflective thinking. This prompted discussions about whether the standard teaching approaches, such as emphasizing memorization in first-year survey courses, were having the desired effect, given student characteristics and developmental levels. Wood began to incorporate this information into the teaching practicum for teaching assistants (TAs) in psychology, for which he was responsible. The results are now used in other departments for TA training, as well. In addition, he now routinely presents at teaching and learning seminars on and off campus. Modeling a scholarly approach to assessment, Wood discovered some limitations in the instrument and scoring protocol after piloting the instrument in 1989. He has since revised the tool several times, building in some internal checks to identify the few students who had difficulty with certain types of items. Wood's good work was recognized by his campus with an award for outstanding departmental assessment.

Institutional Examples of Scholarly Assessment Approaches

Most scholarly assessments of student development are imbedded in institutional student development assessment programs.

Longwood College

Since the mid-1980s, the student affairs division at Longwood College has used the Cooperative Institutional Research Program (CIRP) Student Information Form to assess entering students' characteristics and aspirations, and it has also used the College Student Experiences Questionnaire (CSEQ), as well as some other instruments, to assess students' activity patterns and satisfaction. In response to worrisome retention rates and to further promote Longwood's commitment to student success, the College established the Longwood Seminar for first-year students in 1987. By 1992, retention levels had risen by almost ten points. At this point, Longwood adopted three clusters of collegewide student development goals that cut across and integrate the efforts of student affairs and academic affairs (intellectual development, personal development, social development). In addition, policies were enacted that prohibited first-year students from bringing automobiles onto the campus and deferred fraternity and sorority rush until the spring semester to allow first-year students to concentrate on academics in the fall semester.

In 1997, again in the face of slipping persistence rates and declining freshman satisfaction levels, the First-Year Experience course was revised once more and Longwood established its Office of New Student Programs. Data from two national surveys of alcohol and drug use (CORE Survey and Harvard Alcohol Survey) pointed to the need for a wellness center to help students develop a "balanced and healthy lifestyle," one of the institution's student development goals. Longwood also implemented the On-Campus Talking About Alcohol Program for new students, adopted a "three strikes and you're out" alcohol violation policy, and instituted alcohol-free residence halls for first-year students and upper-class students. Senior survey data indicate that students are well aware that the college aims to discourage a party atmosphere on campus; however, data on alcohol usage in the wake of these changes are mixed. Other institutions, such as Indiana University, Bloomington, and the University of Missouri, Columbia, have also used assessment data to point to the need for changes in student life policies and practices to discourage hazardous use of alcohol and other drugs (see Table 6.1).

Longwood College also uses results from the National Survey of Student Engagement (NSSE) to monitor the extent to which the institution is making progress in attaining its strategic goals and guiding improvement efforts. Results from NSSE 2000 confirmed welcome progress in several areas. For example, the level of engagement of Longwood seniors in cocurricular activities is about twice that of counterparts nationally, and they also score significantly higher on a cluster of items dealing with civic virtue (citizen leadership), which reflects the institution's mission-driven civic virtue emphasis.

Truman State University

The Truman State faculty senate took advantage of positive assessment results as an opportunity to expand its recently implemented portfolio program. All students are now required to develop a portfolio of their best work, which, in the senior year, is accompanied by a reflective essay on what they have learned in college. This material is assessed by faculty on eight dimensions, such as evidence of progress made, interdisciplinary thinking, modes of inquiry, and so on. Originally, the portfolios were going to be used primarily to gauge major field outcomes. However, about a quarter of the work students chose to feature was associated with cocurricular experiences, such as leadership responsibilities for a student club or organization, volunteer service, and other activities.

A particularly distinctive and relevant feature of Truman's student development assessment program is its incorporation of a formative student feedback component. In Spring 2002, Truman academic advisers will begin talking with students about their performance as reflected by results from the CSEQ. First-year students will receive a personalized report on their CSEQ scores that

compares their responses with those of their peers (norm-referenced) and with those of a "Truman Goal" (criterion-referenced).
Academic advisers in the Residential College Program will discuss
these results with students during regularly scheduled advising
meetings. It's expected that these meetings will help advisers work
more effectively with students who are disengaged or dissatisfied
with the institution.

Western Governors University

Western Governors University (WGU) is intentionally building a
culture of evidence in order to promote data-driven decision making and to rigorously assess the quality of degree programs. The
latter is especially important because WGU degrees are competency-
based and are delivered via distance education. Coursework
emphasizes collegiate-level reasoning and problem solving—intellectual skills that underpin practical competencies. The assessment
approach is grounded in the work of King and Kitchener's (1994)
reflective judgment model and Fischer's (1980) dynamic skill theory. Students are challenged with open-ended problems, apply
information from related disciplines, and attend meetings to vet
results. Students can use Web-based tutorials (see www2.apex.net/
users/leehaven) and can seek guidance from a problem-solving
coach throughout the process. Assessment data are analyzed by
major field and in other ways to guide program improvement,
accreditation, and state reporting, and institutional reports can be
obtained in paper form or via the Web. Individual student results
are also shared with the student via e-mail.

After reviewing its student development assessment program,
WGU revised its statement of Collegiate Reasoning and Problem
Solving Competencies to be more responsive and appropriate for
the developmental levels of students. WGU is also piloting efforts
to assess general education competencies in humanities, life and
physical sciences, and social sciences disciplines. In addition, task
forces are puzzling through how to respond to some of the assessment findings. While the results have already begun to influence
institutional policy and decision making, WGU realizes that it will
take more than a few years to institutionalize a culture of evidence
throughout the institution. Toward this end, the university intends

to augment student self-reported learning outcomes with objective measures in order to meet accreditation requirements and to examine the impact of different types of assessment contexts on student performance.

Summary

These institutional examples and others listed in Table 6.1 suggest that key findings and implications from scholarly assessments of student development are typically circulated by sending out reports electronically and via hard copy to various campus constituents. Frequently, data are interpreted in face-to-face open campus forums and posted on the Web. In most instances, assessment managers or teams take stock of the findings with an eye toward implications for institutional policy and practice and, less frequently, for revising assessment processes and tools.

The State of the Art of the Scholarly Assessment of Student Development

Based on our review of current practice in student development assessment, we share some observations about the character of scholarly approaches to student development.

Most schools are assessing some aspect of student development. Colleges and universities are gathering data on a wide range of student development outcomes, from course-based cognitive-intellectual gains to civic engagement, to practical competencies associated with internships and work experiences. However, few schools have a comprehensive, "self-regarding" assessment program in place whereby instrumentation, data collection, and results reporting are continuously monitored and reviewed and are subsequently modified in order to improve the assessment process.

When student development goals are clearly articulated and the assessment questions are sharply focused, the results are more likely to be used for institutional improvement. Scholarly approaches to student development assessment are typically keyed to important learning outcomes that are featured in the institution's educational mission and purposes. Targeted assessments of student development are often more powerful and persuasive than large-scale institution-wide efforts. For example, all aspects of student development do not have to be measured to learn important things about student learning or to identify policies and practices that could be changed to enhance learning. Pennsylvania State University, the University of Southern Indiana, and many other schools conduct telephone surveys of small numbers of students to gauge opinions on current issues, such as whether or not to build a coffeehouse in the student union. The key seems to be to focus assessments on specific, well-defined areas of interest that are consistent with the institution's educational mission and programs.

A scholarly approach to assessment is more likely to flourish at institutions that have cultivated a culture of evidence. All institutional participants, from top-level administrators to faculty and staff members and students, need to discover and support student development assessment by shaping the beliefs, values, rituals, traditions, and language with regard to assessment on the campus. Such a culture cannot be developed overnight. For example, Alverno College, James Madison University, and Truman State University have all invested a great deal of time, money, and leadership to develop a campus culture that celebrates the value of assessing student learning and personal development. Faculty members must be involved in selecting assessment tools if the results are to lead to action. Administrators can leverage the collection and use of assessment data both symbolically and financially. For example, at North Carolina State University, the chancellor and provost provide funding and leadership and have earmarked $330,000 from a tuition fee increase to encourage faculty members to assess the effectiveness of the Inquiry Guided Instruction course.

Many faculty members are socialized into valuing scholarship. A scholarly approach to assessment would be aided if the graduate programs preparing student affairs professionals emphasized the skills and competencies needed for a scholarly approach to assessment, as recently called for by Carpenter (2001) and Blimling (2001).

Student development assessment has both direct and indirect implications for institutional improvement. Left unattended, every curricular offering or student life program will decay over time. In addition, student characteristics and aspirations are constantly changing in visible and not-so-visible ways (Kuh, 2001b). Assessment data can serve as an early warning system by monitoring whether programs and practices are having the desired impact with various groups of students. For example, from its comprehensive student development assessment program, Longwood College twice revised its freshman seminar within a ten-year period. Similarly, Penn State determined from polling students that the importance of certain college goals and outcomes, such as the value of general education and experience with human diversity, needed to be reemphasized (see Table 6.1).

Using results to improve assessment processes and tools is the least well-developed area of scholarship in assessing student development. There is probably more going on in this area than we discovered. Nevertheless, most of the assessment experts with whom we spoke were much more focused on collecting data and using the results than they were on reflective assessment practice. Using a scholarly approach to assessing student development requires members of an assessment team be knowledgeable about student development theory and research as well as the methodological and technical best practices. Assessment specialists must critically evaluate the evidence of student growth as well as the technical quality of the instrumentation and data collection processes. This is the reflective component of the assessment process that ensures that the results are reliable, valid, credible, and trustworthy. Should the data collection tools be revised or replaced? Are there alternative methods (qualitative inquiry, use of technology, observations of existing student records, and so forth) that would produce more accurate and compelling evidence of the aspects of student development being assessed?

Suggestions for Promoting the Scholarly Assessment of Student Development

In this section we offer suggestions to promote the scholarly assessment of student development and to ensure that assessment data are addressing critical needs in the field and will be used to affect educational policies and practices.

Enlist the support of influential constituents before, during, and after data collection. Key faculty members, administrative leaders, and others who occupy gatekeeping roles need to be informed and involved for assessment to achieve improvements in the policies and practices that promote student development. Faculty members often misinterpret the purpose of assessment, fearing that the results will be used to serve a simple accountability agenda rather than identify areas where student engagement and learning can be enhanced. In other instances, faculty members may be skeptical of the assessment tools. For example, they should be given an opportunity to examine and endorse the assessment tools to be used in order for the results to be seriously and fairly considered and to expect that action will subsequently be taken. Faculty members may also be more amenable to student development assessment efforts when these efforts are conducted and conveyed with the rigor, discipline, care, and skepticism associated with their own ideals of scholarship (Carpenter, 2001).

Use multiple assessment approaches that answer the most important assessment questions. A comprehensive student development assessment program requires a complement of quantitative and qualitative measures. For example, like many other institutions, Appalachian State University aims to increase the diversity of its student body. But to achieve this goal and ensure a high-quality undergraduate experience for all students, the university must learn more about the nature of the experiences of its students of color. Information from focus groups and telephone polling of minority students' parents has augmented what the institution discovered from the results of satisfaction surveys and the CSEQ, revealing a richer, more detailed, and nuanced picture of the minority student experience. In this instance, personal stories and anecdotal evidence amplified and enriched the quantitative data.

Collect enough data to be able to disaggregate the results at the academic unit level. Institution-wide averages are typically meaningless to faculty and staff groups charged with improving some aspect of the undergraduate program. One of the keys to promoting increased interest in and use of assessment data is getting department-level buy-in so that the numbers of students participating are large enough to enable dissagregation at the unit level where faculty members can see the performance of their own students. This means that enough students in specific cohorts or major fields must be assessed so that the results can be used at the unit level for policy decisions.

Strengthen feedback loops between assessment processes, results, and changes in policy and practice. Too few institutions routinely provide information to various groups (faculty and staff members, trustees, students) about whether or how they are using assessment data. This may mean several things: they aren't using the data or don't know how to use it, the quality of the data is poor and is therefore not usable, they don't have anything instructive to report, and so on. Several people commented that they have a lot of useful data but too little time to translate it into feedback that will prompt constructive change. Many schools are posting assessment results on the Internet to make them more widely and immediately available. For example, see Indiana University-Purdue University Indianapolis's Web site (www.imir.iupui.edu/imir) or the Web site of the University of Colorado, Boulder (www.colorado.edu/pba/outcomes/). Appalachian State University is a pioneer in the use of database applications and the Internet to report assessment results and has developed an interactive Web site (www.appstate.edu/www_docs/depart/irp/irp.html), from which individuals can obtain survey results by major field, year, or other cross-sections.

Focus additional assessment efforts on the development and experiences of students from historically underrepresented groups. Much more is known about the development of White students than about that of students of color. Fortunately, tools are being developed that focus on the specific needs of minority students. Instruments such as the Multicultural Assessment of Campus Programming Questionnaire can be used to estimate the nature of student relations, cultural accessibility, diversity recognition, cultural integration, and cultural sensitivity (McClellan, Cogdal, Lease, and Londono-McConnell, 1996). The Pluralism and Diversity Attitude Assessment measures the degree to which a respondent possesses positive attitudes toward cultural pluralism and whether an individual is comfortable or uncomfortable with diversity (Stanley, 1996). In addition, existing instruments such as the College Student Experiences Questionnaire, the College Student Survey, and the National Survey of Student Engagement can be used to examine interactions among students from different backgrounds.

Use an internal advisory panel or a consultant and an external advisory panel to maintain focus and momentum. Some schools, such as

North Carolina State University, use an external consultant who is charged with asking important but sometimes difficult questions about the degree to which the goals of the assessment program are being met, for what purposes the data are being used, and how policies and programs are being modified in response to assessment results. In addition to offering expert counsel, the presence of a consultant or advisory panel can act as a form of soft accountability—both for the assessment program and for the institution—by helping the assessment team persuade others at the institution that assessment is a key component of an effective institution and by encouraging them to take assessment results seriously.

National research and assessment programs and allied professional organizations should provide leadership in key areas. To further the scholarly assessment of student development, national research and assessment programs such as the Higher Education Research Institute at UCLA and the CSEQ and NSSE surveys at Indiana University can host user group meetings to provide examples of how to analyze and use assessment data. Collaboration between these survey organizations and professional associations would be especially valuable for raising the level of awareness of good practices in assessing student development processes and outcomes. They can also be helpful in assisting institutions to link the results of multiple surveys that are able to capture longitudinal data. Another area where leadership is needed is in that of developing reasonable and appropriate guidelines that institutional review boards can use to evaluate the merits of projects to assess student development. Many institutions are facing the dilemma of needing information from students to meet the expectations of external authorities—such as accreditation agencies, at the same time that their campus institutional review board is making it increasingly difficult to obtain approvals to do research on students. Suggestions for how to effectively manage this situation to the satisfaction of all parties would be most helpful.

Conclusion

The amount and quality of college student research in American colleges and universities is exceptional. Virtually every institution is assessing one or more aspects of student development for various reasons. However, higher education needs more scholars who can further develop the scholarship of student development assessment (Blimling, 2001; Carpenter, 2001; Schroeder and Pike, 2001). In this chapter we've featured many promising examples that represent but a small fraction of the scholarly work being done in student development assessment. In addition to the issues discussed earlier, others must also be addressed in order to increase the frequency with which practitioners use a scholarly approach in assessing student development. Prominent among these are using technology to measure and monitor student development, being sensitive and responsive to the changing campus and governmental regulations related to college student research (for example, human subjects' approval), and the persistent challenges associated with accurately measuring change or gains in various outcomes domains. Students of all ages change while in college, so something akin to "a maturation effect" must be recognized, because there is no convenient way to control it.

As with other areas of policy and practice focused on improving undergraduate education, the scholarship of assessment will be furthered through collaboration between student affairs professionals who often are knowledgeable about student development theory, survey research methods, and the out-of-class experiences of students, faculty members who are expert in pedagogy and curricular matters, and institutional research and assessment specialists who are familiar with assessment theory, research methods, and technology. Nothing short of a team effort will be required to produce the kind of high-quality information about student learning and personal development that is needed to enhance the undergraduate experience, respond to external accountability demands, and improve the assessment process itself.

Part Three

Methods of Assessment

This section contains three chapters that describe some of the infrastructure that supports assessment methodology.

In Chapter Seven, Gary Pike likens the process of conducting assessment to that of conducting research. Both involve asking good questions, identifying appropriate methods of investigation, selecting representative participants, applying good measures, and communicating results effectively. Basing his discussion on current psychometric theory, Pike describes a number of the technical qualities of good assessment instruments.

In Chapter Eight, Mark Shermis and Kathryn Daniels present some possibilities for using technology in assessment. Computer-based tests using multimedia, Web-based surveys, and electronic portfolios are a few of the technology-enabled methods faculty members are beginning to try. The chapter ends with a listing of Web sites containing assessment-related information.

Program evaluation and outcomes assessment in higher education can be enhanced considerably by the availability on campus of competent institutional research professionals. Victor Borden uses Chapter Nine to present the many dimensions of information support—from knowledge management for classroom assessment to management reports and analysis for comprehensive program review—that offices of institutional research can provide as scholarly assessment and the scholarship of assessment are advanced.

Chapter Seven

Measurement Issues in Outcomes Assessment

Gary R. Pike

Ernest Boyer (1990) poses the question "What does it mean to be a scholar?" In answering his question, Boyer advances a new vision that includes four interrelated types of scholarship: discovery, integration, application, and teaching. From my perspective, effective assessment is closely related to Boyer's concept of the scholarship of application. Parallels between the scholarship of application and assessment can be seen in the questions they address. Researchers engaged in the scholarship of application ask, "How can knowledge be responsibly applied to consequential problems? How can it be helpful to individuals as well as institutions, and how can specific problems themselves define an agenda for scholarly investigation?" (Boyer, 1990, p. 21). Similarly, assessment focuses on important issues that are central to the mission of higher education—student learning and development. Assessment also encompasses issues intended to benefit the institution and the learner, and the agenda for assessment is to identify shortfalls between what is and what is desired in order to create opportunities for improving the quality and effectiveness of higher education.

The relationship between assessment and the scholarship of application extends beyond the conceptual level. The elements of good applied or action research are also the elements of good assessment. In this chapter I examine five elements of research that are essential for effective assessment: asking good questions, identifying appropriate methods, using appropriate measures, selecting representative participants, and communicating results effectively.

Asking Good Questions

Good research involves asking good questions, and good research questions are both interesting and important. For colleges and universities, student learning, as embodied in the mission, goals, and objectives of the institution, is important. Not surprisingly, programs that are considered to be exemplars of effective assessment have tightly coupled the questions being researched with the institution's goals for student learning. Thus, institutions such as Capital University, the University of Colorado at Boulder, and Miami University (Gray, 1999b) developed assessment programs within the context of their existing missions, goals, and objectives. Other institutions, including James Madison University and Union College, revised their missions, goals, and objectives to provide strong foundations upon which to build their assessment programs (Gray, 1999b).

Goals for student learning, along with the research and assessment questions that flow from them, have generally focused on traditional learning outcomes—that is, what students should know and be able to do as a result of the courses they have taken. There are exceptions to this rule. Capital University broadened its definition of student learning to include the development of attitudes and values, and the University of California, Berkeley, included the impact of an increasingly diverse student body (Gray, 1999b).

Because many assessment activities occur at the department or unit level, it is essential that departments develop clear goals and objectives that are aligned with the missions, goals, and objectives of the institution (Pike, 2000b). Alverno College (American Productivity and Quality Center, 1997) and Chicago State University (Gray, 1999b) extended alignment to the learning outcomes of individual courses. Some institutions have translated expectations for alignment into policy. A blue ribbon faculty committee at the University of Colorado at Boulder developed specific guidelines for review of assessment plans in order to ensure alignment of department and university goals (Gray, 1999b).

Because both the scholarship of application and assessment involve action research, assessment professionals must know what the institution wants to accomplish and how it is to be accomplished via the curriculum, cocurriculum, and pedagogy. In other words, effective assessment must focus on process as well as outcomes (Pike, 1999). Both James Madison University and Miami University focus their assessment efforts on students' in-class and out-of-class experiences because they believe both curriculum and cocurriculum contribute to student learning. At Eckerd College, the strategy for student learning relies heavily on interdisciplinary courses and the assessment plan identifies outcomes that are likely to be produced by interdisciplinary studies (Gray, 1999b).

What institutional experience tells us is that having goals for student learning is an essential part of effective assessment. Just as a good research question focuses research efforts, the linkage between assessment and goals for student learning brings attention to what is important to an institution. It is critical, however, that goals fully reflect the institutional mission. By sharpening the focus of assessment, goals necessarily limit the scope of assessment. If what is to be assessed is what gets done, goals must be comprehensive. Experience also suggests that assessment will be most effective when goals are aligned throughout the organization. The alignment of departmental goals and strategies with the goals and strategies of the institution helps ensure that improvement actions within the complex systems of colleges and universities are not counterproductive (Pike, 2000b). Finally, institutional experiences tell us that an emphasis on both goals (outcomes) and strategies (process) is most likely to lead to effective assessment. Moreover, evaluating the alignment between goals and strategies represents one of the most fundamental forms of assessment research.

Because assessment is oriented toward change, it is important that assessment efforts primarily address those things that can be changed. It does little good for an assessment program to focus on enhancing an institution's reputation, because that is how others perceive the institution, and the institution cannot affect those perceptions directly. At the same time, I believe that improving the quality of an institution will improve that institution's reputation, but the focus should be on quality, not reputation. Likewise, it may not be productive for an institutional assessment plan to focus too heavily on policies and procedures that are extremely difficult to change. To be sure, it is important to study and know the effects of policies that are difficult to change, if only to better understand the limitations of improvement initiatives. However, the greatest gains in improving student learning are likely to come from a focus on policies and practices that an institution can directly affect.

Identifying Appropriate Methods

The second element of good research that is necessary for good assessment is the identification and use of appropriate methods. At this point, assessors and researchers are confronted with a variety of choices. Will the approach be cross-sectional (measurement at a single point in time) or longitudinal (measurement at multiple points in time)? Will the approach be normative (designed to make generalizations about a larger population) or idiographic (focused only on the individuals being studied)? Will the research be qualitative (relying more on words than numbers) or quantitative (relying primarily on numerical analyses)? Within the choice of qualitative and quantitative approaches there are other design considerations. Will the quantitative design be experimental, quasi-experimental, or correlational? Will the qualitative design make use of such things as participant observation, grounded theory, and critical incidents?

As complex as this bewildering array of questions and options may seem, it is an oversimplification. There may be a blending of these choices, such as the combination of cross-sectional and longitudinal designs in a quasi-longitudinal design. Likewise, the approach that is selected may make use of both qualitative and quantitative methods. In fact, many assessment programs intentionally make use of multiple methods to provide a richer understanding of student learning and development (Gray, 1999b). It is not the intention of this chapter to delve into the intricacies of methodologies and methods. There are numerous texts that address these subjects, and the interested reader should consult these basic works on research methods (see Denzin and Lincoln, 1994; Kerlinger, 1986; Light, Singer, and Willett, 1990). What is critical is that the approach be appropriate for the questions being asked.

Several institutions have blended cross-sectional and longitudinal designs to provide both snapshots of student learning and gauges of student development. At State University of New York (SUNY) Fredonia, students complete a series of writing assignments to measure reading, reflective thinking, quantitative problem solving, scientific reasoning, and socioethical understanding (Gray, 1999b). To learn more about the effects of maturation on student performance in these areas, the assessment staff also administered the assessments to samples of first-year and graduating students at another university. This type of quasi-longitudinal, quasi-experimental design allows the assessment staff at SUNY Fredonia to compare the performance of their students while accounting for maturational effects through the comparison of freshmen and seniors at the "control" institution.

Appropriateness is also a consideration in selecting an analytical method. When assessment questions focus on the level of student satisfaction or the amount of change in student learning, quantitative analyses of assessment data generally are most appropriate. Thus, the National Survey of Student Engagement has developed a series of quantitative benchmarks that allow institutions to compare the reports of their students with those of students at similar institutions (Pike, 2001). When assessment questions focus on the nature of students' experiences at an institution, qualitative analyses may be more appropriate. King and Howard-Hamilton (1999), for example, made use of qualitative analyses in their assessment of the development of multicultural competence. In some cases, the nature of the available data may dictate the method that must be used. Although the data available from student transcripts at most institutions lend themselves to quantitative analyses, narrative transcripts are used at Evergreen State College, and the appropriate method of analysis is qualitative (Gray, 1999b). In some instances, a blending of qualitative and quantitative approaches may be most appropriate for assessing student learning. Both the Missouri Writing Assessment (Pike, 1999) and the Cognitive Level and Quality of Writing Assessment (Flateby and Metzger, 2001) make use of qualitative methods to evaluate student writing, but a numerical score is used to summarize the holistic judgments of student performance on these assessments.

Institutional practice underscores the importance of research design in the assessment of student educational outcomes. Appropriate research designs are essential to ensuring that the data collected by the assessments are capable of answering the questions being posed. Questions about changes in student learning and development over time cannot be answered by data from cross-sectional research designs. Likewise, quantitative data may not provide a satisfactory answer to questions about *how* students' experiences affect their perceptions of the college environment and learning outcomes. To be sure, quantitative analysis of students' self-reports can demonstrate that experiences are related to perceptions and outcomes, but the questions of how and why experiences affect perceptions and outcomes are difficult to answer by using quantitative analysis alone.

The appropriateness of research designs also affects the confidence that can be placed in assessment results. Recognizing that maturation can play an important role in student learning, assessment staff at SUNY Fredonia attempted to account for the effects of maturation by collecting data on a control group from another institution. In this instance, the identification of a control group from a different institution was critical because it allowed assessors to distinguish between the effects of the curriculum at SUNY and the effects of general education and maturation at other institutions.

In most cases, true experimental designs with random assignment of participants to treatment and control groups is not feasible in assessment research. However, comparison groups—whether they are national norm groups for standardized tests, peer institutions for surveys, or naturally occurring groups on campus—frequently are available and should be used whenever possible. The experiences of the University of Northern Colorado and the University of Hartford (Gray, 2000), as well as the University of Missouri, Columbia (Pike, 2000a), demonstrate that the use of naturally occurring comparison groups has allowed assessment researchers to build strong arguments for the effectiveness of learning communities, and the strength of these arguments has been a critical element in their administrative acceptance on campus. Because self-selection of students into learning communities represents a threat to the comparability of naturally occurring comparison groups, it was also necessary for the assessment researchers at these institutions to account for differences in learning-community and non-learning-community students in their studies.

Using Appropriate Measures

The third area of overlap between research and assessment is in the need for accurate and appropriate measurement. A cataloging of assessment measures is clearly beyond the scope of this chapter. Readers interested in reviews of available assessment instruments are encouraged to consult Nichols's book, *A Practitioner's Handbook for Institutional Effectiveness and Student Outcomes Assessment Implementation* (1995) or Erwin's book, *NPEC Sourcebook on Assessment* (2000). In Chapter Eleven of this volume, Catherine Palomba also describes several measurement approaches that have been used to improve student learning. This section provides a broader overview of the issues to be considered in selecting and developing assessment measures.

In his chapter on educational measurement, Messick (1993) stressed that questions of accuracy and appropriateness do not inhere in the measure (for example, tests, surveys, or portfolios) but, rather, in the interpretation and use of the data resulting from the measurement process. Thus, a measure such as the Scholastic Aptitude Test may allow researchers to make accurate and appropriate inferences about students' entering abilities but may not allow researchers to make accurate and appropriate judgments about the quality and effectiveness of a general education program or the curriculum in an academic discipline. A variety of criteria have been proposed for evaluating the accuracy and appropriateness of measures of students' learning and development (see Banta and Pike, 1989; Erwin, 2000; Messick, 1993). My personal preference is to focus on three central questions: (1) Does the content of the measure address the question being asked? (2) Does the empirical structure of the data produced by the measure answer the question being asked? (3) Are the data produced by the measure sensitive to students' educational experiences and the effects of educational interventions?

Content of the Measure

Examining the content of a test or survey is perhaps the most straightforward and useful step in evaluating an assessment measure.

As a general rule, there should be a high degree of correspondence between what is being measured by an assessment instrument and the institution's or department's goals for student learning. If the content of a measure is not related to the learning outcomes being assessed, the prospect of obtaining useful information will be quite limited. For example, an assessment of the writing skills of business majors should include samples of business memos and formal reports. A literary analysis of a novel or poem would provide little useful information about students' abilities in the domain that is most relevant in the world of business (see Erwin, 2000).

In some cases, changes in the curriculum as a result of an assessment program may render a particular measure inappropriate and require the selection or development of a new measure. Katz and Gangnon (2000) reported that the University of Wisconsin, Superior, originally administered the College Outcome Measures Program (COMP) objective test to students upon completion of the general education program. Based on the results obtained from the COMP exam, several important changes were made in the general education curriculum. As the effects of these changes in general education were made manifest, the COMP exam became less useful as a measure of student learning in general education. As a result, the University of Wisconsin, Superior, has developed a portfolio assessment system that allows for longitudinal assessment of students' general learned abilities through evaluation of samples of performance in each general education course they take. The final portfolio also allows raters to evaluate students' abilities to self-assess, because each sample in the portfolio contains a description, written by the student, of what each artifact represents.

A high degree of content correspondence between goals for student learning and assessment measures is needed for political as well as measurement reasons. Erwin (2000) has observed that the credibility of a measure depends, at least in part, on decision makers' perceptions of the congruence between the content of a measure and goals for student learning and development. Instruments perceived to be highly congruent with goals for student learning tend to be accorded greater credibility than instruments perceived to be less congruent with expected outcomes. Decision makers are more likely to act on information they consider credible than on information from a source they view as less credible.

Structure of the Assessment Data

Questions about the structure of assessment data go to the heart of traditional issues of reliability and validity. Reliability is a necessary but not a sufficient condition for validity (Messick, 1993). That is, a measure that is not reliable cannot be valid, but a measure that is reliable may or may not be valid. A variety of approaches may be used to evaluate the reliability of an assessment measure, and the choice of one approach over another should be based on what is being assessed and how. If an assessment involves a cross-sectional design using students' summed scores on a series of test or survey questions, then a measure of internal consistency (for example, alpha or split-half reliability) is most appropriate. When the assessment design is longitudinal, questions about consistency over time must be added to questions of internal consistency. For example, Strange's Measure of Multicultural Aptitude Scale (2001) is intended to be used in a pretest, posttest assessment of multicultural programs. Consequently, technical information about this instrument includes estimates of test-retest reliability.

Writing and portfolio assessment require more complex approaches to the evaluation of reliability. When multiple raters are used to assess students' writing samples or artifacts in portfolios, evaluations of interrater agreement are needed to ensure consistency in the evaluation process. When a scoring rubric is used in either writing or portfolio assessment, traditional measures of interrater agreement must be supplemented with measures of the agreement between raters and "true" scores on anchor papers that represent categories or points along a continuum in the scoring rubric.

Direct evaluations of the structures of assessment data frequently focus on what is traditionally called construct validity (see Messick, 1993). The question asked in this line of research is whether the test measures what it purports to measure. One method that can be used to evaluate the congruence between the stated structure of a test and the actual structure of data from that test is factor analysis, which examines correlations among scores from a test or survey in order to identify the constructs or factors underlying the instrument. Item-response patterns that are highly correlated will tend to form factors, and the factor loadings indicate the degree to which items are associated with a particular factor. If a test or survey accurately measures what it purports to measure, factor analysis results should parallel the presumed structure of the test.

Sensitivity to Educational Effects

The sensitivity of scores to the effects of an educational intervention is the most important characteristic of an assessment measure. If scores do not reflect students' educational experiences, they cannot be used to evaluate the quality and effectiveness of educational programs or identify possible opportunities for improvement. Evaluating the sensitivity of scores to educational effects actually involves two related sets of analyses. The first set examines the relationships between scores and students' educational experiences, whereas the second examines the sensitivity of scores to factors, such as gender, ethnicity, entering ability, and mode of assessment administration, that are not related to students' educational experiences. Ideally, an assessment measure will be strongly related to educational experiences and unrelated to noneducational factors. Evaluations of the sensitivity of assessment measures to educational experiences and noneducational factors generally have been correlational. That is, measurement specialists have tended to look at the magnitude of the correlations among assessment scores, educational experiences, and noneducational factors in order to determine whether assessment scores are more strongly related to educational or noneducational factors (see Banta and Pike, 1989).

Several new procedures have been developed to examine the influence of students' background characteristics on assessment scores. For many years, commercial test developers have regularly evaluated the cultural fairness of their tests (Erwin, 2000). Cultural fairness, or bias, in test scores is equally important in locally developed measures, although it is not frequently evaluated. At James Madison University (JMU), assessment professionals in the Center for Assessment and Research Studies regularly check for evidence of bias by using techniques such as differential item functioning (Anderson and DeMars, 2000), standardization, item response models, and Mantel-Haenszel procedures. Assessment staff at JMU report that these approaches have been very helpful in identifying inappropriate items and improving the sensitivity of test scores to educational effects.

Rapid advances in computer technology during the last ten years have provided assessment professionals with a variety of new techniques for assessing educational processes and outcomes (see Schilling, 1997). Although these new techniques hold great promise, they create a need to ensure that scores on assessment measures are not influenced by the mode of administration. For one of these new techniques—Web-based administration of surveys—the evidence regarding sensitivity to mode of administration is somewhat mixed. Some researchers have found that computer-administered surveys are more efficient and that mode of administration does not affect participants' responses to survey items (Olsen, Wygant, and Brown, 2000). But other researchers have found that computer-administered surveys are significantly more likely to produce socially desirable responses than paper-and-pencil surveys, particularly when the surveys focus on sensitive topics and students are concerned about the anonymity of their responses (Antons, Dilla, and Fultz, 1997). Although computer administration of surveys is likely to increase significantly in the near future, assessment professionals should carefully evaluate the effects of mode of administration on responses.

Overall, questions related to the selection and use of measures for both research and assessment revolve around the fundamental issue of managing measurement error. No measure of student learning is without error, and errors of measurement can create a variety of alternative explanations for assessment results that call into question the accuracy and appropriateness of conclusions about the effectiveness of education programs. Given the inherently murky nature of assessment and educational outcomes research, the most prudent course of action is to ensure that measures of student learning and development are as rigorous as possible and that knowledge claims are appropriately limited.

Although the discussion of measurement has, to this point, pertained to quantitative assessment approaches, it would be incorrect to presume that rigor is not a concern in qualitative assessments. Indeed, numerous scholars have proposed a variety of safeguards for ensuring that qualitative research yields accurate and appropriate interpretations (see Guba and Lincoln, 1989; Patton, 1990). Morse (1994) summarized these recommendations, noting that ensuring rigor in qualitative research requires that *adequate* data be collected to understand variation, that the selection of information be appropriate to meet the emerging needs of the study, that investigators construct an audit trail so that others can reconstruct the research process, and that the conclusions of the study be verified with informants. What is fundamentally important, however, is that the method of collecting information be appropriate to answer the questions addressed by the study.

Selection of Participants

The fourth element common to both assessment and research is the selection of participants. Two questions that dominate discussions about the selection of participants in both arenas are *How many participants should be included?* and *How should they be selected?* Statistically speaking, the answer to the first question focuses on *power* (that is, the likelihood that a difference will be found to be statistically significant for a given sample size), and a variety of resources are available to assist the assessor in determining the appropriate sample size from a statistical point of view (see Kraemer and Thiemann, 1987; Wood and Conner, 1999). From a practical or applied perspective, however, questions about the number of subjects to be included in an assessment design strike at the very heart of the assessment process. To answer the question *How many subjects?* the assessment professional must understand the purpose of the assessment. If that purpose is to provide feedback to students about their performance, then a strong case may be made for administering the assessment to all students. If the purpose of the assessment is to provide the institution or department with information about the performance of students in general, sampling may be most appropriate. Wood and Conner (1999) point out that questions about the number of students to be included in an assessment activity should focus on two fundamental questions: *What is the question being asked?* and *How large are effects likely to be?*

The ways in which these two questions are answered can affect the statistical power of an assessment dramatically. Using information about expected differences in scores on the Reasoning About Current Issues Test, Wood and Conner explain that if the purpose of assessment is to examine differences in the scores of freshmen and seniors, samples of as few as twenty students in each group will produce an 80 percent chance of finding statistically significant differences between groups. If the purpose of the assessment is to examine differences between the students at the beginning and end of the freshman year, a larger sample (for example, sixty to seventy students in each group) will be needed. When the goal of the assessment is to examine differences in the gains of two groups over time, a dramatically larger sample size is needed. For the latter situation, as many as 500 students in each group may be needed to accurately assess the effects of specific interventions on gains in critical thinking.

Once the question of how many subjects has been answered, the question in both research and assessment becomes *How should participants be selected?* Assuming that a sample of students is being assessed, the answer is straightforward. In order to make accurate and appropriate generalizations about the population from which the sample is drawn, the sample should be representative of the population. The best way of assuring that a sample is representative is to use random selection of students (see Kerlinger, 1986). In most field research, and in virtually all assessment studies, simple random sampling is not feasible. Although most textbooks on research methods suggest a variety of alternative sampling methods, it is important to understand that departures from random sampling violate the assumptions of many of the statistical procedures used to analyze assessment data, and violating the assumption of random sampling can have a profound effect on the accuracy of the statistical procedures being used (Thomas and Heck, 2001).

Although the importance of random sampling of students is generally acknowledged in the assessment literature, the importance of random sampling of student performances is seldom discussed. Statistical analysis of samples of artifacts from portfolios and performance assessments presumes that the artifacts have been randomly selected. Despite the fact that statistical analysis of student artifacts is based on the assumption of random sampling, many portfolio assessments allow students, or assessors, to select purposefully the artifacts that will be included in the portfolios, use numerical rating scales to evaluate the artifacts in the portfolios, and then proceed to analyze the numerical ratings by using traditional statistical methods. Departures from the random sampling of student artifacts are subject to the same statistical pitfalls as departures from the random sampling of students. The purpose of this discussion is not to criticize the many innovative and worthwhile efforts to use authentic examples of student performance to assess the quality and effectiveness of education programs; rather, the inclusion of what many would consider "methodologically picky" critiques of assessment research is included as a reminder that assessment, like most action research, is seldom methodologically pure. If the goal is the responsible application of knowledge to problems of consequence, then we must take reasonable steps to ensure the validity of our conclusions, be honest with ourselves and with our audiences, and openly acknowledge the limitations of our conclusions.

Communicating Results Effectively

Just as there are numerous articles and textbooks on the topic of research methods, the literature concerning effective communication of research results abounds. Bers and Seybert's book *Effective Reporting* (1999) provides a variety of useful suggestions about communicating research findings. Although it is tempting to follow in the footsteps of Bers and Seybert and provide a catalog of specific guidelines for reporting results, this section focuses on three general principles that I believe can help improve the quality of reporting and better ensure that assessment leads to improvement.

The first and most basic principle is that *assessment results need to be communicated frequently*. In their survey of assessment professionals at almost 1,400 colleges and universities, Peterson and Augustine (2000) found that one of the best predictors of the efficacy of assessment is the number of institutional assessment studies conducted and reported. It would seem that communicating assessment results, in and of itself, impels action on assessment. It is certainly true that it is difficult to act on assessment results if you don't know what they are, but, as Burke (1999) notes, the continuing communication of assessment results also helps break down the functional silos within colleges and universities that give rise to decentralization and autonomy, replacing them with a sense of community and common purpose.

The second basic principle of effective communication is to *know your audience.* It is essential to know who the decision makers are and then to ensure that they receive appropriate information upon which to base their decisions. It is also important to know what types of information the decision makers prefer and how they like to have results reported. It is absolutely essential to have the attention of key decision makers if assessment is to result in significant and lasting improvements.

My experiences at the University of Missouri (UM), Columbia, suggest that in some instances it may be necessary to create an audience for assessment. The Student Life Studies advisory board at UM includes administrators, faculty, and staff who have been very helpful in identifying areas of research and in identifying constituencies for the assessment findings. Ownership of these assessment results can be increased by involving audience members (for example, faculty and students) in the design and implementation of a research project. Participants in the design of assessment projects represent another vehicle for communicating assessment results, and their participation tends to enhance the credibility of the findings.

My experience also suggests that the effective dissemination of assessment results requires multiple modes of communication that are tailored to the needs of a given audience. Some audiences may require detailed assessment reports to guide their decisions; other audiences, particularly decision makers at the highest levels of the organization, may not have time to digest detailed reports and may prefer an executive summary of assessment findings. Still other decision makers may prefer that assessment results be presented orally. I almost always try to make oral presentations to senior administrators because these presentations give me an opportunity to engage the audience and to respond to questions about the research. At the same time, I always distribute something in written form—either an executive summary of the study or copies of the materials I use in my oral presentation. The availability of handouts keeps note taking to a minimum, allowing audience members to concentrate on the implications of the assessment results. The existence of written summaries and reports also provides a history and context for assessment actions that can be used to educate new decision makers when there is turnover in an organization.

Electronic forms of communication (the Internet and the World Wide Web) are relatively new modes of disseminating assessment results, and they hold great promise for quickly and efficiently communicating assessment findings to decision makers. These new forms of communication also present new challenges to assessment professionals. For example, creating an assessment Web site may be an efficient method of communicating assessment results, but it can also pose challenges to the security and confidentiality of information. In addition, the World Wide Web seems to be more like a daily newspaper than a book; that is, Web users seem to expect that the information on a Web site will be updated regularly. Web sites that are not updated regularly and contain stale information are less frequently visited. Thus, disseminating information via the Web may carry with it high maintenance costs owing to the need to continuously refresh and update information.

The third principle of effective communication is to *know your information*. As Bers and Seybert (1999) note, some information lends itself to presentation as text, other information lends itself to tables, and still other information is best presented as charts or graphs. An important consideration in deciding how to communicate assessment results is understanding which presentation format most clearly communicates the findings of a study. Personally, I am a proponent of keeping it simple. There is a wide variety of computer software packages that allow multicolor, multidimensional, and multimedia presentations. These software packages can be very useful in designing presentations that catch the attention of audience members. It is important, however, that form not detract from substance. That is, the presentation should not overwhelm the message. Sophisticated data presentation techniques should be used only if they improve understanding of the assessment results. In many cases, less is more. The experiences of both the University of Maryland, Hampton, and California State University, Stanislaus, indicate that simply hosting open campus information sessions can be one of the most effective methods of communicating assessment results (Engelkemeyer and Landry, 2001).

I began this chapter by observing that assessment is intimately linked to Boyer's (1990) concept of the scholarship of application. As such, assessment should focus on the responsible application of knowledge to problems of consequence. Most of the information presented here has described the responsible application of knowledge and the importance of rigor in assessment activities. I conclude with a plea for increasing our focus on problems of consequence and argue that there is no greater problem in assessment than our inability to influence academic decision making with assessment results. I challenge all of us to create a vision for assessment on our campuses that creates new definitions of excellence and renews our commitment to community.

Chapter Eight

Web Applications in Assessment

Mark D. Shermis and Kathryn E. Daniels

The principal problem with writing about technological innovations in assessment is that the developments keep changing. This is a double-edged sword. On the "dull" edge is the comfort and satisfaction that there will always be something interesting about which to write. On the "bleeding" edge is the realization that the contribution one makes will never be lasting because some newer innovation will replace a tool that was just illustrated as a "best practice." Even though there is no perfect resolution to these two tensions, our hope for this chapter is to identify the current state of the art with regard to Web-based assessments. Although it would be impossible to describe all the creative endeavors in this area, we will highlight a few of the newest developments, indicate how they might be used in a comprehensive assessment program, and identify additional resources that the interested reader can pursue.

If there is a lasting component to this work, it is that scholars everywhere are engaged in fusing technology and measurement with the goal of creating assessments that meet the scientific standards of *validity* and *reliability*. An assessment has validity—the cornerstone of any assessment procedure—if one measures that which is supposed to be measured, whether one employs authentic assessment techniques or some sort of standardized test. An assessment possesses reliability—a prerequisite condition for establishing validity—if one measures a construct in a consistent manner. Our hope is that technology will help transform practices from the past. That which was measured poorly several years ago may now be assessed more effectively. That which we couldn't conceive of measuring in the past may now be within our grasp.

The conceptual framework for this chapter borrows from Shermis, Stemmer, Berger, and Anderson's (1991) "research cycle," which shows how computer technology can fit into all aspects of the research or evaluation endeavor. The focus for this chapter will be on step 5, "Data Collection Strategies." The framework is illustrated in Figure 8.1.

First, we elaborate on the concepts of reliability and validity. Next, we identify common strategies for conducting assessments, including tests, surveys, portfolios, and observations. Then we move to Web-based sites or software that illustrate how emerging technology has influenced assessment practice. It should be noted that our selection of a software package for illustration is not meant as an endorsement of a particular product, though, obviously, we

**Figure 8.1. A "Research Cycle" Typically Used
for Research and Evaluation Activities**

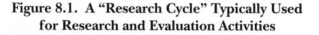

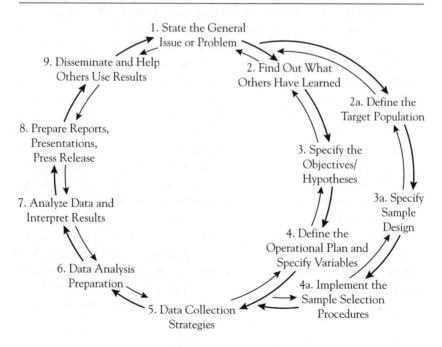

would not have picked something we did not like. Moreover, neither of us has a commercial relationship with any of the products discussed.

Two Basic Considerations: Reliability and Validity

Reliability is associated with the consistency of scores across evaluators and across time. An assessment may be considered reliable when the same results occur, regardless of when the assessment occurs or who does the scoring (Perkin, 1999). Sometimes we say that reliability is a *necessary but not sufficient* condition for establishing evidence of validity. This means that you cannot convince people of the validity of your measure if it is unreliable.

One barrier to establishing reliability is rater bias, which is the tendency to rate individuals or objects in an idiosyncratic way. For example, *central tendency, leniency,* and *severity* biases are names for errors in which an individual rates people or objects by using the middle of the scale, the positive end of the scale, or the negative end of the scale, respectively. A *halo error* occurs when a rater's evaluation on one dimension of a scale (such as work quality) is influenced by his or her perceptions from another dimension—for example, punctuality. Such biases can be reduced by the use of computer data collection strategies, since the computer has the capacity to provide immediate feedback both to the rater and to a supervisor. If the patterns of ratings warrant attention or intervention, this feature can be available *prior* to the collection of all data.

Validity involves establishing that an assessment measures what it is supposed to measure. It also can be thought of as the extent of the relationship between an assessment and the construct the assessment is supposed to predict (Birnbaum, 2001). For example, a math test (a type of assessment) possesses evidence of criterion-related validity when it accurately predicts who will succeed or fail in a math course.

Evidence of construct validity is important when trying to establish that the assessment adequately measures some hypothetical construct, such as intelligence or anxiety. These are constructs that we treat as if they were "real," but in fact they are simply operationalized through scores from an assessment instrument. Research needs to be conducted on assessment instruments to provide evidence of their validity and reliability.

Tests: A Common Assessment Format

Probably the most common assessment of student learning involves the use of tests. Over the past four years, software vendors have adapted their desktop testing software to Web-based mechanisms that typically include a server-administrator and the test generation software. Creation and administration via the Web have a number of advantages, including greater flexibility in testing configurations, reduced costs, instantaneous feedback for students, and the ability of faculty to collaborate on item banks or test construction. Testing formats that are supported include multiple-choice, true-or-false, fill-in-the-blank, short-answer, and essay tests. Most programs provide the capability to automatically grade all of the formats, with the exception of essay tests. However, many programs allow the test administrator to view an extended response and then assign points to it from within the testing package.

One of the primary methods for generating tests is to draw the questions from large item banks. Most assessment software enables the test author to construct a personal item bank or to adopt one that is provided by a textbook publisher. Often, instructors have accumulated many test questions over the years and already have a large question bank from which to draw subsets of questions. Assessment software, such as Perception, by Question Mark Computing, allows for selection of subsets of questions.

One possible solution for the difficulty in generating a large item bank is for academics in the same discipline to pool their resources and collaborate to form a large collection of questions. However, in order for this to be successful, there must be standard formats for storing the questions and agreed-upon standards for the classification of questions. A standard format is necessary so that the questions can be compatible with the assessment software used to generate the tests. Standardized approaches to formatting questions have been proposed by Question Mark Computing, among others, and are based on the standard generalized markup language (SGML) used to write HTML for Web pages (Thelwall,

1999). The software has the capability of classifying both the subject material of the questions and their difficulty (according to Bloom's Taxonomy). To compensate for the fact that questions from different institutions have varying subject material and levels of difficulty, instructors can refer their students to the question bank, explaining that their exam will be taken from those questions. The instructors then can select only the questions that match the subject matter learned in the course. Thus, students can be exposed to a variety of questions over the subject and perhaps benefit from the exposure to relevant subject material, even though that specific matter may not be covered on the exam. Instructors can also easily create practice or makeup exams by using this approach.

Assessing Thinking Processes

A criticism of objective tests is that they may lack authenticity (validity) or may only tangentially tap higher-order thinking skills. Two factors may explain why this occurs: (1) reporting thinking process data is expensive because it is labor-intensive and (2) higher-order thinking is often described in abstract terms, making it very difficult to measure concretely (Schacter and others, 1999). Broad definitions of problem solving have allowed standardized test developers to develop tests to assess problem solving. However, in the future, computer-based performance tests will be able to assess such thinking processes at the same cost as standardized tests. They can be administered, scored, and reported on-line over the Internet. Relational databases that capture student processes, backed by cognitive models of optimal thinking processes and performance, will allow the reporting of outcome and process variables and will increase reliability and validity (Schacter and others, 1999).

A study by Schacter and others (1999) was conducted in which problem solving was assessed in informational environments through networked technology. Students were supposed to construct computer-based "knowledge maps" about environmental topics. Students' problem-solving processes and performance were assessed with the National Center for Research on Evaluation, Standards, and Student Testing's (CRESST's) Java Mapper, a simulated World Wide Web environment and bookmarking applet, which provides students with outcome feedback. The Java Mapper was employed so that students could select concepts and link them to other concepts. The simulated World Wide Web consisted of over 200 Web pages pertaining to environmental science and other topic areas, and the bookmarking applet allowed students to send Web pages found during the search directly to concepts in their knowledge maps. While the students were searching for information and constructing their knowledge maps, they could access immediate outcome feedback concerning whether the links in their concept maps were correct and what additional work was needed. The feedback was based on comparing student map performance with the map performance of experts. Besides reporting to students about performance on the outcome measures, feedback was given about which thinking processes contributed to or detracted from their performance. Those students who searched the Web, browsed the pages to find relevant information, and accessed feedback were told the frequencies with which they employed these problem-solving processes. It was found that the students' scores on the knowledge mapping after this experiment (posttest) improved from the scores before the experiment (pretest). This kind of technology records students' thinking processes and gives them feedback on how well they engage in these processes. By using software and assessments such as this, teachers can benefit from the analysis of the detailed record of student process data.

Computer-Based Tests Using Multimedia

Computerized assessments can be expanded to include multimedia. Types of multimedia might include actual motion footage of an event, firsthand radio reports, and animations. Including these types of multimedia permits the presentation of tasks that are more like those actually encountered in academic and work settings. The ability to present these tasks may aid the measurement of problem solving and other cognitive performances that were previously omitted due to impracticality or the impossibility of assessing with paper-and-pencil instruments. For example, in the discipline of allied health, an assessment could contain the multimedia aspects of a static electrocardiogram strip, a dynamic trace from a heart monitor (that moves left to right), and a heart sound keyed to the monitor display. The student has to use this information to diagnose the patient's condition correctly. For the assessment, making the correct diagnosis depends on the audio information, a skill that could not be tested easily in paper-and-pencil format (Bennett and others, 1999). By using such technology and including multimedia in on-line assessments, students can be assessed in situations that are more applicable to real life.

However, there are important issues to consider before incorporating multimedia in tests, including measurement, test development, test delivery, and concerns about cost. For example, it is important to ascertain exactly what the multimedia are supposed to elicit. Construct distortion and irrelevant factors can creep into the measurement equation if the multimedia are not appropriate. In test development, one needs to determine if the tasks can be "mass-produced" and whether normal development tools and processes should be changed. After considering development, delivery is also an important consideration. Can test centers or testing sites support technology, and what new hardware and software will be required? Security issues and the preparation of test takers for new technology must be addressed (Shermis and Averitt, 2000). Finally, the cost to implement multimedia must be weighed to determine if the benefits of such technology justify its incorporation. After these concerns have been resolved, multimedia can be applied, giving test takers a more realistic type of assessment experience.

Some Available Testing Software

Following is an overview of a few examples of Web-based testing packages. At the end of this chapter is a listing of Web sites that pertain to testing software and related topics.

Perception—Question Mark Computing

Perception, offered by Question Mark Computing (http://www. qmark.com), enables the user to make questions and tests or surveys. It consists of two 32-bit Windows applications and three Web-based applications. The two Windows applications include the

Question Manager and the Session Manager. The Web-based applications include the Perception Server, the Security Manager, and the Enterprise Reporter.

Question Manager allows one to create questions and store them in hierarchically organized topics. It also scores the questions and creates feedback for right or wrong answers. Questions can either be customized or chosen from nine predesigned questions, including multiple-choice, multiple-response, text-match, fill-in-the-blank, numeric, selection, matrix, hotspot, and explanation questions. Within this application, questions and blocks can be tried out in advance and a multimedia wizard is available to help include multimedia within the test. It also allows for the storage of hundreds of thousands of questions and the organization of these questions into hierarchical topic databases.

Session Manager organizes the questions created in Question Manager into tests or surveys, called "sessions." Questions can be selected individually, from a topic as a group, or selected randomly from one or more topics. Links can also be created to another location in the test or survey (or another test or survey), based on individual questions or scores.

The Perception Server is the Web server application. It consists of the software that delivers the session to the participants, Security Manager, and the Enterprise Reporter. It enables one to present questions to the participants one at a time, rather than all on the same page, and allows for the handling of thousands of participants.

Security Manager gives one control over who takes the sessions and who has user rights to use Enterprise Reporter as well as gain access to the software. It enables one to enter a participant's name and password into the system, arrange participants into groups, set up user rights to the Security Manager and Enterprise Reporter, and schedule groups or individuals to take the assessment.

Enterprise Reporter allows one to conduct on-line reporting from anywhere in the world. It runs across the Web and enables analysis of responses to the surveys or tests in an easily accessible fashion. The questions, answers, scores, and other statistics are stored in specialized databases. Customized Web reports can be created and then saved for repeated use.

Surveys

The World Wide Web is a medium that allows for quick and easy collection of survey data. An advantage Web documents can offer is the ability to display "forms." Respondents simply have to click in small circles or boxes to select an option, or they can type responses into a box. After the respondent clicks on a submit button, data are automatically sent to the survey creators so that they can view the forms to see what information the respondent has provided. These forms are simple to complete and are very convenient for the user. In addition, these Web forms are simultaneously available to multiple users. Because of the form feature and time savings, the medium appears to have advantages over traditional paper-and-pencil methods. Other advantages include the elimination of respondent error and data entry errors for the researcher, as well as decreased cost due to the eradication of paper, envelopes, and stamps (Pettit, 1999).

In reference to the application of the survey via the Web, there still are technical issues that need to be considered. Several browsers do not support advanced HTML programming; therefore, it is important to use simple HTML code that most browsers will be able to read. In addition, not every browser is able to read Java and Javascript programming language, so its use may be limited. Finally, it is also very important to consider that the Web is accessible to all audiences, including children. Because of this fact, one needs to ensure that the measures selected for the survey are sensitive to age and maturity factors so as not to offend a wider audience.

SurveyWiz

SurveyWiz is a Web page that facilitates easy placement of surveys and questionnaires on the Web (Birnbaum, 2001). In order to access SurveyWiz, one must go to the Web site (http://psych. fullerton.edu/mbirnbaum/programs/surveyWiz.htm). This program allows the user to add questions with either text boxes for input or scales composed of a series of radio buttons, the numbers and endpoint labels of which can be specified (Birnbaum, 2001).

The survey must be given both a descriptive name (used for the title of the page and heading for the file) and a short name for reference. After the names are written, "Start Form" is pressed to begin survey construction. After the questions have been written, the type of response required selected, and the labels for the radio button scale composed (if applicable), the demographic button is pressed. This button provides preset demographic questions that can be added to the beginning, middle, or end of the form. The "Finish the Form" button is then pressed and one needs to go through and type instructions within the HTML code in the area titled "(put your instructions here)." As a final step, the HTML text is copied and pasted into a text editor and the file is loaded into the intended browser.

Other examples of Web-based survey applications include Zoomerang (http://www.zoomerang.com), which is a division of MarketTools. It allows one to conduct surveys, get prompt responses to questions, and view data in real time. Also available is HostedSurvey.com (http://www.hostedsurvey.com) by Hostedware Corporation. It is entirely Web-based and standardized, so one's survey would be compatible with all browsers on any PC, Macintosh, or other platform. Clients of HostedSurvey.com include those in academic, business, and nonprofit organizations. One final example is Qstation (http://www.qstation.com) by Atypica, Inc., which is a self-service Web site where one can set up (or arrange to have set up) Web-based-structured data-gathering forms such as surveys.

Electronic Portolios

What are they? Portfolios are purposeful organizations of learner-selected evidence of school and nonschool accomplishments. An electronic portfolio is similarly defined except that the evidence is contained on electronic media such as floppy disks, CD-ROMs, or the Web. Usually, the work contained in a portfolio represents the best example of what the learner is capable of doing for a particular class of products. The selection of what to include in the portfolio is made by the student, which means that the student has to develop criteria and expertise to evaluate his or her own work.

Six major premises underlie the use of electronic portfolios. It is desirable that they (1) be learner-centered and learner-directed, (2) serve as a developmental tool to help the learner set goals and expectations for performance, (3) be an instrument that provides a means for the learner to become self-aware and capable of gathering stronger evidence of skills, (4) serve as a basis for documenting and planning lifelong learning, (5) constitute an integration of career planning, counseling, curriculum, instruction, and assessment activity, and (6) be inclusive of the entire program (Stemmer, 1993). The sixth premise relates to the fact that some selections may come from outside the formal curriculum (nonwork accomplishments relating to major field of interest).

Electronic portfolios have advantages in that they typically stimulate greater buy-in from both faculty and students and are useful for other purposes, such as job interviews or application to graduate school. Also, they apply to both individual and program evaluations and historically have correlated well with other outcome measures in disciplines where they have been used (Hatfield, 1997).

Electronic portfolios are not without their disadvantages, however. There is significant time investment for faculty and students, especially during the start-up activities, and faculty and students may not have sophisticated knowledge of the software and hardware needed. Also, electronic portfolios require technical support, and there are varying levels of acceptance from other potential consumers. Figure 8.2 shows a screen shot of an electronic portfolio cover page.

Some academic Web sites provide additional examples of electronic portfolios. One is the portfolio page for Indiana University-Purdue University, Indianapolis (http://eport.iupui.edu). From this Web page, students can log in and revise their portfolios, or visitors may search for a portfolio by typing in a student's last name or ID number. Another electronic portfolio site is http://www.essdack.org/port, presented by Soderstrom Elementary School in Kansas. This site gives tips for creating electronic portfolios as well as providing examples of elementary students' portfolios. Two additional sites include Helen Barrett's On-Line Publications

Figure 8.2. Example of an Electronic Portfolio

(http: //transition.alaska.edu/www/portfolios.html) and the Kalamazoo Portfolio Project (http://www.kzoo.edu/pfolio).

Automated Essay Grading

Automated Essay Scoring (AES) is a new assessment technology
that permits computerized evaluation of written English, and it is
based on empirically derived rating models. Some past studies have
examined the process of automated essay grading with shorter documents under 500 words. Shermis, Mzumara, Olson, and Harrington (2001) conducted a study exploring the feasibility of using
Project Essay Grade (PEG) software (see http://testing.tc.iupui.
edu/pegdemo) to evaluate Web-based student essays serving as
placement tests at a large Midwestern university. The students'
essays were evaluated by six raters drawn from a pool of fifteen faculty and were then evaluated by the PEG software. An interjudge
correlation among the human raters of $r = .62$ and a comparative

statistic of $r = .71$ for the computer provided evidence that the computer model outperformed the multiple human judges in terms of producing consistent ratings.

Another study, conducted by Shermis and others (2002), used PEG to evaluate essays, both holistically and with the rating of traits—content, organization, style, mechanics, and creativity. The results of two combined experiments were reported, with the first using the essays of 807 students to create statistical predictions for the essay-grading software. The second experiment used the ratings from a separate, random sample of 386 essays to compare the ratings of six human judges against those generated by the computer. The automated essay grading technique achieved significantly higher interrater reliability ($r = .83$) than human raters ($r = .71$) on an overall holistic assessment of writing. Similar results were obtained from the trait ratings as well.

Currently, a project supported by the Fund for the Improvement of Postsecondary Education is under way; it is entitled "Automated Essay Grading for Electronic Portfolios" (Shermis, 2000). The purpose of this project is to create national norms for documents commonly found in electronic portfolios. Once norms are established, the project will make available for a period of five years automated software that will grade documents via the World Wide Web. Documents planned for this project include four writing genres: reports of empirical research, technical reports, critiques, and self-reflective writings. This approach uses the evaluation of human raters as the ultimate criterion, and regression models of writing are based on large numbers of essays and raters. To create the statistical models to evaluate the writing, multiple institutions from across the country, representing a wide range of Carnegie classifications, have agreed to participate in the project. Each will provide a large number of documents that reflect the range of achievement in their current electronic portfolios. The documents will be evaluated by six raters employing both holistic and trait ratings. Vantage Technologies, Inc., will provide the Intellimetric (http://www.intellimetric.com) parser for both the model building and the implementation of the project.

Observations

Peer Review

Ratings are forms of observational data that can provide both formative and summative information. Peer review and self-assessment have proven useful for formative evaluation. An advantage of self-assessment is that student motivation often improves when students are respected and involved in the learning process. An advantage of peer review is that feedback from an instructor may not necessarily be interpreted in the appropriate way, while feedback from another student may have a larger impact. There are also benefits to the peer reviewers, in that assessing another student's work forces them to think about the attributes of good work, gives them more of an incentive to learn material, and enables them to see the strengths and weaknesses of their own work, compared with that of peers (Robinson, 1999).

However, for summative assessment, problems arise with peer reviewing. For documents of low complexity, specific criteria to look for can be set for peer reviewers. But for complex documents, it is very difficult to teach an entire class what constitutes an excellent document. Therefore, a review from a single student may not be sufficient to produce a revision that meets the instructor's standards. An additional concern is that peer reviewers may not review a friend as critically as they would a fellow student who is not a friend. These two concerns can be addressed by employing anonymous and multiple-peer reviews.

Multiple-peer reviews protect against subjective judgments and increase the credibility of the evaluation of a document. If reviews are anonymous, biases toward friends may be alleviated and more objective evaluations can be made. One drawback in using this process is the paperwork burden that results from multiple copies of the reviews and revisions contributed by students. The paperwork problem can be addressed by conducting the reviews electronically.

To facilitate electronic self-assessment and peer review, a database network or Web-based system is required. Students produce their documents in digital form and submit the form electronically so that it can be channeled into a database and stored. Multiple reviews of the documents can also be submitted electronically and then sorted with the documents to which they pertain. This Web-based database system permits a double-blind system in which reviewers do not know whose document they are reviewing.

Advantages of this computer-based anonymous peer review system include ease of reviewing and rewriting before the paper is given a grade. Also, the system can allow for team-based writing projects in which the instructor is no longer viewed as a grader but is seen as a facilitator who helps students help one another. Finally, systems can be set up in which students first outline and write a proposal and then exchange comments with peers before writing their papers. This stimulates thought about the process of writing and makes it harder to plagiarize from the large number of documents in electronic circulation.

Automated Data Collectors for Indirect Observation

To facilitate the removal of observer bias (a source of unreliability) from observational experiments, an automated apparatus, or computer setup, may be utilized. Hedden (1997) has evaluated such an apparatus, which allows subjects to collect data on their own experiences. Within his experiment, he uses the apparatus to study subject interaction with computer games, but he believes it can be used for research on practically any type of human-computer interaction. Studies have found that people learn better when they are motivated by interest in the content or in the process of learning (Hedden, 1997). This interest, or intrinsic motivation, can be fostered by a sense that one is in control and acting on one's own will. Hedden found that to create these feelings of autonomy, there should be no limits set on the subject's choice of what to do or how long he or she can keep trying. In addition, the investigator should not be present during the study. To comply with these findings, Hedden removed the experimenter and allowed subjects to collect and record data while interacting with a computer. Hedden's apparatus can be referred to as a computer within a computer. The "outer computer" represents a bias-free observer of the subject while the subject interacts with the software that runs on the "inner computer." The apparatus attempts to ensure intrinsic motivation by forming a context supportive of the subject's autonomy, and it attempts to remove biases by replacing the human observer with a computer.

After the system is operational, but before data collection begins, subjects must be trained on the apparatus. They should understand the experimental procedures as well as the target software/task. It is also highly recommended that each subject practice on the apparatus and view a test recording of his or her performance with the investigator present in order to prevent any effect of the subject's level of comfort on the results of the experiment. After these precautions are taken, both the system and the subject should be prepared for data collection.

Conclusion

The field of Web-based assessment is vast and this chapter provides only a sampling of what is available. We have described the principal data collection procedures as well as a few popular sites offering software to implement such procedures. Because we are not able to offer comprehensive coverage of all the software, we conclude with a listing of Web sites pertaining to assessment that would be helpful to review on a continuing basis. These sites can provide the reader with a sense as to how Web-based assessment may evolve in the future.

Resource List of Web Sites Pertaining to Assessment

Following is a list of Web sites of associations and organizations that are concerned with assessment:

- American Educational Research Association (AERA) (http://www.aera.net)
- AERA Division D Measurement and Research Methodology (http://www.aera.net/divisions/d)
- AERA SIGS (http://www.aera.net/sigs)
- American Evaluation Association (http://www.eval.org)

- The Johnson O'Connor Research Fund—Aptitudes
  (http://members.aol.com/jocrf19/index.html)
- Applied Measurement Professionals, Inc.
  (http://www.goamp.com)
- National Center for Research on Evaluation, Standards,
  and Student Testing (CRESST)—assessment links
  (http://cresst96.cse.ucla.edu/index.htm)
- McREL (Mid-Continent Regional Educational Laboratory)—
  assessment projects (http://www.mcrel.org/products/
  assessment/index.asp)
- "Designing a Sustainable Standards-Based Assessment System,"
  by Don Burger (http://www.mcrel.org/products/
  assessment/designing.asp)
- Association for Institutional Research (AIR)
  (http://www.fsu.edu/~air/home.htm)
- Buros Institute of Mental Measurements
  (http://www.unl.edu/buros)
- College Board (http://www.collegeboard.com)
- Educational Testing Service (ETS) (http://www.ets.org)
- Graduate Management Admission Council—the GMAT
  (http://www.gmac.com)
- Graduate Record Examination (GRE) (http://www.gre.org)
- Journal of Psychoeducational Assessment
  (http://www.psychoeducational.com)
- Law School Admission Council (http://www.lsas.org)
- Association of American Medical Colleges—MCAT
  (http://www.aamc.org/stuapps/admiss/mcat/start.htm)
- National Association of Test Directors (NATD)
  (http://www.natd.org)
- National Council on Measurement in Education (NCME)
  (http://www.ncme.org)

ERIC

Professionals who have assessment responsibilities may be particularly interested in the ERIC home page. Ask ERIC e-mail service is a personalized Internet-based service for educators and professionals associated with education support services. The entire contents of "Resources in Education" and "Current Index to Journals

in Education" are available through the ERIC Database and the
ERIC Digest File, which consists of 1,500-word reports that synthesize research and ideas about emerging issues in education.

- AskERIC: (http://ericir.syr.edu)
- Ericae.net—ERIC clearinghouse for assessment, evaluation,
  and research information (http://ericae.net)
- ERIC/AE Test Locator (http://ericae.net/testcol.htm)
- SearchERIC Wizard (http://ericae.net/scripts/ewiz)

Additional Searchable Indices

- Research Measurement Transactions and SIG Activity
  (http://209.41.24.153/rmt/index.htm)
- Assessment and Evaluation on the Internet
  (http://ericae.net/intbod.stm)

Commercial

- Assessment Systems Corporation (http://www.assess.com)
- Comprehensive Adult Student Assessment System
  (http://www.casas.org)
- Coursemetric—customizable Web-based student evaluations
  (http://www.coursemetric.com)
- Kaplan, Inc. (http://www.kaplan.com)
- NCS Pearson (http://www.ncs.com)
- Question Mark (QM) (http://www.qmark.com)
- Scantron—scanning systems (http://www.scantron.com)

Assessment Tips

- North Central Regional Educational Laboratory—Critical
  Issue: Reporting Assessment Results (http://www.ncrel.org/
  sdrs/areas/issues/methods/assment/as600.htm)

Services Offered and Used by Various Universities

- Instructional Assessment System (IAS) at the University of
  Washington (http://www.washington.edu/oea/ias1.htm)

- Demonstration of Diagnostic Multiple-Choice Test (http://www.nott.ac.uk/cal/mathtest/demon.htm)
- Center for Excellence in Learning and Teaching, Pennsylvania State University—Student Evaluation of Educational Quality (SEEQ) (http://www.psu.edu/celt/SEEQ.html)
- Office of Planning, Budget, and Analysis, University of Colorado, Boulder—Undergraduate Outcomes Assessment (http://www.colorado.edu/pba/outcomes)
- Web-Based Assessment Tools (http://ist-socrates.berkeley.edu:7521/wbi-tools/assessment-tools.html)

University Testing Services

- BYU (Brigham Young University) Testing Services (http://testing.byu.edu/testinghome)
- The IUPUI (Indiana University-Purdue University, Indianapolis) Testing Center (http://assessment.iupui.edu/testing)
- MSU (Michigan State University) Counseling Center—Testing Office (http://www.couns.msu.edu/testing)
- Counseling and Testing, Northern Arizona University (http://www.nau.edu/~ctc)
- Oklahoma State University—University Testing and Evaluation Service, College of Education (http://www.okstate.edu/ed/extension/testing/testeval.htm)
- Old Dominion University—Student Services (http://web.odu.edu/webroot/orgs/STU/stuserv.nsf/pages/test_ctr)
- San Francisco State University—Testing Center (http://www.sfsu.edu/~testing)
- Measurement and Research Services, Texas A&M University (http://www.tamu.edu/marshome)
- UAH (University of Alabama, Huntsville) Instructional Testing Services (http://info.uah.edu/admissions/tstsrv/test.html)
- University of Alaska-Anchorage Advising and Counseling Center (http://www.uaa.alaska.edu/advise/home.html)
- Testing Services, University of South Alabama (http://www.southalabama.edu/counseling/testing1.htm)
- MEC Measurement and Evaluation Center, University of Texas, Austin (http://www.utexas.edu/academic/mec)

Chapter Nine

Information Support for Assessment

Victor M. H. Borden

College and university assessment activities take a variety of forms. Although the targets (students, specific classes, academic programs, support programs, the entire campus) and methods (student tracking, primary trait analysis, portfolios, standardized tests, program self-study) of assessment differ, they have in common the use of information about the results of teaching, learning, and support program processes to make continuous improvements (Ewell, 1984).

The provision and management of information for assessment efforts is becoming an increasingly necessary and complex support process. This chapter explores some of the concepts, organizational contexts, and practices of information support for a range of assessment functions. It is well beyond the scope of this chapter to treat any of these aspects in great depth. The primary objective, therefore, is to suggest a framework that can guide those who are looking at ways to establish or improve the information support infrastructure for assessment within a college or university.

Conceptual Guideposts

Information support describes an even more diverse set of activities than does assessment. Several major paradigms of information underpin differing information science disciplines. For example, from a library information sciences perspective, information support focuses on the processes and skills related to selecting and evaluating textual and electronic documents (Breivik, 1998). The "traditional" management information sciences perspective views information support in terms of the development of computer information systems to support primary organizational processes (Emery, 1987). The emerging knowledge management paradigm describes information support as processes for "producing, maintaining and enhancing an organization's knowledge base" (Firestone, 2000).

The Information Support Cycle

While each of these perspectives on information support is relevant to program and student learning outcomes assessment, the organizational setting (a higher education institution) and the cross-disciplinary and applied nature of assessment activities suggest a more pragmatic approach. One such model is described by McLaughlin, Howard, Balkan, and Blythe (1998). Their "Information Support Circle" includes five functions: identify concepts and measures, collect and store data, restructure and analyze facts, deliver and report information, and use and influence decisions. McLaughlin, Howard, Balkan, and Blythe provide a general description of the organizational resources and specific activities that are required to execute these information support functions.

A similar model presented by Borden, Massa, and Milam (2001) describes the first stage more broadly as a "design" stage, in which one goes through a range of processes (such as library research, professional networking, and local committee work) to determine the scope and operational components of an assessment or research effort. The subsequent stages in the Borden, Massa, and Milam model (data collection, preparation, analysis, dissemination, and application) parallel closely the subsequent stages of McLaughlin, Howard, Balkan, and Blythe but their development emphasizes the kinds of technologies, tools, skills and competencies, and professional roles that are required to "staff" this cycle.

Both of these models are most relevant to the kinds of activities involved in providing centralized (campuswide) support to primarily quantitative assessment efforts. This would be pertinent, for example, to assessments involving standardized general education tests, student tracking studies, and alumni surveys. These stages can also be applied in a general way to more qualitative assessment methods (for example, curricular mapping, portfolio assessment, and senior interviews). In a more distributed or decentralized way, the domain and range of assessment activities requires a broader set of specific technologies and tools, practitioner skills and competencies, and organizational arrangements.

The Domain of Assessment Information

Before we can develop a guiding framework for information support for assessment activities, it is important to outline the kinds of activities that might be considered within the domain of assessment and would therefore be the target of information supports. We consider, in turn, some of the methods described in more detail in the other chapters of this volume, but we do so here with attention to the information support requirements that they engender.

Classroom Assessment

In Chapter Ten, Tom Angelo describes how classroom assessment techniques (Angelo and Cross, 1993) have helped faculty across the country assess their instructional processes and make midcourse corrections to improve student outcomes. One of the major advantages of these self-contained methods is that they require little in the way of information support in the traditional sense. However, one of the inherent limitations of classroom assessment activities—their applicability to a narrow range of the student academic experience—can be addressed through the type of information supports described briefly earlier as those associated with knowledge management.

The intelligence gained through classroom assessment techniques is often considered personal information for the individual faculty member who uses them. This information may be shared, formally and informally, through discussions within departments or with a broader audience through efforts organized by units such as a center for teaching and learning, a center for academic excellence, or an office of faculty development. In effect, these operations serve the function of expanding the organizational knowledge base, that is, the key information support function in knowledge management, as cited earlier from Firestone (2000).

There is a growing body of methods and technologies associated with maintaining this knowledge base and making it available to an organizational or professional community. For example, the Classroom Assessment Techniques section of the Southern Illinois University, Edwardsville (SIUE), assessment resources Web site (http://www.siue.edu/~deder/assess/catmain.html) provides some examples of reflections on the use of these techniques in the SIUE community. The Cyber Cats section of the Eastern New Mexico University Web site (http://www.enmu.edu/users/smithl/Assess/classtech/cat.htm) serves a similar capacity.

Program Evaluation

Karen Black and Kim Kline describe variations in approaches to program review. Information support for program review is often most pertinent to the development of the program of self-study. It is common for an institutional research or other central information support office to provide available management reports and analyses to departments undergoing review. For example, at Indiana University-Purdue University Indianapolis, each program undergoing review is provided with a standard packet that includes reports on basic enrollment and degree trends, program demand (new admits), student progress, student satisfaction, alumni employment and further education outcomes, students' perceptions of their learning gains, and staffing patterns.

However, the primary information support for program review comes not with the provision of this information but with the conversations that ensue about how these information sources relate to the content of the self-study. For example, small programs often cannot benefit from continuing and alumni survey results because of the small numbers of students involved. Special surveys of course enrollees may be more useful to a program that has few majors but that offers service courses. Other assessment methods, such as interviews and focus groups, might be more useful to small departments. Student focus groups can benefit large programs as well in helping faculty understand the meaning and implications of survey results.

Many programs undergoing review also discover that their own information sources on the faculty, courses, and student learning outcomes are not well organized for review, analysis, and synthesis. Program faculty and staff can spend hours assembling up-to-date faculty curriculum vitae, collating results of student capstone course reviews, reviewing results from department-wide tests in introductory courses, and so on.

Thus, departments undergoing program review require more than a set of reports to support their information needs. They may also need assistance in conducting special studies, including follow-up explorations of information provided by a central support office. And they may require assistance in assembling and analyzing or synthesizing information from their own program-level records.

Assessment of Student Development

As George Kuh describes in Chapter Six, the primary way to assess student development is by asking students about their college experience and its impact on their attitudes, cognitive development, and behaviors. The survey methods employed in this activity range from paper-and-pencil instruments to focus groups and one-on-one interviews. Data from these can be supplemented with naturalistic observations and tracking studies that use data from the institution's operational information systems.

A range of instruments for assessing student development can be obtained from commercial and nonprofit groups. Entering student surveys are available from ACT™ (formerly American College Testing Program) and the Higher Education Research Institute at the University of California, Los Angeles. Two popular surveys of enrolled students—the College Student Experiences Questionnaire (CSEQ) and the National Survey of Student Engagement (NSSE)—are available from Indiana University's Center for Postsecondary Research and Improvement. The Educational Testing Service (ETS) provides assessments of student general education outcomes (Tasks in Critical Thinking) as well as learning in the major (Major Field Tests). Petersons now offers the College Results

Survey, developed originally as the Collegiate Results Instrument by Massey and Shaman (National Center for Postsecondary Improvement, 1999).

Borden and Zak Owens (2001) include these instruments and many others in their "survey of surveys" on quality assessments in higher education with an associated searchable database available at the publication Web site (http://www.imir.iupui.edu/surveyguide). They also lay out the kinds of organizational arrangements and conditions that should precede and follow the use of any such assessment instrument to optimize its use for institutional and program improvement. The information supports delineated in these conditions include the technical and methodological expertise required to choose an appropriate instrument, select samples, and package and disseminate survey results in formats that can be used by faculty members and administrators to make improvements in academic and support programs.

Assessment of Student Outcomes in General Education and in the Major

Learning outcomes assessment employs a range of methods—from standardized tests to rubric-based grading of essays and oral presentations, to portfolio assessment and capstone project reviews. Many of these methods use as their data the products of students' academic work. The supports required for designing, collecting, analyzing, and using the results of these assessments are similar in a general way to those described in the information cycle. Assessment of general education outcomes requires that these capacities be made available to programs and offices throughout the institution.

Information support infrastructures for assessment should accommodate program-level needs for assistance with collecting, managing, and using the assessment "data" obtained from student academic work. Current institutional data systems for planning, analysis, and management, such as those called data marts or data warehouses, are not typically developed for this purpose. These systems usually focus on data within the institution's operational information systems. There are some software systems that have been developed to accommodate these data systems, such as those available from Laureate, Inc. (http://www.laureate.net) and Enable

Technologies (http://www.enableoa.com). Winona State University recently received a Title III grant to create a similar type of resource specific to that institution's assessment needs (Hatfield and Yackey, 2000). Several institutions, such as Kalamazoo College (http://www.kzoo.edu/pfolio), Rose Hulman Institute of Technology (demonstration site: http://reps.rose-hulman.edu/demo/register.html), and Indiana University-Purdue University Indianapolis (http://eport.iupui.edu), have Web-based electronic student portfolio systems that can serve this purpose.

These emerging information support systems require some standardization in assessment approaches at the program level. That is, they can accommodate a limited range of methods and are specifically geared toward leveraging common methods across programs to derive institution-wide results. The level of consensus required for these systems is not easily attained, especially at large universities or those with long-standing traditions of program autonomy.

The Scholarship of Teaching

Hutchings and Shulman (1999) suggest that the link between the scholarship of assessment and the scholarship of teaching must be explicit if faculty are to embrace assessment. They identify as a requisite component the fact that the scholarship of teaching "involves question asking, inquiry, and investigation, particularly around issues of student learning" (p. 13). They further stipulate that for the scholarship of teaching to be sustainable, it requires an institutional "culture and infrastructure that will allow such work to flourish" (p. 15). That is, there must be administrative supports for this activity, including rewards and incentive systems, as well as institutional capacity for engaging in systematic research that addresses questions about teaching effectiveness and student learning and development.

A benchmarking study conducted by the American Productivity and Quality Center (APQC)(1998) identified several key components of measuring institutional performance outcomes in higher education institutions that relate closely to the kind of culture and infrastructure issues raised by Hutchings and Shulman (1999). One "cultural condition" specifies that assessment activities should reflect core values of the institution, as exemplified in several of the "best practice" institutions identified in the study. Examples include Alverno College's focus on cross-disciplinary "developmental abilities," Truman State University's attention to "academic quality" as defined by student achievement, and the "student-centered" system that values client feedback for maintaining quality at the University of Central England.

Other findings in the APQC study relate to the balance between providing reward and incentives for such work—whether performance measures or student learning outcomes assessment—while not directly punishing or rewarding units or individuals based on the results of those efforts. For example, at Indiana University-Purdue University Indianapolis, internal grant monies are available to faculty and staff seeking to improve student success in first-year courses. Proposals require an evaluation component with specific guidance as to important outcomes (evidence of improved learning, increase in percentage of passing grades, continued enrollment, and so forth). Results from these studies are shared among faculty across disciplines that teach these "gateway courses," through workshops and forums. Faculty have sufficient intrinsic incentive to adopt successful strategies and to discontinue unsuccessful ones. Moreover, successful programs lend themselves to subsequent budget requests for continuation funds. Most important, faculty and program administrators are not directly penalized or rewarded for the results of their efforts. Rather, an incentive is provided for trying to do something to improve student success and further incentive, in the guise of prospective compelling budget requests, to expand successful initiatives.

Hutchings and Shulman (1999) underscore a dilemma for providing systematic information support for assessment activities. Faculty involvement is essential for assessment success, but obtaining that support usually requires that assessment activities move forward with a substantial degree of program-level autonomy. From an information support perspective, this is served best by a developmental and consultative support structure. However, an integrative approach to assessment is more conducive to systemic reforms that are likely to have a more profound influence on the student learning process. This evokes a more centralized approach to assessment, as is characterized in the literature of organizational assessment (Lawler, Nadler, and Cammann, 1980).

Information support for assessment must strike a balance between these two countervailing forces. In the next section we consider how to extend the information support cycle approach to achieve this balance.

Information Support Requirements for Assessment

The information support cycle, although generally relevant to all assessment tasks, provides an incomplete specification for the range of information supports required by assessment activities in their various forms. In this section we place the cycle within a broader framework in order to address these insufficiencies.

First, it is useful to consider the domain of activities and supports for which the information cycle is most directly useful. The cycle is most relevant to a centralized support office, such as an institutional research or assessment office that develops a capacity for pulling together and managing information from various sources for the purposes of analysis, reporting, and application. This will serve well those components of assessment that employ data from an institution's operational information system for such analyses as student tracking or course-taking patterns. A centralized support structure can also assist with the implementation of campus- or program-based surveys, whether the surveys are developed locally or selected from commercially available ones.

Many institutions also utilize a centralized testing function that is staffed by professionals with expertise in psychometrics. This capacity can be useful for institutions and programs that choose to use standardized testing instruments such as those provided by the Educational Testing Service or ACT™ to assess general education or major field outcomes. This capacity is also useful for programs that seek to develop their own performance assessments.

The review of assessment activities in this chapter suggests several other information support requirements for assessment. These include program-level information management capacity, faculty development and consulting for qualitative and quantitative assessments, knowledge management, and integrative strategies for campus-level planning and external accountability. These require-ments are reviewed in turn and then integrated with the informa-tion cycle into a unified framework.

Program-Level Information Management

The tools, technologies, and professional staffing requirements for information support are growing increasingly sophisticated. In the early days of the assessment movement, the lack of accessible and appropriate data was viewed as a major obstacle to progress. As computing and information system technologies rapidly advanced, the problem shifted to issues about analyzing and interpreting overly abundant, although not necessarily the most appropriate, data (Ewell, 1988).

As assessment activities spread through an institution's aca-demic programs, so, too, do information support issues. Individ-ual departments and programs require information support in all aspects of the information cycle: identifying information needs; collecting and maintaining "data" ranging from quantitative, unit record information on students and faculty to representative sam-ples of student and faculty work; scoring and analyzing these various forms of data, interpreting the results of these analyses; and putting these results to use for program improvement. In sum, the infor-mation support cycle can be conceived separately as a framework for consulting and distributing systems development rather than as a map for developing centralized repositories and institution-wide capacities for analysis and interpretation.

The components of the cycle take on different aspects when applied in this manner. For example, data storage issues now include components of archiving, which requires knowing how long and in what form individual programs should maintain copies of student portfolios or capstone project reports that served as the input to pro-gram assessment efforts. This requires a professional skill set more typically found within an institution's library organization than in an information technology, assessment, or institutional research office. Similarly, the formatting and use of results now becomes embedded within the organizational climate for program evaluation, planning, and resource allocation decision making.

Faculty Development and Consulting

Many colleges and universities have deployed a centralized support staff and a technological infrastructure for the more judgmental and qualitative forms of assessment, such as portfolio assessment and primary trait analysis. These supports are typically consultative in nature, providing guidance to department faculty who choose to use these methods. Development and consulting supports are crucial for promoting and sustaining assessment in colleges and universities, regardless of whether faculty are intrinsically or extrinsically motivated to engage in assessment efforts.

The University of Kansas's Center for Teaching Excellence provides a comprehensive list of "Teaching Centers" around the world (http://eagle.cc.ukans.edu/~cte/resources/websites.html). For the United States, the list includes 241 separate centers at 223 colleges and universities in 47 states and the District of Columbia. Most of these centers focus their activities on efforts to support faculty who seek to improve their teaching effectiveness. Services typically include instructional consultation, course planning and development, and professional development workshops. But some centers, like the Portland State University Center for Academic Excellence (see http://www.oaa.pdx.edu/CAE), include the advancement of assessment as a core objective. The National Center on Postsecondary Teaching, Learning, and Assessment, (http://www.ed. psu.edu/cshe/htdocs/research/NCTLA/nctla.htm), with organized activities at Pennsylvania State University, the University of Illinois, Chicago, Syracuse University, Northwestern University, Arizona State University, and the University of Southern California, epitomizes the integration of faculty development and assessment to assist in the enhancement of the learning environment in postsecondary institutions.

Knowledge Management

Firestone's (2000) on-line paper on knowledge management provides an excellent overview of a rapidly advancing field that fills a great need in the further development of higher education assessment. Knowledge Management (KM) provides a set of concepts and tools for building and maintaining an organization's operational intelligence. KM, in its most comprehensive form, revolves around the organization's ability to create, distribute, and use knowledge about its own operations. The KM model is built around the essence of the scholarly approach: furthering our understanding about a field through in-depth inquiry and the sharing of results throughout the community. In effect, KM epitomizes what Ewell (1984) has characterized as the self-regarding institution.

It is reasonable to cite as examples of early KM efforts in higher education the development of institutional portfolios, which seek to organize the results of institutional assessment as indicators of institutional effectiveness. Examples include the portfolios being developed by the six universities involved in the Urban University Portfolio Project (http://www.imir.iupui.edu/portfolio). Whereas most business and industry KM efforts are aimed at cataloging institutional knowledge for internal management processes, the institutional portfolio is intended as a medium for communicating to external stakeholders the effectiveness of an institution in pursuing its education, research, and service missions. But given the broad and diverse constituencies involved in university operations, it is difficult to distinguish between internal and external audiences. For example, the Portland State University portfolio (http://www.portfolio.pdx.edu) includes guided tours for the business community, faculty, staff, current and prospective students, higher education boards and agencies, and the metropolitan community.

Efforts like those of the Urban University Portfolio Project notwithstanding, higher education institutions have been slow to adopt some of the more promising technology-based approaches to collecting and utilizing organizational intelligence (Edirisooriya, 2000).

A Unified Framework for Information Support to Assessment

One way to extend the information support cycle framework to serve assessment activities is to place it within the context of the organizational supports that serve the various functions. For example, the design stage of the cycle would relate to the kinds of supports often made available at centers for teaching and learning or offices of faculty development. These units support the developmental aspects of assessment efforts, wherein research and evaluation issues are clarified and linked to appropriate methods of inquiry. The data collection and storage part of the cycle can utilize supports available from the institution's information technology department, its library services, and the other centralized offices that support testing and survey administration.

The next stage of the cycle—restructuring and analyzing data—requires the kinds of support usually found in a centralized assessment or institutional research office. However, colleges and universities can also employ faculty with expertise in these aspects of inquiry. These same capacities are relevant to the packaging and dissemination stages of assessment. Using assessment results relates to other aspects of institutional support structures, as well. Administrative offices, committees, and faculty governance structures that oversee policy formulation, resource allocation, and program development can benefit greatly from the "intelligence" that derives from the results of assessment efforts. It is at this stage that the methods and tools of KM would be most useful.

The information support cycle is complete as the intelligence and experience gained through earlier efforts are fed back into the design and development stage. Answers to baseline questions raise additional questions that may require new methods and approaches. Ideally, the system achieves continuously higher levels of sophistication within existing domains (such as general education outcomes) and incorporates a wider array of domains (such as distance learning) leading down the path that W. Edwards Deming (1993) characterized as profound knowledge. Figure 9.1 summarizes the information support cycle within the context of organizational supports.

Elements of this integrative framework are exemplified by efforts like those of the National Center on Postsecondary Teaching, Learning, and Assessment, mentioned earlier in this chapter. The Teaching, Learning, and Technology Group (TLT) (http://www.tltgroup.org), an affiliate of the American Association for Higher Education, provides support across developmental, technical, and analytical aspects of the processes previously described.

Figure 9.1. Information Cycle: Functions and Supports

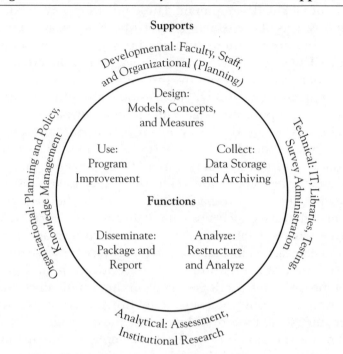

At Indiana University–Purdue University Indianapolis, the Office of Professional Development, located physically within a state-of-the-art technology-based library, works closely with the institution's planning, assessment, and institutional research departments to provide an integrated range of supports for student learning and program assessments throughout the campus.

Challenges to the Integrated Vision

The greatest challenge in assessing higher education programs, especially undergraduate programs, is the nature of the organization as a conglomeration of loosely coupled programs. As Kuh, Gonyea, and Rodriguez note in Chapter Six, the undergraduate student experience is integrated across both the social and the academic milieus of a college or university. Students will experience coherence throughout the various components of their education—such as residence life, student activities, general education, major courses, and electives—only insofar as there is coordination and collaboration among those who administer and implement the various aspects of the experience. Assessment, program evaluation, institutional research, or whatever other forms of self-study occur, can only serve to improve student learning if the organization attains a level of integration that is not commonly found in higher education.

College and university faculty often resist managerial approaches to organizational integration, as exemplified by total quality management and knowledge management approaches. This resistance is justified to the extent that these systematic approaches compromise the richness and variety of learning stimulated by academic autonomy. However, there is ample evidence that quality improvement and knowledge management approaches can have positive influences on institutional effectiveness (see Teeter and Lozier, 1993).

Boyer's (1990) expanded model of scholarship, as applied to both teaching and assessment, provides another possible approach to the integration of program evaluation and improvement efforts in higher education. As Hutchings and Shulman (1999) point out, scholarship is, by definition, a public activity, subject to review and replication by other scholars. If college or university faculty view teaching and learning as an institutional discipline, and participate in the scholarship of that discipline, there is the possibility of creating the kind of integrative approach that will optimize student learning.

Scholarly Assessment

The chapters in Part Four describe scholarly assessment as it is enacted at hundreds of colleges and universities across the United States. This process of planning, implementing, and reflecting on practice undertaken for the purpose of improving the efficiency and effectiveness of assessment takes place in individual classrooms, at the program level, and across the institution. All of these levels are treated in this section.

In Chapter Ten, Tom Angelo notes the popularity of classroom assessment but suggests that classroom research, like other forms of assessment scholarship, has failed to engage large numbers of faculty. His "guidelines for successfully promoting the scholarship of assessment" may assist in increasing the level of engagement in future years.

In Chapter Eleven, Catherine Palomba provides specific examples of scholarly assessment at colleges and universities across the country. Her focus is on the studies that are under way to document the application of assessment tools as faculty attempt to assess student learning in the major and in general education. Particular attention is given to performance assessment, capstone assessment, and the use of student portfolios to document learning.

Comprehensive academic program review is the assessment approach that Karen Black and Kimberly Kline describe in Chapter Twelve. Peer review can encompass all aspects of the life of an academic department—from the credentials and research interests of faculty members to the methods they use to demonstrate student learning—and the collective judgment of peers is the form of departmental assessment most universally accepted by faculty.

Assessment of institutional effectiveness is the focus of Chapter Thirteen. Here, Barbara Wright tells us how regional accrediting associations have shaped and been shaped by outcomes assessment over the past two decades. She also gives an account of the current ferment in the accreditation arena as all the associations attempt to streamline their processes and focus more intently than ever on the assessment of student learning outcomes.

Chapter Ten

Engaging and Supporting Faculty in the Scholarship of Assessment
Guidelines from Research and Best Practice
Thomas Anthony Angelo

Other chapters in this volume explain *why* outcomes assessment should be treated as a legitimate focus for academic scholarship and *why* American higher education needs such a scholarship of assessment (SoA). They also offer definitions and examples of *what* the SoA is and *what* it could become. The range of SoA examples presented runs from large-scale, multiyear institutional research projects led by highly trained professionals to small-scale, short-term studies carried out by the faculty members in their various disciplines. This chapter focuses mainly on the small-scale, faculty-directed end of that range and mostly on *how* and *who* questions. Specifically, it suggests how to evaluate an institution's or department's readiness for an SoA effort and *how* to build in success by learning from prior reform efforts. It considers *who* it is the SoA aims to inform and influence and, consequently, *who* among the faculty should be encouraged to practice the SoA. This chapter also suggests *how* to engage, support, and sustain those faculty practitioners in high-quality, high-impact SoA efforts. While it is intended primarily to help faculty leaders and academic administrators responsible for promoting and leading SoA efforts, this chapter should also be useful to those advancing other innovations, as well as individual faculty.

Underlying Premises

Four premises undergird the arguments and guidelines that follow. The first premise is that the SoA can improve educational quality only if it engages enough of the right "producers" and "consumers." That is, a significant fraction of influential faculty leaders (scholarship producers) must engage and succeed in the SoA. And at the same time, a much larger proportion of the faculty (scholarship consumers) must be convinced to take these activities seriously *as* scholarship and to apply SoA results to their teaching. The second premise is that productive, influential faculty members will engage in the SoA only if they find it intellectually compelling, professionally rewarding, and relatively unburdensome. And the third underlying premise is that, to be intellectually compelling, rewarding, and effective, SoA efforts must be designed and implemented according to the highest, most broadly accepted standards of academic scholarship. The final premise, notwithstanding the focus of this volume and this chapter, is that closely connecting the SoA with existing scholarship of teaching and learning efforts may be a more effective change strategy than presenting it as a new and separate form of scholarship.

Content

The discussion begins by placing the scholarship of assessment within the context of the current teaching and learning reform movement, generally, and within the context of assessment and the scholarship of teaching, specifically. It considers why these two approaches to reform have not yet produced deep and widespread learning improvement. I next present a case study—the dissemination of Classroom Assessment and Classroom Research—to analyze, using these "necessary conditions," then extract possible lessons for SoA proponents and outline a few basic conditions necessary to promote change successfully. Guidelines for successfully engaging and supporting faculty in the SoA follow, and the chapter ends with a proposal to embed the SoA within the scholarship of teaching and learning.

Sources

The necessary conditions and guidelines for success are drawn from four main sources: the previously mentioned efforts to disseminate Classroom Assessment and Classroom Research, the growing literature on the scholarship of teaching and learning, research and best practice studies in higher education assessment and faculty development, and the broader literature on the diffusion of innovations and organizational change.

Background

Over the past two decades, how we think and talk about teaching, learning, assessment, and scholarship in American higher education has changed—and much more dramatically than how we actually teach, assess, or do scholarship. The most consequential of these changes are both cultural and Copernican. That is, the central focal points of academic culture seem to be shifting away from faculty, traditional research, and instruction and moving toward students, scholarship, and learning. Barr and Tagg (1995) dubbed this a shift from the "instruction paradigm" to the "learning paradigm." While changes in behavior typically lag behind changes in concepts, significant changes have already been implemented in the rhetoric, standards, and practices of most accreditation agencies. And there are signs that this paradigm shift in academic culture is beginning to affect decisions regarding budgeting, hiring, tenure and promotion, course design, and instruction on many campuses.

The SoA's "Parents": Assessment and the Scholarship of Teaching

Assessment and the scholarship of teaching are broad-based reform movements that are, at the same time, outcomes and motors of this ongoing cultural shift. The scholarship of assessment is a hybrid of these two movements. Given that the promise of SoA derives largely from its dual parentage, it seems worthwhile to consider the strengths and weaknesses of both lines.

Assessment

According to Palomba and Banta (1999), "assessment is the systematic collection, review, and use of information about educational programs undertaken for the purpose of improving student learning and development" (p. 4). After fifteen years of a widespread assessment "movement," there is now broad agreement among accrediting agencies, disciplinary and professional associations, administrators, and faculty opinion leaders that improving student learning is (or should be) the primary goal of assessment. The fact that all of our accrediting agencies require assessment and that virtually all American colleges and universities claim to be practicing it (El-Khawas, 1995) constitute evidence of its wide and still-growing influence. At this point in its development, assessment is a relatively mature innovation that can claim a range of resources, a growing literature, and a large network of practitioners (see Gardiner, Anderson, and Cambridge, 1997; Banta, Lund, Black, and Oblander, 1996).

The Scholarship of Teaching and Learning

More recently, widespread consensus has begun to emerge among these same leadership groups on the need to expand the range of scholarly activities and faculty roles that are encouraged, evaluated, and rewarded. This notion of an expanded model of scholarship, and of the scholarship of teaching in particular, was first championed by Boyer (1990) and Rice (1991). Building on their work, scholars associated with the Carnegie Academy for the Scholarship of Teaching and Learning (CASTL)—notably Glassick, Huber, and Maeroff (1997) and Hutchings and Shulman (1999)—have developed definitions, examples, and standards for evaluating this form of scholarly activity.

But what is the scholarship of teaching or the scholarship of teaching and learning, since the two terms are used virtually interchangeably? According to Hutchings and Shulman (1999), "a scholarship of teaching is *not* synonymous with excellent teaching.

It requires a kind of 'going meta,' in which faculty frame and systematically investigate questions related to student learning—the conditions under which it occurs, what it looks like, how to deepen it, and so forth—and do so with an eye not only to improving their own classroom but to advancing practice beyond it" (p. 12). Throughout, CASTL materials characterize it as: discipline-based, public ("community property"), open to critical peer review and evaluation, and capable of being adapted and used by other teachers in the same discipline. With support from the Carnegie Foundation, the American Association for Higher Education, and The Pew Charitable Trusts, CASTL has created an impressive infrastructure for developing and disseminating the scholarship of teaching and learning, along with a number of useful publications (see http://www.carnegiefoundation.org). As of late 2001, over 200 campuses were formally involved in these efforts, and many more were engaged in activities influenced by CASTL.

The Limited Impact of Assessment and the Scholarship of Teaching

Notwithstanding these impressive achievements, neither assessment nor the scholarship of teaching has yet to make the deep and lasting impact on teaching and learning quality or academic culture that proponents have hoped for. In their review of the last two decades of reform attempts, Lazerson, Wagener, and Shumanis (2000) assert that "efforts to improve teaching and learning have been supported only in part by faculty and institutions as a whole, with results that are neither significant nor pervasive" (p. 14), and they conclude that "a genuine teaching-learning revolution seems far away" (p. 19). Ewell (in Chapter One of this volume) notes that after more than fifteen years of effort, assessment in higher education "remains established but stuck" and must be characterized as "broad but not deep." The same can be said of the scholarship of teaching at the end of its first decade. If the scholarship of assessment is to succeed, we must find ways to get unstuck and penetrate deeper into academic culture. This requires that we first correctly diagnose the reasons why promising and widely supported academic change efforts, such as assessment, so often fail to meet expectations.

Peter Ewell (1997c) offers a compelling diagnosis of failed academic reforms, noting that they have "been implemented without a deep understanding of what 'collegiate learning' really means and the specific circumstances and strategies that are likely to promote it," and that these reforms "for the most part have been attempted piecemeal within and across institutions" (p. 3). I would add a third, related, reason many academic innovations have failed or have underperformed: They have been implemented without a deep understanding of how faculty themselves learn and develop, how change occurs in academic culture, and what the most effective strategies and approaches are for promoting lasting change.

The Scholarship of Assessment

By all rights, the scholarship of assessment should be an attractive and effective innovation, given that it has the potential to respond to many real, widespread needs in higher education. For example, it has long been recognized that most American faculty members do not in fact engage in the "scholarship of discovery"—that is, in the traditional disciplinary forms of research that result in publication in refereed journals and grants—and that most faculty members do care about teaching and believe that it is undervalued. Partly for these reasons, many American universities are now revising or have already revised their retention, tenure, and promotion policies to include a broader conception of scholarship and to reward a broader range of scholarly activities. A likely expectation of administrators and trustees backing these changes is that a greater proportion of the faculty will engage in documentable and meaningful scholarly activities. Thus, while this broadening of options will benefit those faculty already engaged in less traditional forms of scholarly activity, it may also impel significant numbers to develop new skills and interests.

To respond to changed expectations and take advantage of these wider options, many faculty will need training and support in systematic, straightforward ways to do scholarly work on teaching and learning issues. The SoA can provide such an approach. Academic administrators, in turn, need more valid and useful information on teaching and learning effectiveness for personnel decisions, public relations, program review, and accreditation. But few institutions can afford to invest the additional staff and financial resources needed to generate this information through existing institutional research and assessment processes. Faculty engaged in the SoA could help provide such information, along with the knowledge and judgment needed to make use of it. And those responsible for assessment, faculty development, and accreditation need effective ways to engage and sustain faculty involvement in those efforts. By engaging large numbers of faculty in applied inquiry, the SoA could respond to these organizational development needs as well. Consequently, the SoA holds great promise for engaging faculty in activities to document and improve teaching effectiveness and student learning quality that are both institutionally and individually valuable.

But promising ideas alone—even ones that meet real needs—are not sufficient to change academic culture, as the past half century of attempts to disseminate innovations has amply demonstrated. A short list of promising but largely unrealized reforms might include educational television, programmed learning, mastery learning, writing across the curriculum, computer-assisted learning, and multimedia instruction.

How can the SoA avoid this common fate? First and foremost, realizing the promise of the SoA will require that its "champions" recognize and apply lessons learned from previous academic innovations—both successful and unsuccessful—and from the research on the diffusion of innovations more generally. Second, it will require alignment among three key elements: institutional systems, faculty culture, and leadership for change. In other words, it will require a more systematic, strategic, and scholarly approach to innovation. Taking these hard-won lessons seriously can better the odds that faculty will engage and persist in the scholarship of assessment and thus increase our collective understanding of and capacity to improve student learning.

Classroom Research and Classroom Assessment: A Case Study

Cross and Steadman (1996) define *Classroom Research* as "ongoing and cumulative intellectual inquiry by classroom teachers into the nature of teaching and learning in their own classrooms" (p. 2).

They go on to characterize Classroom Research as learner-centered, teacher-directed, collaborative (between students and teachers), context-specific, scholarly, practical, and relevant (pp. 2–3).

There are at least four reasons Classroom Research (CR) may serve as a useful case study in the scholarship of assessment. First, CR was conceived and developed from the start as a faculty-directed synthesis of applied educational research and outcomes assessment. Second, CR's history and development are largely parallel with those of the American assessment movement. Since K. Patricia Cross first introduced the concept in the mid-1980s, Classroom Research—and the closely linked *Classroom Assessment*—have remained associated with the assessment movement. Third, among existing approaches to faculty-driven assessment, CR is relatively well developed, with a small but rapidly growing literature of theory and practice. And fourth, through more than a dozen years of implementation and field testing, practitioners have learned useful lessons about what works and what does not in engaging faculty in pedagogical research. Thus, the successes and missteps of CR, to date, may be instructive for those promoting other approaches to the scholarship of assessment.

In 1985, K. Patricia Cross first introduced the concept of Classroom Research. A central tenet of her well-received message was that "the intellectual challenge of teaching lies in the opportunity for individual teachers to observe the impact of their teaching on students' learning. And yet, most of us don't use our classrooms as laboratories for the study of learning" (1990, p. 5). Cross urged teachers, in numerous speeches and articles, to take up that challenge by becoming "classroom researchers." In retrospect, Cross's vision can be seen as an early version of the scholarship of teaching. Indeed, four years later, in *Scholarship Reconsidered,* Ernest Boyer endorsed Cross's concept of the "classroom researcher" as a promising approach to the scholarship of application (1990, p. 61).

Soon after I began working with Professor Cross, in 1986, we realized that in order to get started successfully, many would-be classroom researchers needed a clear-cut method and a simple tool kit. To meet those needs, we developed Classroom Assessment (CA) to serve as the method and *Classroom Assessment Techniques* (CATs) to serve as the start-up tool kit (Cross and Angelo, 1988).

The purpose of CA is to provide faculty and students with timely information and insights needed to improve teaching effectiveness and learning quality. CATs are used to gather feedback on a single class discussion, lab, reading assignment, or other learning activity. Faculty use the information gleaned from CATs to make well-targeted adjustments to their teaching plans. They also share feedback on those results with students to help them improve their learning and study strategies. We viewed CA as only one possible method of inquiry within the larger framework of CR, much as CR is only one approach to the scholarship of assessment.

By almost any measure, Classroom Assessment has been a very successful innovation. Over the past fifteen years, tens of thousands of faculty from hundreds of campuses have attended workshops on CA, and many thousands have gone on to adapt CATs to their disciplines and courses. Beginning with Miami-Dade Community College in the mid-1980s, dozens of institutions of all types, and even whole state systems, such as Minnesota's former community college system, have developed their own CA projects. Well over 60,000 copies of the two editions of the CATs handbook (Cross and Angelo, 1988; Angelo and Cross, 1993) have been published since 1988, along with thousands of copies of two related collections of examples (Angelo, 1991, 1998). CA and CATs are cited regularly in the literatures of teaching and learning improvement and assessment and on faculty development Web sites, and they figure largely in faculty development program agendas. Although this chapter is concerned only with U.S. higher education, CA and CATs are becoming increasingly well known and used in Australia, New Zealand, and Britain, as well.

In sum, in the few years since its inception, Classroom Assessment has become a widely diffused, adopted, and accepted method for improving teaching, learning, and assessment. As such, it represents more an approach to "scholarly teaching" than an example of the "scholarship of teaching." On many campuses, CA has penetrated beyond the innovators and early adopters, and on some campuses, it has likely diffused beyond the early majority. This widespread diffusion does not constitute evidence that the proper use of CATs actually does improve student learning. The effectiveness of CA has yet to be established through rigorous, scholarly assessment. Unfortunately, the same can be said of most teaching and learning innovations. But the great majority of indications to date are positive and promising.

Why Classroom Assessment Has Been More Widely Adopted Than Classroom Research

Given that Classroom Assessment was developed as an introductory approach to Classroom Research, it is somewhat ironic that CA has, to date, been so much more widely diffused and adopted. In comparison with CA, the number of faculty who have participated in systematic CR training is probably still in the hundreds, and only a handful of campuses have sponsored ongoing CR projects. Cross and Steadman's comprehensive guide *Classroom Research: Implementing the Scholarship of Teaching* (1996) has yet to reach the wide audience that the 1993 *Classroom Assessment Techniques* handbook has enjoyed. To be sure, CR is often mentioned and praised in the teaching and learning literature, but it remains more praised than practiced.

In retrospect, some of the reasons for Classroom Assessment's much wider diffusion and adoption seem obvious. CA is, by design, a low-risk activity that requires modest time investment and little training, preparation, or planning. Faculty can begin experimenting with CATs after reading about them or attending short workshops. Most CATs fit easily into already established instructional routines and are similar to quizzes and questioning—activities familiar to most teachers. As CA requires relatively low levels of investment, faculty often expect little or no support or formal recognition for engaging in it, although some institutions, particularly community colleges, do include CA among activities that "count" toward tenure, promotion, and merit pay.

Classroom Research, however, requires more training or self-preparation and a greater commitment of time and energy. It also requires more advance planning, deliberate design, and more record keeping than does CA. With greater investments come greater risks. The activities involved in CR are also less familiar because relatively few faculty, even those who have done extensive disciplinary research, have ever engaged in systematic inquiry into teaching and learning in their disciplines. At the same time, there have been fewer opportunities for faculty to develop the skills needed to design and carry out CR. Because of limited budgets, short time horizons, and the desire to maximize involvement, faculty development programs have been more likely to sponsor short, one-shot CA workshops than the systematic, ongoing training required for CR, as have academic conferences and professional organizations.

CR's progress was also hindered by the inherent difficulties of participant research and the challenge of demonstrating that any approach or innovation "causes" better learning. Without accepted definitions of quality, metrics, or measures for student learning in most disciplines, it was, and is, nearly impossible to determine or communicate how well we are doing. Similarly, there was little consensus on how to assess this type of scholarship when CR was emerging, making it problematic for even sympathetic editors and colleagues to evaluate.

In addition to the individual, cultural, and systemic factors previously mentioned, some early implementation decisions may have inadvertently limited the reach of CR. For example, in retrospect, it is clear that I greatly underestimated just how challenging many faculty would find it to adapt and apply disciplinary research skills to teaching and learning questions. As a consequence, the early CR training modules and materials worked well for experienced innovators but often provided insufficient preparation for willing novices. At the same time, hoping to focus faculty attention directly on learning improvement and to involve nonresearch university faculty, the Classroom Research Project sometimes downplayed the importance of publishing the results of CR in disciplinary journals. At that time, there were few venues for publishing this type of scholarship and it was unlikely to be rewarded even if published.

With the concept of Classroom Research, as with other influential ideas, Professor Cross may simply have been ahead of the curve. Today, conditions are much more favorable for the widespread adoption of CR than they were during its first decade. For example, opportunities to present on CR at conferences and publish its findings in journals, both disciplinary and general, have expanded greatly in the past decade. And thanks to redefined policies on roles and rewards, presentations and papers on CR are now more likely to be counted and to "count" in retention, tenure, and promotion decisions than they were in the past. The same changed conditions that favor CR also favor the spread of the scholarship of assessment.

Some Necessary Conditions for Teaching and Learning Reform

To sum up the argument thus far, there are seven interrelated conditions that seem necessary, if not sufficient, for a teaching and learning innovation to succeed. First and foremost, the proposed reform has to meet strongly felt faculty needs *as well as* institutional priorities. Second, it must conform to the values and culture of the faculty. Third, it requires effective leadership *and* followership within and beyond the faculty, including involving influential faculty members from the start. Fourth, it requires long-term planning and a long-term institutional commitment. Fifth, success requires well-aligned support from the multiple systems that affect faculty life, including tenure and promotion, merit, course and faculty evaluation, workload distribution, and faculty development. Sixth, it requires resources, which often means redistribution of existing time, energies, and effort. And last, it requires "scaffolding"—that is, evolving programs and services designed to support faculty members through the difficult process of reflection, unlearning, experimentation, and critique that change requires.

Whom to Involve When

Perhaps the greatest challenge both the assessment and the scholarship of teaching movements face is engaging and sustaining broad and deep faculty involvement. Indeed, this is a problem common to all teaching and learning innovations—and innovations generally. Rogers (1995) provides a useful framework for analyzing this problem. He places members of organizations in the following categories, on the basis of their responsiveness to innovation: innovators, early adopters, early majority, late majority, and laggards (pp. 252–280). Rogers characterizes innovators as venturesome risk- and failure-tolerant cosmopolitans who are well connected to wide networks of innovators outside their organizations. Though innovators are the bringers of change, they are not necessarily highly respected opinion leaders locally. Early adopters, however, are typically well-respected local opinion leaders whose championing of innovations is necessary, if not sufficient, to make change (1995). These two categories generally make up less than a fifth of the total population of any organization. It is the early adopters who convince the next early majority, the next third or so, to try the innovation.

The assessment movement has struggled to expand and sustain faculty involvement beyond the innovators and early adopters. Unless new approaches to scholarship and assessment reach beyond these first two categories of disseminators, neither movement is likely to become an integral part of academic culture. By extension, the same caveats hold true for the scholarship of assessment.

Guidelines for Successfully Promoting the Scholarship of Assessment

The following guidelines are drawn from more than a decade of experience with classroom research specifically, and from the literature of academic innovations generally:

• *Plan for a long-term campaign.* Successful innovations take years to become part of the standard practice of the majority, typically a minimum of three to five years. Consequently, it is critical to plan on a several-stage, multiyear "campaign" (see Hirschborn and May, 2000). This is not to say that a campaign must be complex or costly, only that it must be well planned and able to persevere until the SoA becomes embedded in the local academic culture.

• *Engage and involve opinion leaders from the start.* In general, whom we begin with determines whom we end up with. Thus, it is wise to start by recruiting faculty opinion leaders from the main faculty groups one hopes to involve eventually rather than recruiting the easy and obvious participants. An initiative that starts with graduate teaching fellows and new faculty, for example, is likely to be perceived as being useful only for those groups. Similarly, an SoA effort that begins only with innovators and early adopters will likely be seen as a fad by other, more skeptical faculty.

• *Keep the focus on the main purposes: improving student learning.* There are many reasons to engage in the SoA, and the more reasons a faculty member finds to do so, the better. That said, the main attraction and promise of SoA lie in its focus on improving student learning, a focus that many faculty share. Taking this aim seriously, however, means finding valid and acceptable ways to measure student learning and not just involvement or satisfaction.

• *Identify likely costs and benefits—intrinsic and extrinsic—then lower costs and raise benefits whenever possible, and look for multiplier effects.* Potential practitioners need to know what's in it for them and what it will cost them. The likely costs of engaging in the SoA center around investing time and effort—and suffering occasional setbacks. These costs can never be totally eliminated, but they can be minimized. The likely benefits are multiple and relatively easy to capitalize on. Administrators need ways to get information on student learning without large new investments or expensive hires. Faculty need meaningful research projects for professional development and career advancement. Graduate and undergraduate students perpetually need funded employment and research opportunities. Inasmuch as working with faculty on research projects on campus is one of the most powerfully positive learning experiences students can have, providing support for student apprentices on SoA projects can generate multiplier effects all around.

• *Start with the familiar and make connections.* These are well-supported guidelines for effective teaching from cognitive science, guidelines that apply to faculty as well as to students. In the case of faculty learning the SoA, the familiar elements are the academic disciplines and traditional scholarly activities that they have observed and experienced. For many faculty, making connections between their prior knowledge and experience and the SoA—understanding key similarities and differences—will be critical to their success in changing behavior. Walvoord and Anderson (1998) offer a powerful way to build on the familiar by engaging faculty in the task of turning grading into a rigorous, scholarly form of assessment.

• *Provide scaffolding for novice and intermediate practitioners.* Most projects aimed at changing academic practice begin with training and support for novices, and most end there. Given the long gestation period of most reform efforts, most participants will need ongoing support well beyond the novice phase. As practitioners become more experienced in the SoA, the amount of structure—or "scaffolding"—they require should diminish.

- *Develop and sustain social supports for practitioners.* Changing one's academic practice is much like changing any set of habits or patterns. Support groups demonstrably improve the perseverance and success of those trying to lose weight or stop smoking. In the same way, SoA support groups can increase the perseverance and success of participating faculty.

- *Don't pay participants to do what is to become part of routine practice.* Faculty development projects, particularly those with grant funding, often offer stipends to participants for engaging in the desired innovative behaviors. All too often, faculty stop engaging in these behaviors when the stipends end. And new recruits are often hard to find after the money runs out. If we want faculty to engage in the SoA over the long term, paying them to do so initially is a risky strategy. Instead, use available funds to buy books and materials, provide training, send productive participants to conferences, and the like.

- *Insist on clear criteria and high standards for quality.* If the SoA is to become an accepted and consequential form of scholarly activity, it must be evaluated by scholars against agreed-upon, meaningful criteria. Thanks to Glassick, Huber, and Maeroff (1997) and the Carnegie Foundation, we now have "a powerful conceptual framework to guide evaluation" (p. 25) of the scholarship of teaching in any discipline that can serve the SoA as well. The framework includes the following six evaluative criteria: clear goals, adequate preparation, appropriate methods, significant results, effective presentation, and reflective critique. The challenge for disciplinary associations, institutions, and departments will be to adapt these criteria to their specific needs and circumstances as well as to different forms of the scholarship of teaching, including SoA.

- *Share information on efforts, findings, and successes widely.* To be credible and useful, the SoA must become public and shared. If we think of the implementation of the SoA as a kind of public education campaign, it is reasonable to assume that our audience will require many and various messages before they get the point. For most of us, faculty included, definitions are much less important than examples, and numbers are less compelling than narratives.

Planning ahead and using assessment to gather illustrative examples and stories, then, is a critical step in informing and influencing the early majority.

Why Not a Scholarship of Teaching, Assessment, and Learning?

I end this discussion of conditions and guidelines for success firmly convinced that a separate and isolated scholarship of assessment campaign is *not* likely to succeed. And I fear that adding one more innovation to the already long list may draw faculty attention away from the central aims of all: improving teaching and learning quality. Rather, I propose joining forces with the already widespread and prestigious scholarship of the teaching and learning movement, perhaps by inserting "assessment" between "teaching" and "learning." The scholarship of teaching and learning has opened into a very large umbrella, sufficiently broad to include the majority of examples found in this volume. Whether these two approaches are merged or are simply closely linked, both will gain strength, credibility, and influence.

Chapter Eleven

Scholarly Assessment of Student Learning in the Major and General Education

Catherine A. Palomba

This chapter documents the range of scholarly assessment activities occurring on college and university campuses and demonstrates the thoughtfulness with which faculty and administrators approach their assessment projects. Although primarily success stories, nearly every example shows the willingness of assessment practitioners to reflect on and improve their assessment strategies. Because many assessment methods apply equally well to assessment of student achievement in general education and in the major, examples are presented from both areas. The "reflective assessment work" described in this chapter illustrates the foundational choices that support scholarly assessment, trends in assessment practices, and factors that foster assessment success.

Assessment Scholarship Explored

Programmatic assessment focuses on the impact of a curriculum on the knowledge, skills, and values attained by groups of students. To assess student learning in general education or in the major, faculty work collaboratively to determine their educational goals and objectives, implement appropriate assessment methods, and use assessment results to improve their educational programs. They also evaluate and improve their assessment practices. Thus, the work of assessment practitioners exhibits the "common dimensions of scholarship" identified by Glassick, Huber, and Maeroff: clear goals, appropriate methods, and reflective critique (1997, p. 24). Glassick, Huber, and Maeroff identify effective presentation as an additional standard of scholarship. Assessment practitioners meet this standard when they recognize that their work has implications beyond their own campuses and they share what they have learned with others.

Regardless of their area of expertise, all scholars must be appropriately prepared before undertaking their projects (Glassick, Huber, and Maeroff, 1997). Assessment practitioners typically prepare for their work by becoming familiar with criteria that describe effective assessment programs. One frequently used source is the American Association for Higher Education's *Principles of Good Practice for Assessing Student Learning* (1992), which urge faculty and administrators to pay close attention to educational values and commit to continuity of effort. On a number of campuses, assessment leaders have found it helpful to develop their own guidelines for successful assessment. In the Division of Academic Affairs at Youngstown State University, assessment is expected to enhance the teaching and learning process and play an integral role in planning, budgeting, and allocating resources (Gray, 1999a). An important item on lists of good practice is the recommendation that assessment evidence be used to improve student learning. This provides the "impact" that is the necessary result of scholarly activity (Sandmann and others, 2000).

The Foundations of Assessment Scholarship

Sandmann and her colleagues (2000) identify "attention to context" as an important factor in strengthening the scholarship of outreach activities. To be considered scholarly, these projects need to "make sense in the context for which they are designed" (p. 48). Assessment projects are "primarily problem-oriented and field-based" rather than traditional laboratory research (Gainen and Locatelli, 1995, p. 5). Thus, assessment practitioners must address important contextual issues, such as reaching consensus about goals and objectives for learning and developing coherent plans for data collection.

Developing statements of intended learning outcomes is an important foundational step in the assessment process. These statements help faculty select relevant strategies for gathering assessment evidence. Equally important, clear statements about desired outcomes convey a "sense of direction and purpose for an academic program" (Gainen and Locatelli, 1995, p. 45) and help faculty "structure experiences that will lead to those outcomes" (Huba and Freed, 2000, p. 92). Huba and Freed (2000) encourage faculty to consider both "essential" and "unique" aspects of their academic programs as they begin to develop these statements. Because of their key role in shaping assessment and instruction, agreements about desired goals and objectives for learning must reflect widespread faculty involvement. When assessment leaders in the Mathematical and Computer Sciences department at the Colorado School of Mines were drafting their statement of departmental goals and objectives for learning, every full-time faculty member was interviewed. Faculty were asked what competences they thought students should possess at the end of their mathematical core and major courses. A subcommittee consisting of the department head, a mathematician, a computer scientist, a mathematics educator, and an assessment specialist drew on the faculty interviews, the university mission statement, and accreditation requirements to create a draft statement. After participating in several discussions, the faculty approved a revised statement, which is now available at the department's Web site (Barbara Moskal, personal communication, January 2001).

As the preceding example illustrates, a core group of assessment champions must exist to provide encouragement, support, and momentum as assessment proceeds. In many cases, leadership comes from an assessment committee whose members "facilitate the process and serve in a resource capacity" (Gainen and Locatelli, 1995, p. 18). At the University of Wisconsin-Superior, assessment of the general education program is guided by an assessment team that consists of the assessment committee, the general education subcommittee of the academic affairs council, and the assessment staff. Members of the assessment staff have worked with a small group of volunteers to design a developmental portfolio process for students. Although the assessment staff are responsible for the details of implementing portfolios, the entire assessment team plays a continuing role in portfolio design, periodically reviewing and revising the process (Katz and Gangnon, 2000).

Creating an assessment plan allows faculty to agree on content and direction for an assessment program. In the College of Business at Ball State University (BSU), the Graduate Curriculum and Assessment Committee guided development of a comprehensive assessment plan for the Master of Business Administration (M.B.A.) program. The committee recommended the use of multiple measures in order to verify results and explore alternative methods. Faculty endorsed this recommendation, reasoning that with the simultaneous use of several measures, they could more easily modify or eliminate ineffective techniques. To gather assessment evidence, they implemented a review of taped cases from the capstone course, a pre- and post-objective test, surveys of graduating students, and individual course-based assessment in all courses. After two years of collecting evidence, faculty reviewed the effectiveness of their approaches at an all-day retreat. They concluded that the individual course assessments were very labor-intensive and somewhat uneven in quality. Consequently, they decided to use the most effective course assessments as models for the others and to conduct these assessments in alternate years from the review of taped cases. Faculty also decided to refine the objective test and place the student survey on the Web. In addition to using their initial assessment results to improve their assessment methods, faculty also used them to consider changes in their curriculum. They created one task force to deal with integrating technology into courses and another to reevaluate foundation course requirements (Tamara Estep, personal communication, February 2001).

Like faculty at BSU, those on many campuses find that using evidence from multiple sources enhances their ability to make decisions. In the College of Arts and Sciences at the University of New England, the core curriculum assessment program includes both qualitative and quantitative approaches. A standardized instrument is used to examine reading, writing, mathematics, and critical thinking skills. Information about core curriculum themes is obtained through student focus groups and attitudinal surveys, and data on seniors is gathered through a required fourth-year citizenship seminar. After some experience, faculty modified their assessment program to include longitudinal tracking of individual students and to obtain faculty perspectives through a detailed survey (Paulette St. Ours and Maryann Corsello, personal communication, January 2001).

Assessment in Action

Based on the scholarly work of many assessment practitioners, some consensus about valuable ways to collect assessment information has emerged (Banta, Lund, Black, and Oblander, 1996). The following examples illustrate trends in assessment, such as the use of performance evaluation and capstone experiences. The examples demonstrate the careful attention that faculty pay to selecting, designing, and improving their assessment strategies. Similar to the actions of other scholars, assessment practitioners "think about what they are doing as they carry out their work" (Glassick, Huber, and Maeroff, 1997, p. 35). They engage in "choosing methods wisely, applying them effectively, and modifying them judiciously as a project evolves" (p. 27).

Performance Assessment

Although both locally developed and nationally normed objective tests are still in use for programmatic assessment purposes, faculty attention on many campuses has turned to performance assessment. Performance assessment requires students to display their learning through papers, exhibits, demonstrations, or other activities related to the subject matter, providing an opportunity for students to actively practice their skills, synthesize their knowledge, and engage in self- and peer evaluation (Palomba and Banta, 1999; Huba and Freed, 2000). At Sinclair Community College, nursing faculty use simulated clinical settings and patient problems to assess students' mastery of complex, integrated skills. Students participate in an examination during which actors play patients, and faculty observe student performance using standardized rating scales for evaluation. Nursing faculty at the college engage in a thoughtful approach as they develop this project. Faculty establish content and construct validity of the rating scales through the use of professional standards, feedback from faculty subject matter experts, and input from nurse managers from area hospitals. To ensure reliable results, the actors attend an orientation session to practice their roles, and faculty raters participate in a group training session. Debriefing sessions are held following testing to gather information to improve the examination process. Only after subjecting exam results to tests for interrater reliability and predictive validity do faculty feel confident about using findings to modify their academic program. Thus far, they have added discussion about the importance of critical thinking to various courses and have created additional opportunities for clinical students to participate in decision making (Goldman, 1999).

Because students generally design individual approaches in response to a performance assessment, they are able to display their talents and strengths as learners. Although this is one of the great benefits of performance assessment, the lack of standardization in student performances can decrease the reliability of assigned scores. To increase reliability, assessment scholars pay close attention to the development of scoring rubrics, which identify the aspects of student work that will be evaluated and the rating scale that will be used (Huba and Freed, 2000; Palomba and Banta, 1999). At the Colorado School of Mines, students participate in a four-course sequence, during which they work in teams to solve problems solicited from industry and local businesses. The rubric used to evaluate student projects addresses both technical content and written communication. According to Moskal, Knecht, and Pavelich (forthcoming), a careful study comparing results from fall and spring administrations revealed that, while the scoring rubric was effective, two other factors may have caused scores to be lower in the spring than in the fall. These factors were "the preparation of faculty mentors and the availability of appropriate projects." This insight has led to program improvements and to a decision to continue using the current scoring rubric.

Performance assessment is used to assess student learning in general education as well as in the major, particularly in areas such as speech and writing, where performance activities are traditional. As in the major, general education faculty seek to design assessment projects that provide meaningful learning experiences for students. According to Therese Trotochaud and Judith Dallinger (personal communication, January 2001), Western Illinois University (WIU) faculty recently modified their writing competence requirement "to better match current classroom practices." Rather than receiving one generic prompt at the writing exam, students are now given an article to read in advance. At the exam, students select one of three questions about the article as the basis for their essay. Reflecting real-world practice, this approach allows students to "have background information to work with as they write." WIU's writing center has developed a tutorial to help students prepare for the essay exam, and the new exam format has been adopted by several faculty for use in their classes.

Capstone Assessment

Capstone experiences allow seniors to demonstrate comprehensive learning in the major, as well as proficiency in learning goals that are valued in general education (Wright, 1997; Palomba and Banta, 1999). At Southern Illinois University, Edwardsville (SIUE), the Senior Assignment (SRA) is defined as a "scholarly engagement by the baccalaureate student, under the supervision of a professor, that results in a product" (Eder, 2001, p. 201). The product may be a thesis, poster, performance, design, or other evidence that allows the curriculum to be assessed. Students present their products to faculty, outside specialists, the university community, or the general public, often defending or explaining what was done. As described by Douglas Eder (who is director of undergraduate assessment and program review at SIUE), discipline-specific SRAs provide "a concrete integrative revelation to the faculty of student learning" and the curriculum that generated it (2001, p. 201). Eder encourages faculty to write about their assessment work and to present their results at conferences. Students often contribute to these presentations.

In many cases, capstone experiences occur within capstone courses. At California State University, Los Angeles, seniors who are biology or biochemistry majors participate in a joint senior seminar that enhances their critical and analytical skills. Seniors work in teams to prepare a grant proposal that represents a work assignment that would be encountered upon entry into the workforce. The course design was developed in Fall 1999 by Beverley L.

Krilowicz and Raymond Garcia, who received an Innovative Instruction Grant from the university's Center for Effective Teaching and Learning. Scoring rubrics were carefully designed to evaluate both the written project and an accompanying oral presentation. Students' projects were graded by the two course instructors and by an evaluation team of three "unbiased" faculty. Because panel members raised concerns about individual student accountability and about the quality of oral presentations, the course has been modified to include a peer evaluation process and a practice oral presentation (Krilowicz, Garcia, Oh, and Goodhue-McWilliams, 2000).

On some campuses, assessment information is also collected in freshman-level courses, allowing faculty to examine how students change over time. At the Colorado School of Mines (CSM), all entering freshmen complete a common introductory course that is used to collect baseline data. Then, even if students change their major, departments can still obtain entry-level information about those students who ultimately graduate from their program. (Moskal, personal communication, January 2001). At the Rocky Mountain School of Art and Design, students begin work on a cross-discipline timeline in their introductory freshman courses. As Elisa Robyns explains, assignments in subsequent courses continue to allow students to "integrate knowledge across disciplines and through time with a focus on ethics, diversity, and ecology." The timeline assignment is completed in the senior capstone course and is used to assess student development in integration and cognition (personal communication, February 2001).

Student Portfolios

To create portfolios, students select examples of their classroom assignments and other work and enter them in a collection device such as a folder or disk. Typically, students also include personal reflections about why the items were selected and what the items demonstrate about their learning. Faculty and other evaluators then review the portfolios for evidence of achievement on established learning goals. If done well, portfolios allow students to demonstrate their progress and to examine their personal strengths and weaknesses (Karlowicz, 2000).

Faculty teaching in a variety of majors, particularly professionally oriented subjects such as art and journalism, have found portfolios to be useful. At the Rose-Hulman Institute of Technology, faculty instituted portfolios to instill in their graduates "the skills appropriate to their profession and to lifelong learning" (Rogers and Chow, 2000, p. 4). Faculty designed a portfolio process that met several requirements, including ease of use, access through multiple search criteria, availability of on-line rating systems for faculty, and focus on defined learning outcomes. At the University of Phoenix, counseling students prepare three portfolios. The first is used to demonstrate communication and critical thinking skills and to determine entry into the program. The second demonstrates the ability to assess clients, plan interventions, and apply theory in practice. The third portfolio captures a student's internship experiences and demonstrates that he or she can "perform as a professional in a real-life situation." Faculty periodically update requirements to ensure that the project continues to validly reflect "the essence of what a counselor does" (Patrick Romine, personal communication, January 2001).

According to Karen Karlowicz (2000), the use of student portfolios is a "growing trend in nursing education," even though nursing educators have found it difficult to "correlate portfolio scores to other measures of program effectiveness," such as licensing pass rates (pp. 82–83). Before adopting portfolios at Old Dominion University, nursing faculty reviewed the portfolio literature, obtained portfolio samples from other schools, and sought advice from evaluation consultants. Then, faculty reviewed their courses to identify required elements for portfolios, created additional assignments to reflect portfolio goals, and identified opportunities for students to include self-evaluation materials. Experience with a pilot project led faculty to make several improvements in the process. Students are now encouraged to clarify their portfolio theme and to select contents based on their career path goals. Faculty have created a clinical objectives form to assist students in identifying the competences they wish to obtain in the clinical course, and they have introduced a one-credit-hour portfolio seminar for seniors (2000).

Portfolios are also used to assess learning in general education. At Ferris State University, portfolio review is used to assess writing.

A team of faculty reviews portfolios that are randomly selected from each section of the introductory writing course in order to get a sense of the types of assignments and kinds of writing taking place. Both the portfolios and the essays they contain are reviewed for organizational skills. A similar procedure is used to evaluate portfolios from the next English course, which focuses on research writing. Finally, the work of students in the professional writing course is evaluated for technical writing skills demonstrated through critiques of professional articles. As a result of this project, faculty have revised course objectives and evaluation instruments to focus on desired skills rather than on types of assignments and word requirements (Roxanne Cullen, personal communication, January 2001). At Stephens College, portfolios are used to focus on the whole general education program rather than on just one or two skills. Portfolios are assembled by seniors, drawing on all of their work while in college (Huba and Freed, 2000).

Trudy Banta (1999) has recently noted that portfolios "are becoming the instrument of choice for assessment on a growing number of campuses" (p. 3). Nevertheless, implementing successful portfolios is a difficult challenge, and some campuses have already experimented with and abandoned this approach to assessment. For example, nursing faculty at one campus introduced portfolios with the best of intentions but found that after several years portfolios did not provide sufficient information to justify their cost in faculty and student time. To successfully use portfolios, faculty must develop clear guidelines about their purposes and about the method that will be used to evaluate their contents. Faculty who introduce portfolios without thinking through these issues in advance have found portfolios awkward to use, at best (Ewell, 1999).

Course-Based Assessment Approaches

Because general education programs typically include several learning goals drawn from numerous disciplines, faculty often struggle to find an effective way to assess these programs. On some campuses, faculty have chosen to assess the learning that is occurring in individual courses. In this approach, course instructors use assessment evidence to demonstrate that students in their courses are mastering the knowledge, skills, and values associated with one or more goals from the general education program. Often, faculty use existing or newly designed classroom activities for this purpose, integrating assessment into the teaching-learning process in a way that is minimally intrusive for students (Walvoord and Anderson, 1998). Southern Illinois University, Carbondale, has a large student body with many transfer students who do not take core courses in any particular order. Hence, faculty believe that evaluating individual core courses on a regular basis is the best approach to assessment. For each course, instructors establish learning outcomes that support overall program goals. They also create a longitudinal portfolio for the course, containing syllabi and assessment reports provided by instructors. The Core Curriculum Executive Council reviews these portfolios to ensure that objectives of the course meet core goals, that appropriate indicators are being used to gather assessment evidence, and that assessment results lead to course improvements. Courses that do not meet these standards are put on warning or are dropped from the program. Initial assessment efforts have pointed to areas that need attention, such as creation of appropriate learning goals for interdisciplinary courses (Morey, 1999).

Faculty serving on the University Core Curriculum Committee at BSU have nearly completed their second round of a similar course-based assessment process. The process was not without contention, as some faculty objected to the time involved in preparing their reports and to the control exerted by the committee. The committee found it necessary to convey to faculty that, rather than merely satisfying the committee, "their own learning about the courses and their implementation of improvements were the overall goals of the UCC assessment process" (Hill, 1999, p. 10). The committee's work was facilitated considerably when they updated and improved the worksheet they were using to examine assessment reports submitted by course instructors. The redesigned worksheet highlights the importance of making course improvements. Group meetings with department chairs and faculty also address this issue.

Positive Influences on Assessment Scholarship

A number of factors influence assessment success and create conditions necessary for assessment scholarship. Some factors, such as support from university resources and encouragement from disciplinary accreditors, come from outside academic departments and programs. Other factors, such as a strong link between assessment and program beliefs about teaching and learning, can be directly influenced by faculty. Examples of how these factors promote scholarly assessment are shared here.

University Resources and Support

University resources and support reflect an institutional commitment to assessment and are mandatory in fostering assessment success. Southern Illinois University, Edwardsville, has provided substantial financial resources for assessment, primarily through the Senior Assignment Fund, which facilitates assessment projects in the major. The fund is used to foster student-faculty academic relationships and to help embed assessment activities within the teaching and learning process (Eder, 2001). Nonfinancial resources are also useful. Assessment leaders at California State University, Bakersfield, have created a Program Assessment Consultation Team (PACT) of local faculty and staff, who provide consultation and assistance for assessment. Members help departments develop learning goals and objectives. They also conduct focus groups and interviews and have written an assessment handbook. A well-trained group of students helps PACT carry out qualitative assessment projects (Mary Allen, personal communication, January 2001).

The existence of university-wide requirements provides support for assessment by stimulating related activities in academic departments. At Youngstown State University, departments must submit annual reports that include intended student outcomes, activities to assess these outcomes, results and conclusions drawn from assessment activities, and an indication of how the results will be used to improve the curriculum (Gray, 1999a). At the University of Massachusetts, Amherst, the program review process focuses on assessment of student learning. Departments must describe their assessment process in their self-study, and external evaluators are asked to critique this process (Martha Stassen, personal communication, January 2001).

Disciplinary Accreditation and a Professional Focus

Faculty and staff in professional fields are often campus leaders in assessment of student learning (Palomba and Banta, 2001). In several professional areas, disciplinary accreditors provide a strong and positive influence on assessment of student achievement in the major. These accreditors expect their members to assess general education skills such as communication and critical thinking, encourage the use of performance assessment, and urge their members to use assessment results to improve student learning. The American Council on Pharmaceutical Education, for example, asks members to engage in continuous improvement that is driven by data (Zlatic, 2001). Specialized accreditors and professional associations use Web sites, written materials, and conference sessions to support these activities. Additional factors, such as opportunities for active learning and close faculty ties with external stakeholders, have also fostered assessment in professionally oriented disciplines.

On many campuses, pharmacy education faculty have developed thoughtful and creative approaches to assessment. Faculty from Creighton University, the University of Arkansas, and Shenandoah University have worked together to develop the Pharmaceutical Care Encounters Program, a valid and reliable system used to assess whether students can perform competences expected of pharmacists. At the University of Georgia's College of Pharmacy, faculty questioned the validity of surveys designed to determine whether learning objectives had been achieved during the year and added student focus groups to their assessment program to help obtain this information. Pharmacy faculty share the results of their assessment work in publications such as the *American Journal of Pharmaceutical Education* and the *Journal of Pharmacy Teaching* (Zlatic, 2001).

Nursing is another discipline in which faculty engage in scholarly assessment activities and publish their work in disciplinary journals. In a recent review of assessment practices among nursing faculty, Donna Boland and Juanita Laidig write that "the greatest challenge faculty have faced is how to develop valid assessment plans" to determine "both individual student competences and group competences for learners" (2001, p. 85). In addition to identifying overall competences, nursing faculty have struggled with how to define particular outcomes such as critical thinking. Faculty from the Medical Sciences College of Nursing at the University of Arkansas conducted a national survey to examine practices in assessing critical thinking. The authors concluded that "definition and measurement are major problems" for nursing faculty as they attempt to assess critical thinking, but faculty are motivated to deal with these issues (O'Sullivan, Blevins-Stephens, Smith, and Vaughan-Wrobel, 1997, p. 28). At Linfield College, for example, nursing faculty developed a measure to evaluate the competence of senior nursing students to apply theory and think critically. Results from this measure were examined for their psychometric properties and were correlated with results from other instruments (May and others, 1999).

Involvement of Stakeholders

Many of the previous examples illustrate the key role faculty play in carrying out assessment and the actions that assessment leaders take to ensure their involvement. Faculty development efforts are particularly useful in engaging the interests of faculty in assessment. At the University of Massachusetts, Amherst, staff from the Office of Academic Planning and Assessment and the Center for Teaching have collaborated to create "faculty work groups on assessment" with members from across campus who collaborate on assessment issues. Topics have included the development of writing objectives and the use of course-embedded assessment strategies in large general education courses (M. Stassen, personal communication, January 2001).

External stakeholders such as employers, internship supervisors, and alumni provide valuable perspectives that strengthen the assessment process. At Kean University, Carol Williams and Dorothy Rizzo reviewed information gathered from external agency-based field instructors when they assessed the Bachelor of Social Work (B.S.W.) program. Based on a content analysis of field instructors' evaluations of student work, faculty developed a required learning contract for students and initiated a training program for field instructors. Williams notes that, over time, assessment practice in the B.S.W. program "has become more in-depth," maturing from an impressionistic alumni survey to concrete information about the "learning process that students experience" (personal communication, January 2001). Faculty in Tufts University's School of Veterinary Medicine benefit from a survey project that obtains information from alumni, employers of veterinarians, faculty, and students. Feedback from alumni has been particularly helpful in identifying the need for more clinical training. Each year, the assessment committee reviews survey instruments for clarity, brevity, and function, and they have designed additional instruments to follow up on some survey results (Terkla and Armstrong, 1999).

Current students are important stakeholders in assessment. To participate effectively, they need faculty support. When faculty in teacher education at Providence College designed their portfolio process, they included several strategies to assist their students, including a series of seminars conducted across the four years of preservice teaching. Each student is provided with a portfolio partner with whom he or she can consult, as well as an upper-class mentor. Departmental advisers review progress with their advisees on a periodic basis, but formal assessment of student work is conducted by teams consisting of an education faculty member, a noneducation faculty member, and a practicing classroom teacher (Thibodeau, 2000).

In addition to demonstrating their learning, students can contribute to assessment in a number of other ways, such as articulating learning goals, evaluating assessment instruments, and providing feedback on educational experiences (Palomba and Banta, 1999). In the art department at California State University, Northridge, the department chair conducts at least one town hall meeting each semester for students only. Any information obtained about achievement of learning outcomes is then provided to the entire department (Madison, Fullner, and Baum, 1999). Psychology students in the social and behavioral sciences department at the University of New England have made a unique contribution to that department's assessment efforts. As part of an upper-division psychology assessment course, students critiqued the department's assessment model. Drawing on the theory and practice they were studying in the course, students provided several suggestions about how to improve the assessment program and presented their findings at the university's annual research symposium. Through their research methods class, students in the department participate in collaborative assessment work with academic and cocurricular units throughout the university, helping faculty and administrators design instruments and analyze and report findings. As Maryann Corsello and Paulette St. Ours point out, these students "serve as consultants to units who would otherwise not have the resources or expertise to conduct such assessments" (personal communication, January 2001).

Relationship to Teaching and Learning

Assessment is most successful when it is part of a larger context of teaching and learning. At Alverno College, assessment scholarship reflects the educational values of the faculty. In their recent book, *Learning That Lasts,* Mentkowski and Associates (2000) describe Alverno's learning and action principles for assessment design. Each principle is linked to a campuswide view of teaching and learning. For example, the view that learning is integrative and experiential leads to the principle that "assessment must judge performance" (p. 60). The view that learning should be characterized by self-awareness leads to the principle that "assessment must include expected outcomes, explicit public criteria, and student self-assessment" (p. 60).

Reflecting the assessment-as-learning principles that originated at Alverno, pharmacy educators on several campuses have adopted an ability-based curriculum plan and have integrated assessment into the entire teaching and learning process. For example, in the Division of Pharmacy Practice at the St. Louis College of Pharmacy, faculty identified seven abilities to be addressed in all division courses. Then, working in ability subcommittees, they examined performance expectations for each course and developed criteria for three levels of student performance correlated with the curriculum. Faculty "painstakingly developed, shared, and revised self-, peer-, and expert-assessment forms" to be used to provide formative feedback to students, as well as to generate summative assessment information (Zlatic, 2001, p. 58). Incorporating the assessment-as-learning principles developed at Alverno College provided a coherent framework for assessment efforts in the division.

Patience

Although it is intangible, patience is an important factor in creating effective assessment programs. Faculty on many campuses work for several years to develop such programs (Palomba and Banta, 1999, 2001). In 1995, a workgroup of faculty, administrators, and librarians from California State University began its systemwide efforts to assess the general education skill of information competence. After examining existing definitions available through other universities and professional organizations, the group formulated six core competences that collectively identify the "ability to find, evaluate, and use information effectively." Lorie Roth notes that the quest to find an appropriate method to assess information competence "evolved through a series of stages." Initial efforts focused on a multiple-choice test that was piloted and improved. Next, questions about information competence were incorporated into an already existing and well-established systemwide survey instrument. Then a telephone survey was instituted in which more than 3,300 students were asked to respond to hypothetical scenarios, such as seeking information for a planned trip. Students were assigned both a "breadth" score to reflect the comprehensiveness of their answers and a "depth" score to rate their ability to elaborate on specific issues. Only now has the working group embarked on its ultimate goal, which is to develop and administer a performance-based assessment technique to every student (personal communication, January 2001).

At Truman State University, assessment efforts in general education began more than twenty years ago with the use of nationally normed exams. Careful thinking about the results led faculty to introduce two major qualitative assessment projects, one focusing on writing and self-assessment skills and another focusing on the use of portfolios to evaluate the liberal arts and sciences curriculum. Faculty continually revise these projects, based on student self-reflections and artifacts. At Truman State, assessment projects are considered major faculty development efforts that lead to improvements in teaching, curriculum, and student learning (Shirley Morahan, personal communication, January 2001).

Flexibility

Although continuity is an important characteristic of successful assessment, flexibility is also important. As in other areas of scholarship, flexibility allows scholars to "respond to change, to pick up a clue and follow it as a project proceeds" (Glassick, Huber, and Maeroff, 1997, p. 29). Richard Seymann (2000) writes about how assessment of honors college students at Lynchburg College in Virginia was redesigned after faculty identified open-ended problem solving as their educational objective. After an informative visit from Cindy Lynch and Susan Wolcott, faculty adopted the view that successful problem solving involves a four-stage development process that begins with the ability to identify problems and recognize uncertainty. Once faculty recognized this developmental sequence, they realized that they needed to link the freshman year experience more explicitly to the senior year. They have introduced a first-semester freshman group research project that helps develop the skills students need as they complete their programs.

In their book *Developing Reflective Judgment* (1994), Patricia King and Karen Strohm Kitchener describe the strong reliability and validity of the Reflective Judgment Interview, which is used to examine complex problem-solving skills. However, the time and expense involved in using this interview protocol has led Kitchener, Philip Wood, and others to develop a new instrument that contains both discrimination and recognition items—the Reasoning about Current Issues (RCI) Test. Research results from a cross-sectional and longitudinal study of the RCI indicate that it is measuring outcomes that are quite distinct from those measured by currently popular critical thinking instruments. The willingness of these scholars to develop the RCI should result in a valuable new assessment approach for faculty who include problem solving as an outcome in their academic programs (Kitchener, personal communication, February 2001; Phillip Wood, personal communication, February 2001).

Challenges to Assessment Scholarship

To begin their assessment efforts, faculty often ask, *What do we want graduates of our program to know, do, and value?* Then, faculty work together to establish learning goals and objectives and to agree on an approach to assessment. Unlike scholarly inquiries in many other areas, this is not a question that can be answered by one or two faculty working independently. Faculty in assessment must work collectively to design and carry out their agendas. The need to work collaboratively is both a strength and a weakness for assessment scholarship. Faculty who traditionally have worked alone to develop assessment methods for students in the classroom now have to work with others to make decisions. Reaching agreement on goals and objectives for learning and development may take months or years. Designing and implementing assessment techniques can be just as time-consuming. Issues of responsibility—who will do what and when?—can provide difficult challenges. Yet the chance for faculty to work collectively can be exhilarating. Faculty in the College of Business at Northern Arizona University (NAU) found that their culture was transformed when they recognized that the core curriculum "belongs to the faculty as a whole rather than [to] an area" (p. 6). Course instructors drafted syllabi containing student outcomes statements for each course. The statements were later approved by the full faculty and synthesized into a set of seven learning outcomes for the entire business core. Such efforts to "break down functional blinders" created an "environment of change" at NAU (Tallman, Jacobs, and Jacobs, 1999, p. 28).

Faculty on other campuses report similar kinds of results from engaging in assessment efforts. Philip Wood describes how faculty in the psychology department at the University of Missouri are often skeptical of assessment results, questioning data that are posttest only or that do not control for differences in student abilities. Nevertheless, assessment evidence about student approaches to problem solving has shown faculty that "careful consideration about complex reasoning has a place in the design of their coursework and major." Faculty have become more aware that how and what they teach makes a difference in student learning. They have created more opportunities for students to write intensively, to engage in problem-based learning, and to work with faculty on research. In addition, department assessment efforts have led to a "shift in commitment of resources to the improvement of undergraduate instruction" (personal communication, February 2001).

Overcoming challenges to assessment scholarship may be most difficult in general education when faculty must come together across several disciplines to decide on learning goals and objectives and agree on strategies for assessment. Tom Lowe confides how several faculty at BSU initially resisted the course-based approach to assessment developed by the University Core Curriculum Committee. For example, faculty in some disciplines were reluctant to assess the development of values within their courses. Only after the committee instituted a series of week-long faculty development workshops and provided advice on conducting assessment did those individuals who were most resistant to assessment begin to see its value and become supporters of it (personal communication, January 2001). Over time, the efforts of these and other faculty involved in assessment of general education contributed to a successful cross-disciplinary effort in organizational learning at BSU (Hill, 1999).

Conclusions

Although some faculty and administrators are new to the challenges of assessment, others are experienced practitioners. As scholars, these individuals pay close attention to context, seeking widespread involvement in developing statements of goals and objectives for learning and in implementing assessment strategies. Similar to nursing faculty at Sinclair Community College and Old Dominion University, as well as scholars in other fields, these practitioners "show an understanding of existing scholarship in the field" and "use methods recognized in the academic community" (Glassick, Huber, and Maeroff, 1997, pp. 27–28). Assessment practitioners learn through trial and error and are willing to modify their programs. Thus, on many campuses today, assessment processes are quite different from what they were when they were introduced. As do scholars in other disciplines, those in assessment benefit greatly from reflective critique.

Much evidence exists that faculty use the results of assessment to modify their academic programs, as well as their approaches to assessment, providing the "impact" necessary for scholarship. However, few assessment practitioners can clearly demonstrate that these changes have improved learning. Because assessment projects rarely involve controlled experiments, demonstrating cause and effect is particularly difficult. In spite of this challenge, many assessment practitioners view assessment as a legitimate area of research and routinely communicate their work with others through disciplinary journals, *Assessment Update,* conference presentations, and other outlets. From scholars like Kitchener and Wood, who devote much of their energy to understanding a particular area of learning, to campus experts who focus on helping their immediate colleagues, many stakeholders are involved in scholarly assessment efforts. As at California State University, Bakersfield, and the University of New England, students themselves often contribute to assessment in unique ways.

With so much assessment activity occurring across the country, much knowledge exists that has yet to be shared. Those who are working locally should be encouraged to tell their stories, perhaps on their own Web sites. Not unlike other areas of research, more is known about how successful programs have been modified than about what does not work at all. Thus, scholars need to write about their failures as well as their successes. Much is left to learn—particularly about what works best in what circumstances. For example, why do portfolios fail on some campuses? Under what circumstances do they work best? Huba and Freed (2000) suggest that portfolios may allow for more effective reflection if they extend beyond the period of a single course. Is this the case?

With respect to particular methods, performance assessment is increasingly widespread, particularly in those areas where it grows most naturally out of the curriculum. Indeed, faculty use the methods that are best suited to their disciplines. Case studies are frequently used in business, while clinical observations are used in nursing. Portfolio usage, which can involve all kinds of assessment evidence, has branched out from traditional areas such as art to less traditional areas such as business and engineering.

General education faculty use assessment methods that are similar to those used by faculty teaching in the major; however, faculty engaged in assessment of general education programs struggle with greater organizational issues. Course-based approaches, which are sometimes used to assess major programs, are becoming more popular as a way to assess general education programs. These approaches maximize faculty involvement in assessment but can be very labor-intensive. Campuses such as SIUE—which use senior assignments to assess achievement in general education, along with achievement in the major—have adopted a model that should be useful on many campuses. To insist that general education always be assessed separately from the major may make assessment more of a burden than it needs to be.

In all, the examples included in this chapter demonstrate that the work of assessment practitioners reflects common dimensions of scholarship, including attention to goals, careful preparation, appropriate methods, communication, impact, and reflective critique. Faculty do not merely purchase an instrument, put it in place, and then forget about it. They carefully evaluate whether or not their methods and approaches are effective. They develop assessment programs that are thorough, clever, engaging, and evolving. Thanks to their contributions, many scholars of assessment have been able to improve their own assessment practices.

Chapter Twelve

Program Review

A Spectrum of Perspectives and Practices

Karen E. Black and Kimberly A. Kline

This chapter traces some trends in evaluation and program review and provides an example of one institution's attempt to study and improve the program review processes on each of its eight campuses. This three-year study produced a literature review and a matrix identifying common and varying practices used in the conduct of program review across the eight campuses.

History and Trends in Evaluation

While program (or peer) review and program evaluation have similar meanings, *program review* is a term used almost exclusively in higher education, while *program evaluation* tends to be used in the P–12 education, education, business, and not-for-profit sectors. We use these terms interchangeably in this chapter. Program evaluation is a systematic field of inquiry that has formed the historical and philosophical underpinnings of what we refer to as program review.

Some scholars have noted that program evaluation in education, particularly higher education, has evolved from what it was in the 1960s and is just beginning to reach a point of institutionalization. During the 1980s, some researchers suggested that evaluation was "making the transition from late adolescence to adulthood" (Conner, Altman, and Jackson, cited in Worthen and

Sanders, 1987, p. 11). However, practitioners who wish to use evaluation models to inform their program review process can trace these models back to the 1800s in K–12 settings. In the mid- to late 1880s, studies by educators Horace Mann, Henry Barnard, William Torrey Harris, and others provided empirical support for matters of concern to educators (Travers, 1983). Horace Mann expressed his concerns to the Board of Education of the Commonwealth of Massachusetts in a series of annual reports between 1838 and 1850. Mann's reports contained information on issues such as geographic distribution of schools, teacher training, financial support for poor students, and selection of an appropriate curriculum—issues that are prevalent today (Travers, 1983). These studies provided some of the first records of empirical work in the field of education and served as a precursor to models of program evaluation, and later, program review.

One of the outgrowths of the educational evaluation movement in states like Massachusetts and Connecticut was the attempt to undertake large-scale assessments of student achievement. Students were tested within the Boston school system on their comprehension of several subjects, including geography, writing, and math. These assessments took place in 1845 and 1846 but were abandoned in 1847 because the results were never used (Travers, 1983). Later, between 1895 and 1905, Joseph Rice made a similar call for standardized examinations at the national level for elementary and secondary schools. Rice had claimed that faculty were not properly and efficiently engaging students and set out to employ wide-range assessment testing as a way to support his assertions. He discovered that there were large differences in test scores among students in certain subjects, such as arithmetic. Based on these findings, Rice proposed the creation of standardized tests (Travers, 1983).

A few years later, Rice's *The People's Government: Efficient, Bossless, Graftless* (cited in Travers, 1983) made a significant contribution to the development of evaluation in the United States. Rice addressed a process for resolving policy conflicts within education. It was an early acknowledgment of the role that politics plays in education, and it provided the underpinnings of what would become the judicial or advocate-adversary approach to evaluation (Travers, 1983).

Another event in the development of evaluation took place during the same time period, from about 1906 to 1915, in Gary, Indiana. Superintendent William Wirt was recruited to Gary from Bluffton, Indiana, for his innovative vision. This vision, coined "The Gary Plan" or "Work-Study-Play Plan," called for an integration of academics, school, and community, whereby academics would be intentionally applied to the everyday life of the student (Travers, 1983).

In their 1915 book, *Schools for Tomorrow,* John and Evelyn Dewey (cited in Travers, 1983) included a description and endorsement of the changes that were taking place in the Gary School System (Travers, 1983). Many advocates viewed the Gary model as the wave of the future, but there were some opponents, mainly conservatives, who viewed the model as a passing fad. Superintendent Wirt was determined to refute this view. With new evaluation tools available, Wirt approached the General Education Board and asked that a comprehensive evaluation of the Gary School System be conducted. The General Education Board agreed and appointed Abraham Flexner to conduct the study (Travers, 1983).

The appointment of Flexner was unusual because he was a conservative and in favor of traditional forms of education. The results of his comprehensive review seemed to reflect his negative opinions toward the progressive, community-based schooling offered by the Gary School System. Flexner concluded that:

- Gary students were academically inferior to students from comparison groups.
- Gary students did not respond to tests that required drill, recall, and memorization.
- The Gary Plan's innovative, community-based style was not effective when compared with the efforts of other school systems, because "academics" were compromised (Travers, 1983).

What the Flexner report did not point out was that when tested on problems that required critical thinking skills, Gary students scored as high as the average established by the other students tested. Also, Travers (1983) noted that Gary was not representative of many other Midwestern towns of the time. There were many first-generation Americans living in Gary who were bilingual, using their families' native languages when in the home. Thus, it is suspected that the children of Gary may have scored significantly better than their first-generation peers in other locations. The situation in Gary, Indiana, was an obvious exercise in political might that can be characterized as a difference in ideological beliefs. It paints a telling picture in the history of evaluation, one that illustrates the damage that can come from evaluation taken out of context.

Between 1932 and 1940, Ralph Tyler conducted the Eight-Year-Study, which measured the effectiveness of different types of schooling available at the time. Tyler's research focused on "learning outcomes instead of organizational and teaching inputs, thereby avoiding the subjectivity of the professional judgment or accreditation approach" (Madaus and Stufflebeam, 2000, p. 9). Many believe that Tyler made some of the first formal linkages between outcomes measures and desired learning outcomes, and evaluation made significant progress in what came to be known as the Tylerian Age (Madaus and Stufflebeam, 2000). Later, scholars steered the conversation regarding higher education away from entrance test scores, numbers of students enrolled (Astin, 1985, 1991), and faculty rankings (Conrad and Blackburn, 1985) toward "educational outputs such as knowledge, skills and values" (Palomba and Banta, 1999, p. 5). Pioneers such as Tyler have provided a foundation for scholars in the field of assessment to develop further the use of student learning outcomes.

The War on Poverty and Great Society programs that followed World War II were not evaluated for several years. As the years progressed, however, some federal officials became more concerned about the millions of dollars that were being spent on these two initiatives. Officials' and taxpayers' concerns become more pronounced and resulted in the Elementary and Secondary Education Act (ESEA) of 1965. Title I of this act required educators, for the first time, to submit evaluation reports that demonstrated the results of their efforts (Worthen, Sanders, and Fitzpatrick, 1997). The federal act awarded thousands of dollars to schools, state governing agencies, and universities to help elementary and secondary schools comply with the mandate in Title I. This national assessment requirement served as the precursor to the calls for formal assessment that are ever present in higher education today.

More recently, colleges and universities in the United States have implemented peer review as a means of developing the quality of academic programs. In the 1980s, groups concerned with accountability embraced program review by respected peers as a tool, and the two entities have been connected ever since. In 1982, Barak reported that over 82 percent of higher education institutions were using some form of program review. Program review has held different meanings, depending on the goals of a particular organization. Arns and Poland (1980) defined program review as a "searching, comprehensive evaluation of an existing coherent set of academic activities" (p. 269). Because of the multiple goals of program review and the uniqueness of each program, a single model for program review that can serve all programs has not emerged (Arns and Poland, 1980; Barak and Breier, 1990; Clark, 1983; Conrad and Wilson, 1985; Craven, 1980).

Evaluation Models

A review of current literature indicates that various evaluation models are used by colleges and universities. These models influence the policies and procedures set forth for peer or program review. The models here outlined have their roots in the field of program evaluation, which predates peer or program review. Although not specifically referenced, some of the most commonly employed models or approaches reflected in program review guidelines nationwide are the input model, comprehensive approaches, the connoisseurship model, the goal-based approach, and the hybrid approach.

The Input Model

Traditionally, institutions have relied upon inputs or resources for assessing quality. These factors include faculty reputation, student admission data, facilities, and size of the endowment. The rankings of faculty reputation are ambiguous at best and are not adequate for assessing undergraduate programs in particular because the entire institution influences the student, not just departmental faculty members (Conrad and Blackburn, 1985). Most colleges include input data in their planning and reporting efforts, but it is not appropriate to use input criteria alone, because they do not reflect the impact of the institution.

Comprehensive Approaches

Some universities employ a decision-making model that uses a matrix of data as a tool to enhance academic decision making. The Context-Input-Process and Product (CIPP) model balances the amount of data assessed with the degree of change that is needed. This model considers four contexts for decisions: planning, structure, implementation, and recycling. Stufflebeam and others (1971) introduced CIPP in 1971; however, it has not gained widespread popularity among college and university leaders (Craven, 1980).

The Connoisseurship Model

An outside evaluator who serves as the primary instrument of measurement may be called a connoisseur. Acting in a fashion similar to that of a music or art critic, the connoisseur utilizes a combination of professional expertise and distinct case study style to complete an evaluation. Madaus and Kellaghan (2000) describe it as being able to "discriminate the subtleties . . . by drawing upon a gustatory, visual, and kinesthetic memory against which the particulars of the present may be placed for purposes of comparison and contrast" (p. 30).

The Goal-Based Approach

The goal-based approach is one of the most commonly applied approaches to evaluation in education. A goal-based process includes the following steps: 1) goals are clarified; 2) indicators of goal attainment are defined; 3) achievement data are collected, and; 4) results are compared to the pre-set criteria. This process is sometimes referred to as Goal-Based Evaluation (or GBE) (Madaus and Kellaghan, 2000). If used alone, goal-based models can omit important unintended outcomes because of their exclusive look at goal achievement. In addition, in this model the appropriateness of goals is not assessed.

The Hybrid Approach

Several institutions currently use a hybrid of goal-based outcome measures and process measures. Hybrid evaluations use both objective data and participant perceptions (Craven, 1980). The hybrid approach is probably the best model currently available for conducting program reviews. Process or goal-based evaluation alone is inadequate, but the combination provides a more comprehensive evaluation (Craven, 1980). The majority of institutions emphasize more quantitative measures. While qualitative measures are not likely to be used exclusively, these measures are often part of an external review and emphasize process aspects of the hybrid approach.

Recommendations for Successful Program Review

Even though there is no agreement on the best form of peer review, a review of literature offers some recommendations for those institutions that have a clear vision of what they would like to accomplish.

Locally Based Review

The literature indicates that the best reviews are locally based and congruent with the environment, history, culture, and needs of the institution. Four national panels composed primarily of representatives of colleges and universities, including the Carnegie Council on Policy Studies in Higher Education (1980), the Sloan Commission on Government and Higher Education (1980), the National Commission on Higher Education Issues, sponsored by the American Council on Education (1982), and the Carnegie Foundation for the Advancement of Teaching (1982) have recommended that the best locus for program review is at the institutional rather than the state level.

The Education Commission of the States (1980), however, suggested that state and institutional cooperation can produce the best result. Creamer and Janosik (1999) studied program review practices in the United States and eight other countries and regions and categorized state program review practices in three approaches: independent institutional review, interdependent institutional review, and state-mandated review. Earlier, Barak (1991, cited in Creamer and Janosik, 1999) reported that thirty-four state agencies have processes for reviewing some existing post-secondary programs.

Illinois provides an example of such a statewide process. The Illinois Board of Education has established a practice in which "similar programs . . . at the 12 state universities are reviewed simultaneously. That is, in a given year all engineering programs at public universities are reviewed" (Smith and Eder, 2001, p. 2). The Illinois Board of Education (IBE) conducts these reviews and reports on the educational and economic viability of the reviewed programs to the appropriate governing board. As a part of this overall review, the state universities are asked to address questions organized around the following criteria: student demand, occupational demand, centrality to instructional mission, breadth, success of graduates, costs, quality, and productivity. In 1998–99, the IBE began asking state universities to respond to the following questions: "(1) What has the program done since the last review? (2) What opportunities for program improvement have been identified? (3) How have assessment results been used? and (4) What has been learned from the review?" (Smith and Eder, 2001, p. 14).

Reviews Linked to Mission

A strong institutional mission statement provides a focal point for assessment (Banta, Lund, Black, and Oblander, 1996) and thus program review. Program reviews linked to the mission of the institution ensure that reviews contribute in fundamentally important ways to attainment of the campus mission and that warranted recommendations for improvement stemming from them are carried out.

By way of example, the mission of Indiana University-Purdue University Indianapolis (IUPUI) is to provide for its constituents excellence in teaching and learning; research, scholarship, and creative activity; and civic engagement. Each of these core activities is characterized by collaboration within and across disciplines and with the community, a commitment to ensuring diversity, and the pursuit of best practices. With the mission in mind, IUPUI constructs teams designed to increase community connections by inviting a community representative to join each team. To increase collaboration among IUPUI departments, two faculty members outside the department are asked to join the team. Finally, two (or three) faculty in the discipline being reviewed, who have no Indiana University or Purdue University connections and can contribute to the enhancement of excellence in the department, also are asked to serve.

Purposes for Review

Program review has been used to enhance the quality of an academic program by pointing out strengths and weaknesses and by providing recommendations for more targeted allocation of resources. Planners for program review at an institution should consider the desired goals of the review, the tradition and values of the institution, the availability of resources and time, the expertise of involved staff, and the integration of program review in the institution (Clark, 1983). When quality enhancement is the goal, program review is usually initiated internally and is referred to as a formative review (Madaus and Kellaghan, 2000). Summative reviews are typically initiated in response to the requirements of an external entity such as a department of the state or an accreditation agency (2000). In general, summative reviews are designed either to ensure accountability on behalf of public stakeholders or to determine the worth of a given program.

Generally, formative reviews have more institutional ownership, and implementation of the recommendations is easier to accomplish. While reviews required by external stakeholders such as governing boards are concerned with quality, they generally assess achievement of minimum standards rather than make recommendations for the best possible allocation of resources and peak performance (Conrad and Blackburn, 1985; Scott, 1980). Sound program review is conducted in coordination with external accreditation reviews to ensure that the processes complement each other rather than duplicate efforts or overburden the faculty. Quality enhancement and external accountability do not have to be mutually exclusive purposes if the institution's culture and communication systems are strong.

Involvement of Stakeholders

An essential characteristic of successful program reviews is involvement of and ownership by all stakeholders in the institution. Of significant importance is concurrent ownership by the faculty and administration within that institution. Reviews are most successful if individuals affected by those reviews have been involved in their development and implementation (Barak and Breier, 1990). Top-down evaluation and responsive changes are difficult to achieve (Mets, 1995). Ideally, the program review design adopted should facilitate interaction among reviewers and those being reviewed during all phases of the process (Conrad and Wilson, 1985).

Systematic Program Review

In addition, program review should be systematic, comprehensive, and ongoing (Barak and Breier, 1990; Conrad and Wilson, 1985). Most institutions follow the advice of Barak and Breier (1990) and conduct reviews using a five- to seven-year cycle. This type of scheduling, on a regular basis, allows departments to anticipate and plan for their program reviews, removes any appearance of bias, and ensures that all programs are reviewed in the cycle. Northwestern University (see http://adminplan.crown.northwestern.edu/progrev/intro/introlnk.htm), Indiana University-Purdue University Indianapolis (see http://www.planning.iupui.edu), and Radford University (see http://www.runet.edu/~senate/96_97/progrev.html) have review cycles ranging from five to seven years. In contrast, in a screening model, basic data are evaluated for all departments, and the results flag departments for a comprehensive review. A version of the screening model is in use at Eastern Kentucky University (see http://www.academicaffairs.eku.edu/planning/DocsProgramReview/ApprovedSept21.doc). While reviews are scheduled on a regular basis (on a five-year schedule), Eastern Kentucky University monitors indicators that will "trigger early program review." These triggers include decreases in enrollment, lack of a critical mass of faculty, loss of accreditation, and lack of evidence that a program is achieving its goals. The University of Colorado's program review system (see http://www.cusys.edu/~policies/Academic/implementrew.html) is guided by the

Colorado Commission on Higher Education's Existing Program Review Policy of March 1998. In part, this policy requires that new academic programs be reviewed by the Board of Regents after the fifth year of operation if original enrollment and/or graduation estimates are not met or if special conditions have been attached to the approval.

Use of Program Review Results in the Larger Institutional Context

Program review scholars (Conrad and Wilson, 1985) and assessment scholars (Astin, 1985; Erwin, 1991; Ewell, 1991b; Study Group on the Conditions of Excellence in American Higher Education, 1984; and Palomba and Banta, 1999) have suggested that for assessment and program reviews to be effective, the results must be used for improvement. Ewell (1991b) aptly stated that assessment "must more fully 'enter the institutional bloodstream' to be effective" (p. 12). Likewise, Larson (cited in Satterlee, 1992), Craven (1980), Mets (1997), and Barak (1982) believe that a critical aspect of successful program review is the full integration of review into institutional processes such as planning and budgeting. Barak and Breier (1990) recommend that reviews be fully integrated to ensure the implementation of recommendations. Northwestern University, the University of Wisconsin system (see http://www.uwsa.edu/acadaff/acps/acps1.pdf), and Drake University provide examples of policies that explicitly state that program review will be used to set priorities for allocating or reallocating resources. Drake University recently reviewed all academic programs and made recommendations to "enhance, maintain, redesign/reduce/restructure, or phase out/eliminate" (http://www.drake.edu/review/guide/recommend.html).

A Study of One University's Program Review Process

In January 1996, Myles Brand, president of Indiana University, presented the collective work of task forces of faculty, staff, students, and friends of the university in the form of a document entitled "Indiana University: The Strategic Directions Charter: Becoming America's New Public University." This document set a course for all eight campuses of Indiana University, and the president provided funds for a grant competition to carry out the initiatives it contained. One project receiving funds was entitled "Assessing the Effectiveness of Indiana University's Academic Program Review Processes."

Although in 1996 Indiana University had only a brief history of using program review as a comprehensive assessment tool, nationally and internationally, peer review was understood to be a widely accepted and highly effective method for assessing and improving programs and curricula (Banta, Rudolph, Van Dyke, and Fisher, 1996). The Strategic Directions project was designed to ascertain whether program review was being used to its fullest advantage on the campuses of Indiana University.

Early in 1993, the Indiana University (IU) faculty chose peer review as a primary tool in academic program assessment (by action of the University Faculty Council, April 13, 1993), and each campus instituted its own process. By 1996, it was time to take stock of the various approaches and make each one as efficient and effective as it could be. Because each campus had to evaluate its assessment program for its next North Central Association (NCA) reaccreditation process, and program review is the comprehensive assessment mechanism that brings together all other assessment data in a unit's self-study, the investigators argued that the peer review of program review processes at IU could serve as an evaluation component for reaccreditation. That is, using the results of this project could not only lead to stronger, more meaningful program reviews but could also address the NCA requirement that each campus assessment program be evaluated.

As a part of this internal grant, IU assessment representatives from each of several campuses conducted a joint three-year study of good practice in academic program review. No attempt was made to standardize the various campus approaches; instead, the aim was to enable each campus to implement its own approach as efficiently and effectively as possible.

This study produced the following:

- A literature review on best practices in peer review
- A review of the purposes of program reviews as implemented on each of the participating IU campuses

- An internal audit of the program review processes employed on each campus
- A systematic study of the uses made of reviewers' assessments and recommendations
- An external peer review of Indiana University's program review processes

During the first year, the investigators conducted a literature review that consisted of a traditional library search as well as contacts with professional groups. In addition, they consulted with other colleges and universities (such as Northwestern University and the University of Colorado) that have substantial experience in conducting program reviews and successful records in implementing change based on the information gathered during the reviews.

In developing a better understanding of the various purposes of program review on the IU campuses, assessment committees and other appropriate faculty groups were consulted. The investigators anticipated that program review was being implemented to achieve at least one of the following three purposes: to solve perceived problems in particular units, to improve programs generally, or to place excellent programs in a spotlight. A common purpose of program review was to gather data, have others outside the program make judgments, and then use the information to make improvements. How campuses went about this varied.

The internal audit of campus processes facilitated an evaluation of the use of best practices in program review. This audit was conducted by assembling information in response to a set of questions. Some of those questions were:

How are units selected and scheduled for program reviews? One campus reported that it reviewed only units without external accreditation and those with an immediate need, while others reported that all units were on a five- to seven-year cycle, with some noting that the reviews coincided with accreditation visits.

What guidelines are provided to units scheduled for review? Do the guidelines establish a strong connection between assessment of student outcomes and determination of overall program quality? All campuses were guided by the broad statement that the University Faculty Council issued, requiring that some sort of review take place. Most campuses reported that their reviews were influenced by their own mission and goals. Some campuses provided guidelines suggesting that units provide information on resources (faculty, physical facilities, equipment, budget, and learning resources), the instructional program, general education, career counseling and overall assessment, demand for the program, special features of the program, and comparative data from previous reviews.

What kinds of data about program processes (such as admissions and advising) and outcomes (such as evidence of student learning and success of graduates) must be in the self-study? The data reported included purposes, reputation, aspirations, resources, program process (content, student support), student learning outcomes, mission, faculty curriculum vitae, syllabi, student handbooks, advisement sheets, admissions information, enrollment data, evaluation measures, cost analysis, diversity of faculty, staff, and students, and the extent of service a unit provides to other units.

How are reviewers selected? Does the unit being reviewed have a role? Are reviewers compensated? Campus representatives reported that reviewers were selected through consultation with specialty accreditation boards, the campus administration, campus administration in consultation with the faculty, or by the responsible dean. In most cases, the unit being reviewed recommended reviewers. In all cases in which external reviewers were used, the external reviewers were compensated.

What processes are in place to ensure that the results of program reviews are used to make needed improvements? In most instances, the academic dean of the school in which the department is located is responsible for ensuring that the review is used. One campus reported that it had the department chair present a mid-cycle follow-up report to the faculty committee responsible for program review oversight.

What improvements can be attributed to program reviews? Improvements can be categorized as informing decisions made about faculty and staff hires and development, curriculum, and resource allocation.

- Campuses reported that mentoring programs for junior faculty were developed or strengthened. One campus invited a selected adjunct faculty member to become a visiting full-time faculty member for one semester to provide opportunities for her to become better integrated into the department, to give students greater access to a scholar with specific areas of specialization, and to add diversity to the department. New faculty hires will reflect a change in area of specialization, augmenting existing expertise. The departments will focus on hiring faculty to build on the strengths of the department, the campus community, and the location. And, finally, one reported hiring a student development specialist for the department.

- A multitude of curricular changes was reported. For example, one campus created an interdepartmental curriculum committee to revise courses. Some departments have identified inadequacies in curriculum and adjusted course content; others have found a need to increase time spent on some topics and have split courses accordingly. Systematic reviews of undergraduate curriculum resulted in one department continuing to probe for more effective ways of integrating lecture and laboratory content.

- Special allocations were made to libraries to increase holdings. In addition, equipment was purchased, resources were increased, and allocations were made to improve facilities.

Based upon conversations with department chairs, who admittedly were somewhat reluctant at first to devote the time to such a review, the self-study process was found to be one that challenged faculty to take a serious look at the curriculum, student learning, and themselves. These same department chairs have now been invited to make presentations at national meetings to discuss the benefits of such a review. One campus reported that the process led to creative thinking about ways to use tools of the discipline to complete the self-study.

As a final step in the project, the investigators arranged a site visit, inviting two experts on evaluation to the Indianapolis campus to meet with representatives from all of Indiana University's campuses as well as interested individuals from other local universities. The initial plan was to invite external reviewers to each campus to conduct a review of the individual processes; however, during discussions, the investigators determined that all would benefit from a more public conversation about the practices. Thus, a daylong visit with two external reviewers was held. In preparation, the reviewers were provided with individual campus program review guidelines, the internal audit, and other pertinent information. The focus of this symposium was to find ways to improve processes and to respond to questions raised by the IU Board Of Trustees. An overall panel discussion opened the day, with follow-up discussion in small groups focused on individual campuses and ways to improve practices. Following the visit, each reviewer submitted final reports that provided overall advice as well as specific advice to each campus. The reviewers' overall recommendations included relating program mission and goals to data collected, providing reviewers with a clear purpose for the review, developing plans for follow-up, involving faculty and staff more fully in reviews, and linking plans to budget recommendations.

Following the Project

As a follow-up to the study initiated in 1996, we queried campus representatives about changes that have been made to the review process since the project concluded in 1999. One representative reported that in connection with his participation in the project, he was assigned to chair a task force of the Faculty Senate to look at division and program reviews. Using information gained from the grant project, the task force proposed significant revisions to the campus review process that subsequently were approved by the Faculty Senate.

The Senate then recommended that a group of appropriate faculty and staff develop benchmarks, examples, exemplars, and other indicators of good practice. Later, the faculty body appointed a more broadly based Assessment/Review Task Force, including both faculty and staff to develop and recommend an assessment program for nonacademic offices and programs.

Although not specifically attributed to the work of the funded project, another participant in the project meetings reported developing a list of lessons learned and a series of workshops for the campus faculty. A workshop for department chairs included sessions that (1) described the process departments had used, explaining how decisions had been made, and offering advice based on what they wish they had known before they started, and (2) provided an overview of the principles specified in the campus program review document.

Finally, one campus that previously had conducted program review as an exclusively internal (to the campus) process now has an external component. Each department initially prepares a self-study for internal evaluation during the fall and then has an additional review by an external evaluator during the subsequent spring.

Conclusion

For program review to be taken seriously and used as a credible improvement activity, each institution must determine the purposes of program review and clearly link the review process to its mission. Senior campus leadership must support program review, both financially and symbolically. It is important that leaders emphasize the program review's improvement aspects. By involving faculty and staff and unit- and program-level administrators early in the program review process—for example, asking them to identify peer reviewers and indicators of performance that they would like to have reviewed—campus leaders can elicit buy-in to the purposes, processes, and outcomes of program review.

Finally, the results of program review must be linked to ongoing improvement efforts at the campus level and to regional and discipline-specific accreditation activities. Although not an end unto itself, effective program review can serve to unite disparate assessment activities, while providing a comprehensive vehicle to evaluate, communicate about, and improve a program.

Chapter Thirteen

Accreditation and the Scholarship of Assessment

Barbara D. Wright

Assessment and accreditation have intersected powerfully over the past fifteen years. One consequence is that accreditation has had a significant effect on the evolution of assessment and on the emergence of a scholarship of assessment. The purpose of this chapter is to reflect on the dynamics of this interaction—that is, how assessment has strengthened accreditation, how accreditation has helped sustain the assessment movement, and how well the synergy has worked, particularly with respect to the strengthening of assessment as a scholarly field. Finally, this chapter will address some of the tensions in the relationship between assessment and accreditation and will close with a vision of where this dance might take us.

Before plunging in, however, let us think for a moment about what we like *least* about contemporary college students. As educators, we believe in our students' potential for intellectual and personal growth. But sometimes student attitudes about learning trouble us. We are dismayed when students ask, *Is this going to be on the test?* or *What do I have to do to get an A?* We wish they would work harder and spend more time studying. Why do these things bother us so much? Perhaps because they embody such a superficial, instrumental attitude toward what we as educators consider very serious business. The sort of student described here is aiming not for the joy of substantive, deep learning; instead, the student seems to model rational choice theory with painful directness: *How can I get the highest grade for the least investment of effort?* As educators, we want higher learning to transform students' minds and hearts, whereas students want to pass the course and get on with their lives. They know they cannot afford to rebel, so they offer compliance—but no more.

The interesting thing is that faculty, professional staff, and administrators do not behave so very differently. In workshops on assessment, I often begin with a cynical but commonly held definition of assessment: *It's simple. You figure out what they want, find the quickest, least damaging way to respond, send off a report, and then forget it.* The problem with this definition is that it takes such a superficial, compliance-oriented view of assessment as a required activity without connection to anything the institution values, without integrity or deeper learning or the promise of transformation. "They" are most often an accrediting agency, and the institutional response has too often been, *All right, what do you want from us? What do we have to do to get an A, or, at least, not fail?* There are intermediate phases, too, at the level of the individual program or faculty member: *What do we have to do to get that faculty line?* or *How many articles do I have to publish to get tenure?*

All this reminds me of fractals, which I first encountered in the book *Leadership and the New Science* by Margaret Wheatley (1992). Fractals can be created through chemical reactions or computer-generated repetition of mathematical formulae, but they are also found everywhere in nature—in cloud formations, in heads and branches and florets of broccoli, in trees and respiratory systems, and in rocky landscapes that repeat their geological formations infinitely in boulders and rocks and particles of sand. Fractals are also a useful metaphor for understanding organizational culture and the difficulty of effecting change. Small, local deviations are up against the power of the overriding design of the fractal. Conversely, if the nature of the design can be changed, it has repercussions all up and down the line.

One of the accepted principles of the assessment movement is that its ultimate purpose—beyond improving student learning, beyond understanding how programs work—is to change institutional culture. We frequently hear about the need for higher education to develop a "culture of inquiry" or a "culture of evidence." More recently, we have heard about the need to become "learning organizations," and it has been humbling to realize that our institutions of higher learning have not been able to transform themselves into learning organizations any more readily than banks or manufacturers or trucking companies have.

The Intersection of Assessment and Accreditation: Some History

In June 1990 at the American Association for Higher Education's (AAHE) annual assessment conference, Ralph Wolff, then associate executive director of the Western Association of Schools and Colleges' Commission for Senior Colleges and Universities, delivered a talk entitled "Assessment and Accreditation: A Shotgun Marriage?" He noted that the explosive growth of the assessment movement since 1985 had forced all the regional accrediting associations to revise their procedures and place greater emphasis on assessment as a form of institutional accountability. He anticipated increasing involvement of accrediting associations in assessment, and he posed the question how accreditation and assessment could work together most effectively for reform. Wolff concluded that the link between assessment and accreditation was neither a shotgun marriage nor a match made in heaven. Ideally, it should become a fruitful partnership.

Wolff's predictions turned out to be wildly understated. A great deal happened between 1985 and about 1992 to link assessment and accreditation, and even more has happened in the period from about 1996 to the present, as a second wave of accreditation activity centered around assessment gained momentum. The linkage has caused accreditors to be increasingly insistent about their expectations for assessment, and it has forced campuses to raise their level of assessment activity. The key question is whether the linkage has contributed on both sides not merely to increased *practice of* assessment but also to increasingly sophisticated *thinking about* assessment. In other words, has the collaboration between assessment and accreditation led to new theories of assessment, to systematic investigation of the merits of particular instruments or methods, to improved practice? Has the synergy between assessment and accreditation brought us closer to a discipline-like scholarship of assessment?

In 1985–1986, the Southern Association of Colleges and Schools (SACS) took the lead when it began to enforce a new standard on institutional effectiveness linked to outcomes assessment, and the Western Association of Schools and Colleges (WASC) followed shortly thereafter. In 1989, the North Central Association weighed in with a new policy requiring all institutions to assess student achievement as part of self-study. Although the Middle States Association had been asking for evidence of "outcomes" since 1953, enforcement was lax until the word assumed new importance in the context of the late 1980s. In the early 1990s, the Northwestern Association adopted a policy on assessment, and in 1992 the New England Association (NEASC) threaded assessment into all eleven of its standards. All the regionals followed up with workshops, regional conferences, publications, and presentations at AAHE assessment conferences.

Where had this come from? The mid-eighties were a time of widespread dissatisfaction with higher education that was expressed in published reports from both inside and outside the academy, including *A Nation at Risk* (U.S. Department of Education, 1983), *Involvement in Learning* (Study Group on the Conditions of Excellence in American Higher Education, 1984), *Integrity in the College Curriculum* (Association of American Colleges, 1985), and *Time for Results* (National Governors' Association, 1986). These reports criticized the state of baccalaureate education and demanded reforms. Conspicuously absent was any discussion of the role accrediting agencies could play in promoting improvement. Accreditors were stung by this oversight; apparently, they had fallen victim to their own invisibility, thanks to policies of confidentiality that prevented them from going public either with success stories or problem institutions.

Then in 1988 the U.S. Department of Education established new criteria for recognition of all accrediting bodies, calling for a focus on "educational effectiveness." Commissions were to systematically consider information on educational effectiveness as part of accreditation and determine whether institutions or programs "document the educational achievement of their students." In this way, federal policymakers drew accreditation more directly into the process of holding institutions accountable for graduates' performance (Wolff, 1992, p. 40). The accreditation community's response went far beyond mere accommodation, however. Accreditation seized the opportunity to redefine itself and refocus its processes.

More radical steps have been taken in the second wave of accreditation activity, which followed closely upon the federal government's abortive flirtation with "state postsecondary review entities" (SPREs) and subsequent founding of the Council for Higher Education Accreditation (CHEA). For example, after several years of study, in 2001, WASC finalized a new framework for accreditation that is organized around two "core commitments": institutional capacity and educational effectiveness (crudely put, inputs/processes and outcomes) and moved to a two-part review cycle. The capacity review focuses on institutional policies, structures, and resources but also asks how effectively these support teaching and learning. The goal is to develop more efficient models for presentation of data and evaluation, to keep data routinely updated and available, for example on a Web page, and to significantly reduce the investment institutions must make in collecting capacity data specifically for self-study.

The educational effectiveness review occurs a year after the capacity review and focuses on the institution's educational vision, its organization for learning, and evidence of student learning. WASC's goal here is to increase its utility to the institution by building capacity for educational effectiveness and facilitating improvement. All participants in the process are to be supported with special training in best practices. Ralph Wolff, now executive director of WASC and initiator of these changes, has argued that only by severing the capacity review from the issue of educational effectiveness can the spotlight be fully trained on student learning; otherwise, institutions will revert to the old input model.

But even before the adoption of the new process, WASC institutions were taking advantage of the opportunity to carry out focused self-studies that put special emphasis on the institution's own priorities. Assessment has been a popular choice, and at institutions such as the University of the Pacific (Stockton, California) or the University of San Diego, the focused self-study has inspired significant progress on assessment. The University of Hawaii, Oahu, offers another example.

The North Central Association (NCA) has also undertaken two initiatives that push the envelope of traditional accreditation practice. In late 1989, the Commission issued its first assessment report, entitled "Statement on Assessment and Student Academic Achievement," which declared that student achievement was a critical component of institutional effectiveness and that "assessment is not an end in itself but a means of gathering information" about improvement (López, 1999, p. 5). A decade later, in 1999, Associate Director Cecilia López led a study of 432 team reports written between 1997 and 1999. The purpose was to determine how much progress member institutions had made in realizing the expectations stated in 1989 and in implementing an effective assessment program. A report of the findings (López, 1999) describes assessment programs along a continuum from "beginning implementation" to "some implementation" to "ongoing implementation." The report also details common obstacles to implementation and institutional learning. López concludes that ten years later implementation is partial at best. "Many [institutions] have yet to realize a level of on-going assessment that could position them to become a student-centered learning organization committed to continuous improvement" (p. 42). At the same time, she finds that NCA team reports do provide institutions with a rich array of good practice in assessment. Her research into characteristics of successful programs is a significant contribution to the scholarship of assessment on a practical as well as theoretical level.

Meanwhile, in the summer of 1999, North Central launched its Academic Quality Improvement Project (AQIP) under the leadership of Stephen Spangehl. The goal of this three-year, Pew-funded undertaking is to make accreditation a more powerful force for reform by melding the continuous quality improvement principles of such thinkers as Walter A. Shewhart, W. Edwards Deming, Joseph H. Juran, and Kaoru Ishikawa with accreditation. AQIP Quality Criteria also map readily onto the Malcolm Baldrige National Quality Award criteria for postsecondary institutions. Institutions that sign on with AQIP are expected to participate in the required workshops, carry out assessments and other activities, and develop processes for continuous improvement of the systems they use to provide education to students. According to the Web page on AQIP processes, reaffirmation of accreditation will be "a simple validation process, resting upon an institution's established pattern of continuing involvement in AQIP. No special visit or report will be required" (http://www.aqip.org/processes.html). The institution is expected to make a considerable investment in AQIP activities; the payoffs are that (1) the institution is clearly investing in *itself,* rather than in an accreditation process to satisfy an external entity, and (2) the cost and intrusiveness of traditional accreditation are virtually eliminated. With regard to scholarship, AQIP Criteria 1 and 2 specifically mention the need for institutions to conduct scholarly research on teaching and learning, while Criteria 7 and 8 address the resources needed to support such activity (http://www.aqip.org/OldAQIPpages/atob.html).

Currently, fifty institutions are listed on the North Central Web site as participants in AQIP, up from twenty-eight less than one year ago (http://www.aqip.org/AQIPmembers.html). One of them is Southern Illinois University, Edwardsville (SIUE). According to Douglas Eder, associate professor of neuroscience and director of both undergraduate assessment and the Undergraduate Research Academy, SIUE began its assessment activities in 1988, thanks to enlightened presidential leadership, and since then assessment has flourished. Two years ago, the university became a pioneering member of AQIP; for Eder, this is a logical development because "we began to hold ourselves to higher standards, such as those revealed through the Malcolm Baldrige Award." Eder sees a natural synergy between assessment and the Carnegie Scholarship of Teaching Initiative, in which SIUE also participates: "We both . . . practice notions of scholarly peer review in our institutional activities. This includes assessment both as an object of and a participant in peer review" (personal communication, March 2001). Beyond that, however, SIUE has taken practical steps to promote the scholarship of assessment. In 2000, for example, competitive Assessment Fellowships were offered by the Undergraduate Research Academy to faculty interested in investigating the question *To what extent and by what mechanisms do students at SIUE improve their writing?* The RFP calls for scholarly inquiry that results in a manuscript suitable for peer review and publication.

The U.S. Air Force Academy in Colorado used the principles of total quality management to structure its assessment effort even before joining AQIP. Training workshops and activities led to a series of campus publications that were controversial but revealed opportunities to improve. Then in 1997 the Academy developed a comprehensive "assessment catalogue" of departmental assessment activities. According to Marie Revak and David Porter, the catalog records all course and program assessment efforts. It facilitates the flow of assessment ideas among departments; identifies sources of data; tracks use of both quantitative and qualitative methods and gives utility ratings; lists decisions based on assessment data; links assessment tools to the seven USAFA Educational Outcomes; and provides names of contacts. Unlike more traditional scholarly reference works, the catalog is primarily an in-house resource. But since the document is on-line, it is also widely available. This very open process has not been without controversy, but in Porter's words it "unfroze" the institution and forced it to question assumptions about authority, tradition, and culture—an ultimately healthy and productive process (personal communication, April 2001).

Other regional accreditors are engaged in equally serious if less radical endeavors. The Middle States Association is rewriting its sixteen standards, known as *Characteristics of Excellence* (completion expected in 2002) and at the same time is engaged in an extensive effort to identify and train educators in the region with an interest in assessment so that they can serve as highly qualified visiting team members and bring their new expertise to bear at their home institutions as well.

William Patterson University (WPU) provides an example of a campus with a long-term, evolving commitment to assessment. The university's Assessment Committee was formally constituted in 1986, in anticipation of an assessment mandate from the New Jersey Department of Higher Education. The department was subsequently abolished as a cost-cutting measure during the early 1990s, but assessment was picked up as a priority by Middle States and other accreditors. Remaining responsive to that pressure, WPU has made steady progress over the last decade, and that is reflected in its 2001 self-study, according to Associate Provost Stephen Hahn. The campus has not engaged in a conscious scholarship of assessment, but in Hahn's view the groundwork for such scholarship is being laid. In this regard, WPU models the progress of hundreds of campuses in the Middle States region and beyond (personal communication, April 2001).

Kean University of New Jersey offers a related example of the dynamics at work among state boards of higher education and regional and professional accreditation. Kean, too, became involved in outcomes assessment in the mid-1980s, largely due to state pressure, and faculty from Kean became regular contributors at assessment meetings. As "first-wave" departments began to formulate assessment plans, the university's social work program developed a model for performance assessment. Data from field supervisors' reports were analyzed to gauge student progress in three key areas: knowledge, values, and skills. When the Council on Social Work Education developed its current accreditation standards in the mid-1990s, drawing a clear line from mission to goals to program outcomes, Kean's social work program already had years of experience doing just that. The data collected for program assessment subsequently became useful for the regional self-study, and assessment has survived despite administrative turnover on campus and turmoil on the political front in New Jersey. Carol Williams, a professor in the social work program and leader of assessment efforts, welcomes this meshing of regional and professional accreditation standards. In Williams' view, scholarship clearly occurs, but it is first and foremost an applied scholarship for domestic consumption (personal communication, April 2001).

The Southern Association of Colleges and Schools' (SACS) call for assessment predated the federal government's 1988 directive by several years, and that fact, combined with early state mandates for assessment in the south, led to the emergence of leaders in the national assessment movement, such as the University of Tennessee, Knoxville, and Winthrop University. A southern institution, James Madison University currently offers the best-known doctoral program in postsecondary assessment in the United States. With its "The institution must . . ." statements and its rigorous enforcement, SACS acquired a reputation for being the most onerous of all the regional accreditors; yet a close reading of SACS's guidelines reveals that while institutions must *do* assessment, *how* they shall do it is not dictated. Nevertheless, SACS is currently reviewing its standards. They are expected to become more streamlined (going from over 400 statements to about 80), less prescriptive, and more focused on the use of assessment data for improvement. Another goal is to make accreditation more efficient and less intrusive.

How will these developments play out? Interestingly, they have met a mixed reception in a region where an understanding of assessment that is particularly strong on testing and measurement has had a longer period of time to take root. Institutions that have invested in a structured assessment strategy and in the institutional research to support it may well be reluctant to change. There may also be implications for the scholarship of assessment. Offices of institutional research have served as home base for a great deal of data gathering and analysis that serve a particular institution but that can also contribute to assessment scholarship when more widely shared at professional meetings.

Angela Roling, of the Office of Institutional Research, Planning, and Effectiveness at Troy State University in Alabama, for example, expresses concern that the revised SACS criteria lack specificity and rigor and that the role of institutional research is being downplayed (personal communication, April 2001). Like Roling, Barbara Boothe, director of planning, research and assessment at Liberty University in Virginia, credits SACS with creating the motivation for better assessment and planning practices. However, she welcomes SACS's proposed criteria. Like others, Boothe sees the scholarly discussion and peer review of her assessment efforts as largely limited to her campus community. Meanwhile, in her own research, she is developing a model for linking assessment, budgeting, and strategic planning, a model that the Transnational Association of Christian Colleges and Schools (a DOE-approved accrediting body) may adopt. Boothe's example illustrates how individual, institutional. and organizational contributions to assessment can become interwoven (personal communication, April 2001).

The New England Association of Schools and Colleges revised its standards to include assessment in 1992, but it has been ambivalent about enforcement. In part this has occurred out of deference to elite institutions that the association is reluctant to antagonize, and in part it reflects a spirit of parsimony that says, *Let's wait and learn from the mistakes of others.* Yet member institutions have not been insulated from developments in the rest of the country or in their professional accrediting organizations. In 1998, then-associate director Peggy Maki surveyed the membership to determine the state of assessment at New England colleges and to identify needs. The survey revealed considerable consternation, along with a strong desire to learn more. In 1998–1999, ten training workshops were organized and were attended by over a thousand participants. During 1999–2000, Maki convened a task force to develop an academic assessment protocol, a nonprescriptive, improvement-oriented list of questions that would help institutions implement assessment and document their efforts in an institutional portfolio. In 2001–2002 the protocol is being pilot-tested on eight to ten campuses in the region. Meanwhile, NEASC finds itself being overtaken by its membership.

For example, Rivier College (Nashua, New Hampshire) has been working at assessment for over a decade. Under the leadership of Paul Cunningham, coordinator of the assessment program, the college has developed a wide range of activities and even served as a case study during the 1998–1999 NEASC-sponsored workshops. Suzanne Tracey, another member of the Rivier faculty, became a founding member of the New England Educational Assessment Network (NEEAN), a consortium of New England colleges. Cunningham locates the scholarly aspect of assessment in activities designed to help faculty and administrators understand the state of the art, relate work on their own campuses to the larger universe of assessment, and use findings for improvement of teaching and learning. Other lead institutions in the region include Tufts University, which, according to Dawn Terkla, was motivated above all by its culture of "wanting to know" (personal communication, April 2001), and Providence College, where assessment was put into the hands of seasoned faculty member Raymond Sickinger.

Since 1992, the Northwestern Association of Schools and Colleges has not had a particularly high profile in assessment, but commissioners reportedly take their assessment policy very seriously, to the point where some 70 percent of the region's focused interim reports are called for solely because institutions have failed to show that they are meeting expectations for assessment. The association hopes to introduce more flexible, less data-driven, and more qualitative approaches, and, above all, it hopes to help institutions move from planning for assessment or collecting data to actually *using* the data for improvement.

At Portland State University (PSU), the president took the initiative, creating an Assessment Council and the position of Faculty-in-Residence for Assessment. The university is part of the Urban University Portfolio Project, supported by The Pew Charitable Trusts and AAHE, and, according to Terrel Rhodes, vice provost for curriculum and undergraduate studies, Portland State plans to embed assessment within its electronic institutional portfolio, then use the portfolio as its self-study for reaccreditation five years hence. Rhodes says that the self-study has been the critical motivating force for these efforts. Echoing what is happening in the western and north central regions, Portland State's portfolio will become part of a streamlined, continuous process of self-reflection that will make the decennial self-study much simpler, since most of the necessary information will already have been collected. For Rhodes, the change is not merely a matter of putting the traditional self-study into an electronic format; rather, a moving picture of decision making based on data and experience is being created.

As for scholarship, Rhodes reports that as a general practice, when faculty members become involved in assessment on campus, their work is described as the scholarship of assessment, and this "has provided [a] needed avenue of benefit for some faculty who were reluctant to be engaged." In addition, the PSU Center for Academic Excellence sponsors discussions on the scholarship of teaching and assessment, and campus activity has led to at least one published article. Rhodes does not see the regionals directly encouraging or discouraging the scholarship of assessment; however, accreditors' emphasis on assessment has provided an indirect impetus for scholarship by creating previously nonexistent data sets (personal communication, April 2001).

The Impact of Assessment on Accreditation

With prodding from the U.S. Department of Education and the cooperation of accreditors, assessment has proven to be an extremely useful tool that accreditation has used to recast itself, making it both more effective and more credible. Assessment has been a means—not the only one, but a hugely important one— for giving accreditation new purpose and increasing its clout. Assessment allowed accreditation to zero in on the crux of the matter, student learning, after decades of fixation on surrogates: the resources and processes that were assumed to lead to quality education—an assumption that proved indefensible in the rough climate of the 1980s.

Now, more than a decade later, assessment has provided the cross-fertilization and energy for a second generation of accreditation reforms. Accreditation has never been more intellectually vital, more service-oriented, or more useful to its member institutions than it is today, and efforts are still in full swing. Today, accreditation is still borrowing ideas from assessment, encouraging more qualitative and innovative approaches, and learning from its member institutions. Good assessment practice has demonstrated, if there ever was any doubt, that education is a complex process impossible to capture in a simple formula or single test score. This is a useful message for accreditors confronting popular demands for ranking, rating, and other forms of invidious comparison. Not least of all, accreditation has both contributed to and inspired an emergent scholarship of assessment.

The Impact of Accreditation on Assessment

Just as assessment revitalized accreditation, accreditation's insistence on assessment has kept the assessment movement alive and thriving. But accreditation has been a sleeper in this role, its importance little noticed and certainly not anticipated in the early years of the movement, when more sensational developments such as state mandates, public outcry about costs, tales of all the things college graduates could not do, mean-spirited state budget battles, and performance funding seemed to be the primary external drivers of assessment.

The contemporary postsecondary assessment movement began in earnest in 1985, and in 1990, AAHE's president Russ Edgerton declared the movement at "half time" with perhaps another five years left. Since then, demand for the AAHE Assessment Forum's services and conference attendance have only grown stronger. To what can we attribute this longevity? It helps that assessment has been a point of confluence for a raft of issues in education: new understandings of teaching and learning, critiques of traditional methods of testing and evaluation, new definitions of the disciplines, a search for durable knowledge in a time of epistemological instability, concern about affective as well as intellectual development, and so on. It has helped to have pioneering successes like Alverno College (Milwaukee, Wisconsin) or King's College (Wilkes Barre, Pennsylvania), as well as models for the institutionalization of assessment, such as the Office of Planning and Institutional Improvement at Indiana University-Purdue University Indianapolis.

Arguably, though, the single most powerful contributor to assessment's staying power has been its championing by regional and professional accreditors. Accreditation has supported development of human capital in assessment—both directly, through its own training and literature, and indirectly, by motivating countless institutions to implement assessment. To finance educational effectiveness-related activities, accreditors have received sizable grants: from the Fund for the Improvement of Postsecondary Education (FIPSE) in the early days, and more recently from Davis, Knight and, above all, The Pew Charitable Trusts. Institutions, too, have applied for grants and made their own budget allocations. Thus, millions of dollars in funding have flowed into assessment as well as into accreditation. Accreditation has provided the external push that could be leveraged by institutional leadership to set its own internal assessment efforts in motion. Accreditation has set parameters for assessment that reinforce assessment's own principles of good practice (American Association for Higher Education, 1992).

Though accreditation standards may seem so generic as to allow all sorts of wiggle room, though self-studies and visiting teams vary in quality and the rhythm of fifth-year reports, and decennial reaffirmation may seem so sluggish as to be utterly ineffectual, the influence of accreditation on campus assessment has been powerful over the last ten or fifteen years, like the flow of a glacier. Glaciers do move, albeit imperceptibly, and in their path they transport boulders, scour valleys, and carve new river beds. Related to that epic pace, there is the constancy of accreditation. While administrators, legislators, or state boards may become distracted by other issues, accreditation keeps coming back, even if it does take five or ten years to do so. There are institutions that have been asked two and three times now what they are doing about assessment and why it is taking them so long. Their faculty and administrators are beginning to get the message that assessment matters and is not going away.

Accreditors have engaged in their own scholarship of assessment, and at the same time they have helped create the conditions for a scholarship of assessment on campus. To the extent that the scholarship of assessment aspires to systematic sharing of findings, peer review, replication of results, development of new approaches, or articulation of new research questions, it behaves like traditional scholarship in other fields. Indeed, the enormously successful Harvard Assessment Seminars, led by Richard Light, were conceived as research seminars into teaching and learning. But as a scholarly field, assessment is still very young, still defining itself, still doing the foundational work of creating databases, defining methods, clarifying assumptions, assembling its canonical writings, still debating whether it should have its own professional society.

At the same time, the scholarship of assessment is not identical to traditional scholarship, and it is worth asking whether it ever should be. Thus far, at least, the intellectual work that has gone into assessment has been primarily in-house, applied, and shared with only a local audience. The results most often appear not in journals or books but in ephemera: reports, memos, the minutes of a senate meeting, the appendix to a self-study. They are difficult to access and unaccounted for in standard bibliographies. Published assessment scholarship is scattered across many disciplines. Thus, a "review of the literature," a standard first step in traditional research and a helpful way for scholars to trace the evolution of a field, becomes difficult or impossible.

The problem of scattered or inaccessible literature may be exacerbated by the motivations of those who carry out assessment on campus. Most of them take on the task out of idealism, intellectual curiosity, or necessity rather than personal careerism. Thus, they may have less incentive to prepare documents for traditional publication to begin with, and such efforts may even be viewed as a distraction from the "real" purposes of assessment, for example, to gain reaccreditation and to strengthen programs. Ted Marchese reflects this view when he argues that if we really want to move the educational reform agenda forward, accreditors should write up a campus not for "weaknesses in assessment (the means)," but rather for "its inattentions to improving undergraduate learning (the ends)" (Marchese, 2000, p. 4).

Ironically, while accreditation has provided critical support to assessment, it could ultimately hinder the development of a scholarship of assessment, at least in the traditional sense. Experience has shown that if campus practitioners are to identify weaknesses or make improvements, they need to be able to do so without fear of repercussions. But there is a tension between this condition for successful assessment and public presentation of research findings. Similarly, there is a tension between the tradition of free exchange of information in scholarship and accreditors' tradition of confidentiality. Despite external pressure, neither institutions nor accreditors are ready for full public disclosure, though institutions that develop a more mature culture of assessment tend to become much less fearful of disclosure.

Some Challenges

A major concern, shared by all the regionals, is that assessment findings could be used inappropriately—for example, tied to performance funding or used punitively by politicians or policymakers. Another possibility is that assessment may become the new orthodoxy, as formulaic and reified as the old audits of finances, numbers of books in the library, or PhDs on the faculty, as capricious and anecdotal as old-style fact-finding interviews. From the campus perspective, there is the "practice what you preach" problem. Accreditors need to walk the talk. If the quality of a visiting team is poor, if there are no rewards for an exemplary job, no disincentives for procrastination, institutions will lose respect for both assessment and accreditation.

Beyond all that, though, there is the more serious question of why, after a decade and a half of intensive effort and the strong support of the accreditation establishment, assessment has not had a more dramatic impact. The problem was brought home most recently by the National Center for Postsecondary Improvement's survey of postsecondary institutions (see Chapter Two). The overwhelming majority reported collecting assessment data. However, only about a third assess higher-order learning or complex outcomes, and such data reportedly are seldom used for program improvement or decision making. North Central's review of over

400 institutions' reports revealed similarly spotty and superficial implementation.

Has the assessment movement stalled? Has it run out of intellectual steam? The answer is no, there are plenty of pockets of energy and creativity percolating on individual campuses. But assessment does need to move beyond its current level of conceptualization, its fixation on method, and mature into an accepted core component of faculty work as well as organizational structure. In organizational terms, assessment must permeate the institution; for example, it must be structurally linked to planning and budgeting, included in job descriptions, and routinely mentioned in communications ranging from the view book or catalog to unit mission statements and employee handbooks. If assessment is to mean anything at all to faculty, it has to be treated not as an add-on but as a legitimate contribution to scholarship, and it must become an integral part of expectations for promotion and tenure. Currently, there is unwillingness to do this at the institutional level for both practical and more intangible reasons. If productive faculty turn their attention from traditional research to the scholarship of assessment, institutions face the loss of research funding and the dollars from indirect costs that grants bring in, dollars that research institutions in particular are dependent upon. Institutions may also fear that intellectual prestige will be lost, and with it, tuition or development dollars. In other words, a decision to reward assessment may look to institutional leadership like unilateral disarmament.

Similarly, faculty may be unwilling to take a chance on the scholarship of teaching, learning, and assessment, even if there is institutional support for it, because they fear that they will lose status or be unable to get a position elsewhere. After all, traditional research and publication remain the coin of the realm, while the scholarship of assessment has been very campus-specific. In other words, devoting oneself to assessment becomes unilateral disarmament at the personal level. And this begins to sound like another fractal.

Perhaps assessment and accreditation, working together from the macro- and the micro level, can push toward a *multilateral* acceptance of assessment as important scholarly work. That would be consistent with what has made the collaboration of assessment and accreditation so powerful up to this point. The two have not merely worked together on a discrete "project." Instead, approaching student learning from different angles, assessment and accreditation have done something more complex: they have begun to build a whole new *infrastructure* for teaching and learning, for improvement and accountability. That infrastructure requires people, training, structures, and financial resources, along with the intellectual contributions of the scholarship of assessment. Building that infrastructure takes time. It progresses at a glacial pace. But it reshapes the whole landscape.

Conclusion

Where do campuses and accreditors go from here? If we are working hard at assessment and generating rivers of data, will we not drown in ever higher waves of information? How will we survive, assaulted as we already are by what seems like far too much information? What kind of scholarship can possibly help us to make sense of it all? In closing, let us return to Margaret Wheatley and fractals. Like Wheatley, I believe fractals can illuminate not only natural formations but also human endeavors. For example, it is impossible ever to know the precise measurement of a fractal. Wheatley explains how Benoit Mandelbrot, to whom we owe the concept of fractals, presented colleagues and students with a simple but provocative fractal exercise. He asked, "How long is the coast of Britain?" As his colleagues quickly realized, there is no final answer. The closer one gets to the coastline, the more there is to measure. Wheatley writes, "Since there can be no definitive measurement, what is important in a fractal landscape is to note the *quality* of the system—its complexity and distinguishing shapes, and how it differs from other fractals. If we ignore these qualitative factors and focus on quantitative measures, we will always be frustrated by the incomplete and never-ending information we receive. . . . What we *can* know, and what is important to know, is the shape of the whole" (Wheatley, 1992, pp. 128–129).

This is an extraordinarily important lesson—for the assessment movement, for accreditation, for all the institutions and individual scholars dedicated to strengthening postsecondary education. The cultural change we all seek cannot be achieved by more measurement alone. But if we step back from data gathering to engage in a qualitative interpretation of the data, at *all* the levels of scale embodied in our system of higher education, if we work together to define that new culture, if the process and scholarly findings of assessment that have proven so powerful on campuses can be carried out at larger levels of scale, then perhaps all of us together, from individual units or schools or colleges or campuses, to associations and accreditors, have a chance at transformation.

Acknowledgments

My sincere thanks to all those who so generously responded to my request for information. They include Barbara Boothe, Liberty University; Paul Cunningham, Rivier College; Douglas Eder, Southern Illinois University; Sandra Elman, Northwest Association; Stephen Hahn, William Paterson College; Libby Hall, George Washington University; Laura Joseph, State University of New York; Gitanjali Kaul, Ohio University; Ernie Oshiro, University of Hawaii; David Porter, U.S. Air Force Academy; Barbara Olds, Colorado School of Mines; Oswald Ratteray, Middle States Association; Marie Revak, U.S. Air Force; James Rogers, Southern Association of Colleges and Schools; Terrel Rhodes, Portland State University; Angela Roling, Troy State University; George Santiago, Middle States Association; Dawn Terkla, Tufts University; Nancy Travers, New Hampshire Technical Institute; Carol Williams, Kean University; and Ralph Wolff, Western Association of Schools and Colleges.

Toward a Scholarship of Assessment

The two chapters in Part Five summarize what we currently know on the basis of two decades of scholarly assessment and they suggest an agenda for future work in the scholarship of assessment.

In Chapter Fourteen, Trudy Banta, the editor of this volume, describes seventeen characteristics of effective outcomes assessment that have been drawn from the literature and the practice of scholarly assessment. These characteristics are illustrated in the experiences of nine institutions that are engaged in scholarly assessment. The chapter concludes with the suggestion that a fundamental component of the agenda for assessment scholarship in the near term is to apply all that we have learned from the literature of organizational development, program evaluation, and other fields to the task of encouraging our colleagues on the faculty and in student affairs to embrace assessment as part of their work and use its findings to improve the educational experience for students continuously.

In the concluding chapter, Trudy Banta looks at the calls that have been issued over the past two decades for colleges and universities to become true learning organizations, using outcomes assessment as a tool for providing evidence to guide continuous improvement. Some of the reasons for scant progress toward this transformation are explored, along with some strategies for moving us forward. The chapter concludes with a synthesis of the suggestions contained in previous chapters for advancing the scholarship of assessment.

Chapter Fourteen

Characteristics of Effective Outcomes Assessment
Foundations and Examples

Trudy W. Banta

What do we know about outcomes assessment so far, and how have we learned it? Most published articles about assessment practice attempt to point to some learnings about the process. Thus, we have a wealth of knowledge about assessment that is based on the experiences of those engaged in implementing it. In the preceding chapters in this volume, the authors have related assessment to scholarship in fields with longer histories and stronger philosophical and theoretical underpinnings, such as cognitive development, organizational change, and program evaluation. In addition, a number of publications have been developed that attempt to summarize the learnings about assessment derived primarily from practice but actually drawing upon a variety of sources, including the literature of learning and program evaluation. Some of these works are identified in the next section of this chapter, which begins with a set of seventeen characteristics of effective outcomes assessment. Each of these characteristics will be illustrated with some examples from current practice. Finally, these principles will be related to some underlying theoretical perspectives, and some questions for future scholarship in assessment will be raised.

Characteristics of Effective Outcomes Assessment

Roughly two decades of practice in assessing outcomes in higher education suggest a number of characteristics that distinguish effective implementation. The primary sources from which these characteristics are drawn appear in the list that follows.

Effective outcomes assessment begins with a *planning* phase that is characterized in the first four principles. Then comes careful attention to *implementation,* as set forth in principles five through twelve. Finally, there is the *improving and sustaining* phase of assessment, characterized by principles thirteen through seventeen.

Planning

1. Involves stakeholders (faculty members, administrators, students, student affairs professionals, employers, community representatives) from the outset to incorporate their needs and interests and to solicit later support.
2. Begins when the need is recognized; allows sufficient time for development. Timing is crucial.
3. Has a written plan with clear purposes that is related to goals people value—to a larger set of conditions that promote change. Assessment is a vehicle for improvement, not an end in itself.
4. Bases assessment approaches on clear, explicitly stated program objectives.

Implementation

5. Has knowledgeable, effective leadership.
6. Involves recognition that assessment is essential to learning, and therefore is everyone's responsibility.
7. Includes faculty and staff development to prepare individuals to implement assessment and use the findings.
8. Devolves responsibility for assessment to the unit level.
9. Recognizes that learning is multidimensional and developmental and thus uses multiple measures, therefore maximizing reliability and validity.
10. Assesses processes as well as outcomes.

11. Is undertaken in an environment that is receptive, supportive, and enabling—on a continuing basis.
12. Incorporates continuous communication with constituents concerning activities and findings. Effective outcomes assessment produces data that guide *improvement* on a continuing basis.

Improving and Sustaining

13. Produces credible evidence of learning and organizational effectiveness.
14. Ensures that assessment data are used continuously to improve programs and services.
15. Provides a vehicle for demonstrating accountability to stakeholders within and outside the institution.
16. Encompasses the expectation that outcomes assessment will be ongoing, not episodic.
17. Incorporates ongoing evaluation and improvement of the assessment process itself. (Hutchings, 1993; Banta and Associates, 1993; Banta, Lund, Black, Oblander, 1996; American Productivity and Quality Center, 1998; Jones, Voorhees, and Paulson, 2001)

Examples That Illustrate the Characteristics of Effective Outcomes Assessment

For the purposes of this volume, we have defined the scholarship of assessment as systematic work that involves carrying out assessment, determining what methods work best over time, and adjusting practice accordingly, then reassessing to see if the desired ends were achieved and sharing the findings with colleagues. Faculty in nearly every institution are currently carrying out some outcomes assessment activities, and most are making adjustments in their methods as they find out what works and what does not in their settings. But it is still quite rare to identify an institution where systematic effort sustained over time is under way that involves not only adjustments in methods but also reassessment designed to improve the technical quality of instruments and to determine whether improvement initiatives have achieved the desired ends.

During Fall 2000, I wrote to some 800 individuals who were presumed to be involved in outcomes assessment by virtue of their attendance at one or more national conferences on outcomes assessment in higher education. I asked them to identify contact persons at institutions they considered to be engaged in the scholarship of assessment as previously defined in this chapter. I also asked that respondents choose from a list of a dozen alternatives in one or more areas (for example, assessment in general education or in the major, institutional effectiveness, or collaboration between academic and student affairs) in which the institution(s) might be considered to excel. Of course, the respondents were free to identify their own institutions. From the 145 institutions named in the responses I received, I derived a list of 14 that may be considered distinctive in terms of their overall approaches to assessing institutional effectiveness.

In January 2001, I sent a questionnaire to the designated contact person at each of the fourteen institutions, asking that individual to describe the scholarship of assessment at his or her institution in terms of the campus planning that provides direction for assessment, methods of implementation, and outcomes of the process over time. Nine of the fourteen questionnaires were completed and returned. Taken together, the institutions represented in the response pool provide a broad cross-section of institutional types: large and small, public and private, research-oriented and teaching-oriented. These institutions, information from which will be used to illustrate the seventeen characteristics of effective outcomes assessment, are identified in Table 14.1.

Characteristic 1. Involves Stakeholders

In beginning to think about assessment, a first principle must be to identify purposes by consulting with as many as possible of the constituencies that have an interest in the program or institution being assessed. In a university, faculty members and administrators must take responsibility for leading any assessment initiative, but students know how they are experiencing and being affected by a program or the campus in general, and thus can provide valuable perspectives on design, content of instruments,

Table 14.1 Characteristics of Effective Outcomes Assessment

Institution	Location	Institutional Type
Ball State University	Muncie, IN	Public, Doctoral/Research universities—Intensive, 20,700 students
Liberty University	Lynchburg, VA	Private, Christian, Master's colleges and universities I, 6,700 students
Ohio University	Athens, OH	Public, Doctoral/Research universities—Extensive, 19,600 students
Pennsylvania State University	State College, PA	Public, Doctoral/Research universities—Extensive, 40,600 students
Rivier College	Nashua, NH	Private, Master's colleges and universities I, 2,600 students
Southern Illinois University, Edwardsville	Edwardsville, IL	Public, Master's colleges and universities I, 11,800 students
Syracuse University	Syracuse, NY	Private, Doctoral/Research universities—Extensive, 18,500 students
Truman State University	Kirksville, MO	Public, Master's colleges and universities I, 6,200 students
University of Illinois	Urbana-Champaign, IL	Public, Doctoral/Research universities—Extensive, 38,800 students

and interpretation of results. As Kuh, Gonyea, and Rodriguez point out in Chapter Six, program and institutional effectiveness can be enhanced if student affairs professionals help extend student learning, and even the assessment thereof, beyond the classroom. Academic and student affairs professionals should work together to plan and implement outcomes assessment. Educators also need to know how their work is perceived outside the academy. Alumni, employers, and other community representatives can provide essential insight about the qualities that society needs in future graduates. These external stakeholders can contribute not only to the goal-setting phase of assessment but also to the processes of collecting data—serving as partners in assessing student assignments and performance, for instance—and interpreting the findings.

According to John C. Ory of the University of Illinois, "Evaluation isn't worth doing if it isn't used, and one of the best ways to get evaluation results used is to have the different audiences buy into the process" (personal communication, February 1, 2001). At Syracuse University, a committee of faculty and staff members "facilitated discussions within academic units and across campus about learning outcomes . . . both within and outside the classroom" (Peter J. Gray, personal communication, February 9, 2001).

At Ball State University, "students serve on both the Senate Academic Assessment Advisory Committee and on various project committees" (Catherine A. Palomba, personal communication, February 13, 2001). At Rivier College, the Student Government Association annually appoints two students to serve on the campus assessment committee (Paul F. Cunningham, personal communication, February 2, 2001). Most of the nine institutions listed in Table 14.1 routinely survey their graduates to obtain information about the perceived quality of their academic programs and student services. They also involve employers and community representatives as advisers for some of their program evaluations. At Rivier College, the campus service learning coordinator combines information derived from interviews with community service providers with that obtained from faculty and students in assessing the success of the service learning program.

Characteristic 2. Begins When Needed and Allows Time for Development

Many outcomes assessment initiatives are developed in response to an impending visit by a regional or disciplinary accreditor, as Barbara Wright notes in Chapter Thirteen. All of the nine institutions featured here acknowledged that accreditation was an important factor in their decisions to implement assessment. Nevertheless, the naming of a new chief executive was also a precipitating event on several of these campuses. Charles McClain chose to employ assessment as a primary strategy for improving the quality of Northeast Missouri (now Truman) State University when he became president in 1970. At Ohio University, assessment began in 1980 "with questions from the President (Cornelius Ping) about evidence for quality" (Gitanjali Kaul, personal communication, February 20, 2001). And at Syracuse, newly appointed chancellor Kenneth Shaw called for the establishment of an assessment program in 1991.

All of the survey respondents would agree that effective outcomes assessment takes time and sustained effort to develop. The assessment initiative at Northeast Missouri (now Truman) is more than thirty years old, and with one exception, the others have been under way for at least a decade. Even at the University of Illinois, where explicit attention was not focused on outcomes assessment until the late 1990s, John Ory's Office of Instructional Resources—the chief source of support for work in assessment at Illinois—had been working for many years on strategies for collecting data and using the findings to improve teaching and learning.

Characteristic 3. Has a Plan with Clear Purposes Related to Valued Goals

Outcomes assessment that is undertaken just for the purpose of satisfying an accrediting agency or responding to the priorities of a new president cannot survive long enough to produce lasting effects on a campus unless it becomes associated with goals and ongoing processes that are really valued by faculty and administrators. Effective assessment is not a process undertaken for its own sake, existing independently without connection to other important institutional functions.

At Liberty University and Rivier College, assessment is explicitly linked with institutional planning and evaluation of effectiveness. According to Barbara Boothe at Liberty, there is "an ongoing process of strategic planning, assessment accountability, and a link to the budget process . . . in the process of strategic planning, there is an opportunity to validate that (regional accrediting) criteria are being regularly maintained" (personal communication, February 7, 2001). At Rivier, the objectives of each academic and support unit are explicitly linked to elements of the institutional mission statement, so that assessment becomes a means of evaluating institutional effectiveness.

No less fundamental is John Ory's statement that at Illinois "we believe that the quality of a student's education will be improved if a department collects assessment information (information about student achievements or accomplishments), and then uses the results to improve its academic programs." A guiding principle for assessment at Syracuse is to use it "as a means to improve the educational outcomes for our students . . . expanding the scope of assessment beyond the classroom to entire programs and learning outside the classroom."

At Ball State, assessment encompasses the academic major and general education as well as institutional effectiveness. At Penn State a principal focus of assessment is a new general education curriculum adopted in 1997. A part of the plan for general education is "to institutionalize a process for formative assessment that is based on measurable outcomes and informs continuous curricular improvement" (Michael J. Dooris, personal communication, January 29, 2001). Assessment at Ohio University is regarded as an important component of program review, general education, survey research, teaching portfolios, faculty development, and ongoing improvement of nonacademic programs and services.

Characteristic 4. Bases Assessment Approaches on Clear, Explicit Program Objectives

At Rivier College, academic and student services units are asked to identify for each of their programs the most important educational outcomes for students and at least one means of assessing each outcome, including the criteria they will use to determine success in achieving the outcome. At Syracuse, Peter Gray reports that academic and student affairs units complete reports in which they specify learning outcomes that are "educationally important, reasonably specific (not too vague or general), and nontrivial (not just focused on behaviors) and include different levels of knowledge, higher-order thinking skills, values, personal/professional development, etc."

Many of us who provide faculty and staff development in connection with assessment introduce Bloom's Taxonomy of Educational Objectives (1956) and the action verbs that can be associated with each level in the taxonomy as a very helpful concept for getting started. If student outcomes can be stated clearly, using action verbs, it becomes relatively easy to identify appropriate assessment methods. For example, if an important outcome, or objective, for a course or curriculum is to enable students to speak clearly and confidently, then systematically observing students making speeches is an ideal form of assessment.

Characteristic 5. Has Knowledgeable, Effective Leadership

A truly supportive chief executive and/or provost can strengthen assessment immeasurably. At Truman, even the institution's governing board has provided leadership. Ruthie Dare-Halma states, "Our Board of Governors has always been highly supportive of assessment data use. It is used in the President's evaluation presented to the Board. The VPAA uses it in his evaluation of Division Heads" (personal communication, February 20, 2001).

At each of the nine campuses featured here, a member of the faculty and/or administrative staff has been given at least a part-time appointment to coordinate assessment activities for the institution. While the support of top leadership is essential in establishing outcomes assessment and in sustaining it over time, knowledgeable individuals at other levels really make it happen. Directors of centers for faculty development or institutional research offices, coordinators of general education or program review, and chief planning officers or accreditation self-study directors often assume the role of campus assessment coordinator.

Leadership within each academic and student services unit also must be cultivated. "Faculty assessment liaisons" have been appointed at Rivier College. As is typical at most institutions, at Penn State, these faculty representatives meet with the coordinator of assessment in a steering committee. At Ohio University and at the University of Illinois, coordinators of assessment in student affairs also have been appointed.

Characteristic 6. Recognizes That Assessment Is Essential to Learning

Motivating individuals to evaluate the effectiveness of their efforts is a difficult task indeed. No one enjoys learning that they have not been successful, and most of us think our time can be spent more productively *doing* our work rather than *evaluating* it. Nevertheless, most faculty and staff associated with higher education share an interest in helping students learn as much as possible while they are in college. Enabling these individuals to see that outcomes assessment really can improve student learning is the key to motivating them to engage in it. Gray, Wright, and Angelo provide fuller discussions of this crucial point in their chapters in this volume.

According to John Ory at Illinois "we believe that the quality of a student's education will be improved if a department collects assessment information . . . then uses the results to improve their academic programs." If this belief is widely shared there, outcomes assessment at the University of Illinois is on firm ground indeed.

At Southern Illinois University-Edwardsville (SIUE), assessment findings are being used to suggest ways to improve the persistence of student athletes. Learning Outside the Classroom is the title of a subgroup of the assessment committee at Syracuse. This group is studying the knowledge, skills, attitudes, and values that students learn outside the classroom in intentionally designed programs offered by student affairs units. Both cases illustrate recognition of the premise that assessment can improve student learning and thus should be a fundamental component of everyone's work within an institution.

Characteristic 7. Includes Faculty and Staff Development

Most faculty have had no formal training in psychometrics or evaluation. Student affairs professionals often take courses that emphasize data-gathering techniques, but few have had experience in applying these methods to evaluate and improve their programs. Thus, ongoing faculty and staff development is needed to prepare individuals for their roles in assessment.

At SIUE, Doug Eder, in his role as assessment coordinator, initiated groups in which faculty members and student affairs professionals studied literature focused on improving student learning. This activity fostered interest in assessment and in attending assessment conferences as a group. Later, workshops on special topics were developed, sometimes with an outside facilitator and sometimes with SIUE faculty and staff providing the leadership. Now, assessment scholarship is truly under way there: According to Eder, "We have an extensive faculty development initiative . . . to identify emerging campus leaders, cultivate their interest, and fund their development both on and off campus. By inviting these individuals to copresent either at local or national forums, understanding grows. So do enthusiasm and acceptance" (personal communication, February 8, 2001). At Rivier, assessment committee members organized an event during which faculty and students shared with other faculty and students "highlights of teaching and learning that excited them."

Characteristic 8. Devolves Responsibility for Assessment to the Unit Level

Learning is an individual activity. So the most important sites for assessment are those where students are learning on their own or with other students or with faculty members. Assessment often has its greatest impact as faculty in individual classrooms adjust their instructional methods on the basis of feedback from students about what helps them learn. Faculty then come together in a program area or department, share assessment findings, and thereby improve the curriculum, advising, and placement, as well as other student services that extend beyond the classroom. Representatives of the departments that make up a college or school may share information that can help improve student activities and services that are even more broadly based. At the campus level, faculty and staff development and institution-wide surveys can contribute in important ways to the implementation of assessment in colleges, departments, and classrooms. But assessment is most powerful at the unit level, so responsibility for it must be devolved to the college, to the department, and, ultimately, to the individual classroom. Assessment is everyone's responsibility.

At Ohio University, assessment is "built around faculty participation in designing assessment strategies at the course/department level." At Illinois, where departments were asked to "collect information that would be useful to them," all eighty-three academic units enrolling undergraduates submitted assessment plans and most also have posted to an assessment Web site the ways their findings have been used to make improvements. At Syracuse, Peter Gray reports that "each program must devise appropriate expressions of goals and means for assessment. Meaningful results depend in large measure on the majority of faculty, staff, and administrators *buying into* the purposes and process of assessment. This is the essence of our collaborative model of assessment."

Characteristic 9. Recognizes That Learning Is Multidimensional and Requires Multiple Measures

Each of the programs featured here has developed a multidimensional approach to assessing institutional effectiveness. Recognizing that learning is multidimensional, faculty at Ball State include assessment of general education and learning in the major, as well as assessment of student development conceived more broadly. Assessment activities in the major include pre-post tests, case studies in capstone courses, portfolios, observations of performance during internships, and surveys to assess satisfaction and perceptions of progress toward identified learning outcomes.

A guiding principle of assessment at Syracuse is to "recognize that university-wide assessment must accommodate multiple systems of thought." And Gitanjali Kaul at Ohio University says that "multiple methods—survey, observation, journaling, focus groups—are used to allow for triangulation." Knowledgeable leaders on all these campuses recognize that our measurement methods are imprecise; none will yield perfectly reliable or valid results. Thus, we must use multiple measures and look for confirming evidence among the collective findings as we seek guidance for our improvement efforts. For more information about appropriate assessment measures, please consult Chapter Seven by Gary Pike.

Characteristic 10. Assesses Processes as Well as Outcomes

In outcomes assessment the primary focus must be on what we achieve—our outcomes. And the ultimate outcome is student learning. But as we collect evidence of student achievements and institutional effectiveness, we also need information about the processes that have helped produce the outcomes. For instance, the information conveyed in a test score alone will not help us improve student learning. Among other things, we also need to know what teaching methods were used, how students perceived those methods in terms of their effectiveness in promoting learning, and how much each student invested in studying the material presented.

At Ball State, assessment tools such as student tracking and satisfaction surveys are used to gather information about the effectiveness of the processes involved in providing learning communities for freshmen. At Ohio University, assessment of student writing and the process of writing instruction are key components of evaluating the effectiveness of a new approach to general education.

Brent D. Ruben at Rutgers University has developed an assessment model based on the Baldrige criteria that he calls Excellence in Higher Education. He identifies seven contributors to the effectiveness of a college or university: leadership, planning, stakeholder focus, information and analysis, faculty/staff focus, process effectiveness, and excellence levels and trends (outcomes, trends, and comparisons with peer and leading institutions) (personal communication, January 18, 2001). Only through careful analysis of the processes associated with each of these areas of institutional functioning could one arrive at an educated judgment about the overall effectiveness of the institution.

Characteristic 11. Is Undertaken in a Supportive Environment

At Liberty University, outcomes assessment is viewed as a component of an ongoing process of strategic planning, budgeting, and evaluation. Regional criteria for accreditation are integrated in the university's strategic plan so that information for demonstrating accountability is available continuously and is documented in annual reports.

Faculty members at Truman, Ball State, and Syracuse have opportunities to apply for small grants to support focused work in assessment. The assessment committee at Rivier has an annual budget to spend on workshops, trips to conferences, and materials. At SIUE, faculty are encouraged to visit institutions exhibiting excellence in assessment practice and are recognized for the scholarship of assessment when they write papers and make presentations based on their studies.

All of these institutions are providing the kind of environment for assessment that is receptive, supportive, and enabling. And since, as Tom Angelo emphasizes in Chapter Ten, good work in assessment requires years to take root and grow, this environment must be sustained over time.

Characteristic 12. Incorporates Continuous Communication with Constituents

Recently, the Rivier College catalog has been revised to include learning objectives for students and means of assessment. In annual reports, faculty members report the findings derived from assessment and describe improvement actions. Four of the nine featured institutions now post annual assessment reports on Web sites.

At SIUE, faculty in every discipline devise a senior project for their majors. After the projects are graded, faculty take a second look across all the students' work to detect strengths and weaknesses that might reflect on teaching or curriculum design. Then they meet with colleagues to discuss the implications of findings across courses. According to Doug Eder, faculty "re-engage publicly to celebrate and share what works well and to improve what merits improving."

At Truman, students were interviewed about their best and worst learning experiences. Findings were disseminated in the campus newspaper and discussed in various committees. In the early 1990s, an assessment newsletter was developed to disseminate assessment definitions, methods, and models, as well as information on assessment projects funded through a small grant program. In 1997, a new assessment coordinating committee named three subgroups that interviewed faculty and administrators to find out what each was doing in assessment and to listen to their concerns.

One of the groups considered learning outside the classroom. Group discussions were held and findings were summarized on a Web site.

Students, faculty, and administrators need to read and hear about outcomes assessment in a variety of formats so that they can begin to understand what it is and why it's important. Of particular importance is publicizing in written and oral reports assessment findings and how the findings are being *used* to effect improvements. Chapter Seven, by Gary Pike, contains additional information about communicating the results of assessment effectively to various constituent groups. Assessment cannot be sustained unless stakeholders—including parents, employers, and legislators—are convinced that it is producing substantive positive change.

Characteristic 13. Produces Credible Evidence of Learning and Organizational Effectiveness

Paul Cunningham at Rivier reminds us that "faculty want data that they can believe in (i.e., are accurate, valid, and reliable)." For Rivier faculty, this desire is addressed most satisfactorily by using a nationally standardized exam to assess student achievement in general education. For faculty at many other institutions, credibility comes only with the use of instruments designed locally to match the course and curriculum objectives they have developed. Unfortunately, the state of the art of measurement is such that neither nationally standardized nor locally developed instruments are yet capable of yielding the levels of reliability and validity we all desire. So we pay our money (and invest our time) and live with our choices—and through the scholarship of assessment we must continue to improve the technical quality of our measures.

SIUE faculty members are deeply engaged in this process of continuous improvement. They believe in the capacity of their senior projects to deliver credible data, they continue to improve them, and they have used their findings for years to increase learning and to document institutional effectiveness. In fact, they have done this so well that SIUE was cited recently for "best practice" by the American Association of State Colleges and Universities. As Doug Eder puts it, "the payoff for acquiring and presenting assessment evidence in a peer-reviewable, scholarly way is huge."

As Black and Kline point out in Chapter Twelve, peer review is the most widely accepted and respected method of evaluation in all of higher education. This respect underlies the use of peer evaluators in disciplinary and regional accreditation processes. Many institutions also have their own review processes that have earned credibility through conscientious implementation over the years and provide the most comprehensive evaluation of programs possible. With the addition of outcomes assessment, peer review takes on added value and importance in demonstrating institutional effectiveness. Gitanjali Kaul tells us that at Ohio University "the Seven-Year Program Review process results in specific recommendations for each unit, and the chair of the department, with support from the administration, is actively involved in implementing continuous improvement."

Characteristic 14. Ensures That Assessment Data Are Used to Improve Programs and Services

All of the institutions featured here can provide evidence that assessment data are being used to improve programs and services. Improvements noted range from streamlining the process of placement testing for freshmen at Penn State to modifying Ph.D. qualifying exams at Illinois. Most also employ an annual reporting requirement for departments to ensure that the expectation for use of data is explicit and ever present across the institution. At Liberty, the president asks vice presidents in their annual reviews to report on changes they have made using assessment data.

In keeping with the spirit of the scholarship of assessment, three institutions reported not only actions taken but also the effects of these actions. At Truman, survey results suggested changes that were made in science programs, and now science students are demonstrably more competitive in the graduate school admissions process. At Ball State, students' scores on a standardized general education exam prompted the math department to place greater emphasis on applied mathematics in introductory courses. Now, scores on the math section of the exam are higher. Senior and alumni survey responses convinced the Ball State faculty to increase computer competence requirements. Subsequently, students' survey responses showed greater perceived gains in this area.

At Rivier, the Graduate Record Exam (GRE) is used as the final exam in the capstone course in psychology. Seniors' scores indicated weaknesses in two areas for which the department had no requirement. After designating these courses as requirements, GRE scores went up. Quality of research questions and literature reviews was less than satisfactory in senior research proposals in nursing. Since students have been encouraged to work in groups, some of the research proposals have been judged good enough to receive external funding. Also, as a direct result of responsive actions, student and faculty satisfaction with library support services has increased and internship supervisors no longer send negative feedback about the ability of paralegal studies students to perform title searches.

Characteristic 15. Provides a Vehicle for Demonstrating Accountability to Stakeholders

Corporate universities and for-profit providers of higher education market the learning opportunities they offer by specifying the knowledge and skills students will develop as a result of taking their courses. Until recently, faculty members in traditional colleges and universities have tended to state in rather vague terms the intellectual benefits of completing their courses and degree programs. This is changing as faculty and administrators begin to recognize that higher education has become a competitive enterprise and that even the oldest and largest colleges and universities are increasingly dependent on external sources of income to keep their doors open.

The institutions featured here acknowledge the importance of their stakeholders and the potential of outcomes assessment in demonstrating the benefits to be derived from the postsecondary experience at a traditional college or university. All recognize the need to keep internal constituents apprised of findings related to program and institutional effectiveness. Truman routinely reports assessment results and responsive actions to its Board of Governors. Truman, Ohio University, and SIUE have state requirements for data from assessment that they must satisfy annually. Liberty and Syracuse incorporate assessment timelines and criteria in their campus approaches.

Several institutions consult regularly with external stakeholders, even involving them in the assessment of student work. A survey of Penn State alumni was instrumental in planning changes in the approach to general education there. University of Illinois departments conduct employer surveys and consult departmental boards of advisers as they conduct assessment activities. In sharing findings and describing responsive actions, department faculty demonstrate accountability to these external stakeholders. At Rivier, faculty and staff members interview the community providers of service learning opportunities, thereby gaining information to guide program improvement but also providing evidence of accountability within the community. In Chapter Three, Peter Gray discusses some advantages of defining assessment for both improvement and accountability.

Characteristic 16. Encompasses the Expectation That Assessment Will Be Ongoing, Not Episodic

In the mid-1980s, when accrediting associations were just beginning to require some assessment evidence and few states were using institutional performance as one of the bases for determining budget allocations for public institutions, many faculty members and administrators assumed that outcomes assessment would likely fade away like so many other fads in the management of organizations. In those days it was not uncommon for institutions to gear up for accreditation visits by collecting some data to report to the visiting team but to drop the data collection efforts after attaining reaccreditation. Now, most colleges and universities recognize that assessment requirements are not a passing fad but are here to stay. Thus, outcomes assessment must become an ongoing activity.

The annual unit assessment reports required by most of the institutions featured here constitute one important means of ensuring that assessment efforts will be sustained. SIUE instituted its senior project requirement in 1988 and expects department faculty to meet every year to discuss student performance on these projects and to derive guidance for improvements. At Syracuse, Peter Gray reports that the assessment committee has been at work since 1997 facilitating "the institutionalization of assessment."

Aligning unit assessment plans with those of disciplinary accreditors and appointing subgroups of the campus assessment committee to facilitate widespread assessment-related discussions are two components of the strategy to maintain assessment as an institutional priority at Syracuse.

Characteristic 17. Incorporates Ongoing Evaluation and Improvement of Assessment Itself

The scholarship of assessment would be incomplete without a reflective phase that brings faculty and staff members together to determine the strengths and weaknesses of the assessment process itself and to improve that process continuously. Peer review is a particularly appropriate method for assessing assessment.

The assessment committees at Syracuse and Rivier plan to use unit annual reports to determine how well assessment is being conducted and how it might be improved at both the unit and campus levels. At SIUE, faculty Assessment Scholars are appointed and given funding to conduct meta-analyses of assessment processes using the tools of their own disciplines. Each scholar is expected to produce a manuscript suitable for publication in a peer-reviewed journal. "Our Assessment Scholars take peer review of assessment to . . . its highest level," observes Doug Eder.

Using a Theoretical Framework

Most of what passes for wisdom in the practice of outcomes assessment is derived from reflection on their experiences by those attempting to carry it out. Moreover, since these practitioners generally were schooled in fields other than outcomes assessment itself, they tend to apply their own ways of knowing as they think and write about assessment. Thus, we have great variety in the frames of reference that are brought to bear in the study of this relatively young field.

The foregoing chapters give some hint as to the variety of fields of inquiry that provide bases for the complex practice of assessing educational outcomes. Peter Gray conceives of assessment as planned change. Vic Borden has used organizational development to frame his presentation. Gary Pike has used measurement theory.

While it is still relatively rare to use a theoretical framework for one's work in assessment, we hope to stimulate more of such use with the publication of this book. All of the participants in this project recognize the value of applying a specific model as we undertake assessment activities. As Hausser (1980) has pointed out, a theoretical model "can effectively guide the entire assessment process from planning through analysis" (p. 133). By providing a common set of terms and frame of reference, a model can facilitate communication among all who are involved. It makes clear which factors and relationships are important and defines what should be assessed. The model can suggest hypotheses for testing and thus the analytic techniques to be used. The model provides guidance for organizing and interpreting the findings and communicating them to others. Use of a model can even help us predict future events.

I asked the assessment coordinators associated with the programs featured in this chapter if assessment at their institutions had been based initially on a theoretical model or conceptual framework. Most said no, but a few said that after some time they had arrived at the conclusion that they were implementing Alexander Astin's Input-Environment-Output (I-E-O) model (Astin, 1991).

Astin (1991) proposes a concept of institutional excellence as talent development—defined as the capacity to develop the talents of students and faculty as fully as possible: "The fundamental premise underlying the talent development concept is that true excellence lies in the institution's ability to affect its students and faculty favorably, to enhance their intellectual and scholarly development, to make a positive difference in their lives" (p. 7).

Astin's I-E-O model posits that educational assessment projects should include data on student inputs, student outcomes, and the educational environment to which students are exposed. *Inputs* refer to the personal qualities, including level of developed talents, that the student brings at entry to a program, *environment* refers to the student's experiences during the program, and *outcomes* refer to the talents the program is aimed at developing (Astin, 1991, p. 18).

Astin has used "natural experiments to study naturally occurring variations in environmental conditions to approximate the methodological benefits of true experiments by means of complex multivariate analyses" (1991, p. 28). Unfortunately, the number of additional users of these complex analytic techniques has not been sizable. While talent development has widespread appeal as an intellectual concept, in practice, Astin's theoretical model has guided very little outcomes assessment on campuses.

I join John Ory of Illinois in expressing a preference for Michael Quinn Patton's work (1997) in utilization-focused program evaluation as a framework for outcomes assessment. This is not surprising since my own educational background is in educational psychology, measurement, and evaluation. Patton's experience has convinced him that the most significant problem in conducting program evaluations is getting people to *use* the findings. His "utilization-focused evaluation" model is designed to narrow "the gap between generating evaluation findings and actually using those findings for program decision making and improvement" (p. 6).

In almost any audience gathered to consider outcomes assessment, one of the first questions will be *How do we get faculty involved in assessment?* And within groups of experienced practitioners, a persistent question is *How do we get people to* use *assessment findings?* Patton's model addresses these questions directly. He focuses on preparing and encouraging people to become engaged so that they will use the results of program evaluation—a term that for many is synonymous with assessment in higher education.

Patton's model is based on fourteen "fundamental premises" (Patton, 1997, pp. 381–383). These premises can be summarized as follows: "Commitment to intended use . . . should be the driving force in an evaluation." From the beginning, "strategizing about use is ongoing and continuous." "The personal interests and commitments of those involved" contribute significantly to use. "Primary intended users" should be identified through "careful and thoughtful stakeholder analysis." "Evaluations must be focused" and the best focus is "on intended use by intended users." This focus "requires making deliberate and thoughtful choices" about how findings will be used and designing and adapting the evaluation to fit the given context. The "commitment to use can be nurtured and enhanced by actively involving" intended users "in making significant decisions about the evaluation." "High-quality participation is the goal, not high-quantity participation," so

evaluators "must be skilled group facilitators." Since "threats to utility are as important to counter as threats to validity," evaluators
must help intended users understand methodological issues so that
they can be involved in selecting among design and methods
options. As evaluators are "active-reactive-adaptive," their "credibility and integrity are always at risk"; thus they must be guided by
the stated standards and principles of their professional association, the American Evaluation Association (Shadish, Newman,
Scheirer and Wye, 1995). Evaluators "have a responsibility to *train
users* in evaluation processes and the uses of information." Use
(making decisions, improving programs, changing thinking) "is
different from reporting and dissemination." "Serious attention to
use involves financial and time costs" but "the benefits of these
costs are manifested in greater use."

Many of the "characteristics of effective outcomes assessment"
outlined earlier in this chapter reflect Patton's emphasis on use
and the intended user, for example, (1) on involving stakeholders,
(2) on beginning when the need is recognized, (3) on basing purposes on goals people value, (7) on developing faculty and staff for
their work on assessment, and (14) on ensuring that data are used
in improvement. But perhaps his emphasis—on use and the intended user—is not as explicit in this listing as it could be or
should be.

In Patton's model (1997), involving the stakeholders and
preparing them to make decisions not only about how an evaluation is designed and carried out but also about how the findings
are to be used is worthy of more attention than are the mechanics
of implementing the evaluation and disseminating the results. If
those of us working on outcomes assessment focused more of our
attention on facilitating the engagement of stakeholders, we might
be able to supply more powerful responses to those two pervasive
questions *How do we get faculty involved?* and *How do we get people to
use assessment findings?*

Questions for Future Scholarship in Assessment

In these first two decades of the history of outcomes assessment in
higher education, we have, understandably, spent much of our
time and effort on developing definitions, plans, and approaches,

as well as designing or adapting measuring instruments. But now that our toolbox is filled with the designs and methods for accomplishing the task at hand, we must turn to the even harder job of winning the hearts and minds of our colleagues, bringing them to an appreciation of the value of assessment for improving teaching and learning.

Now, in addition to answering such questions as *Which works better, standardized tests or course-embedded assessment? Should we use classroom tests, group projects, or portfolios?* and *How can we improve our survey response rates?* we must ask ourselves *What are the best ways to determine the personal interests and commitments of our stakeholders? How can we educate stakeholders in making informed choices among design and methods options that will keep them engaged in assessment and committed to using its findings? How can we reduce costs and maximize the benefits of assessment?* and *What ethical principles should guide our work as facilitators of assessment focused on utilization?*

These are some of the questions that will guide the scholarship of assessment for the next two decades of its development. As the contents of this volume illustrate, our methods are well grounded in the research of other disciplines. Now, we must apply all that we have learned from others to increase the *use* of our designs, methods, and outcomes.

Chapter Fifteen

A Call for Transformation

Trudy W. Banta

In this book and elsewhere the word *transformation* keeps coming up in discussions about assessment. In Chapter One, Peter Ewell suggests two fundamental changes that will be needed "to transform assessment from a movement into a culture." One of these involves shifting the conceptual understanding of assessment on the part of faculty from that of "checking up on results toward an emphasis on assuming active and collective responsibility for student attainment." In this connection, increasing interest in problem-based learning and the use of technology in instruction are catalysts for helping faculty members move from the tradition of awarding credits on the basis of seat time to thinking about performance-based attainment and ability-based credentials. A second needed change is at the administrative level, "evolving a largely top-down, management-oriented use of information in planning and decision making toward a culture that more freely embodies the principles of a learning organization." Here, competition from corporate providers and continued external pressures for higher education to become more efficient and effective are the potential catalysts for the needed change.

Peterson and Vaughan report in Chapter Two that while assessment activity is widespread—95 percent of the more than 1,300 institutions responding to their survey reported that two or more types of assessment were under way on those campuses—the use of assessment data in decision making is limited, and very few institutions are systematically monitoring the impact of assessment. They conclude that the overall influence of outcomes assessment on higher education has been small, at least on the dimensions they have used to measure it. These authors also call for a cultural transformation that will encourage faculty members and administrators to make assessment their own, to view it as a mechanism for directing internal improvement rather than as a series of activities to be undertaken just to comply with some external mandate. They describe three conceptual models for promoting and supporting assessment. The first is an institutional assessment strategy in which assessment becomes an integral part of the mission and planning for improvement at both campus and unit levels. The second is a rational information and analysis strategy that focuses data-gathering and information systems on identifying factors that improve student performance. A third model encompasses a human resource or developmental strategy that enhances the capacity of faculty, staff, and students to contribute to assessment and provides incentives for participation.

Brent Ruben (2001), whose Excellence in Higher Education model I describe in Chapter Fourteen, has written on "excellence beyond the classroom." He urges us to work to transform our campus cultures by improving "service excellence," the services we provide for our constituents, and "organizational excellence," the effectiveness and efficiency of the way we do our work. Specifically, we should study the needs and perceptions of those we intend to serve, identify gaps between what we think we are doing and how we are perceived by our constituents, and take action designed to reduce the gaps. Similarly, we should study and improve our internal operations. Then, in the spirit of a true learning organization, we should share our best practices with colleagues.

Barbara Wright concludes Chapter Thirteen with her own call for transformation: "The cultural change we all seek cannot be achieved by more measurement alone. But if we step back from data gathering to engage in a qualitative interpretation of the data . . . if we work together to define that new culture, if the process and scholarly findings of assessment that have proven so powerful on campuses can be carried out at larger levels of scale, then perhaps all of us together . . . have a chance at transformation."

For almost two decades informed leaders in higher education have been calling on colleges and universities to become learning organizations—to be systematic in defining our missions, as institutions and as units within an institution; to be mindful of the needs and expectations of our stakeholders as we set goals and organize to deliver services; to collect systematic evidence concerning our processes; to use this evidence to improve our work; and to share our successes so that others can build on those without having to repeat our failures. Many in the academy have come to recognize that the curriculum should be more than a series of unconnected courses taught by a collection of individuals who seldom talk to each other about their teaching. We can't just work in our own silos and expect the organization around us to flourish. Nor can we really move forward in increasing and enriching student learning if we fail to apply to our work with students the same principles of design, data-gathering, analysis and interpretation, and sharing of findings that we apply in our disciplinary scholarship.

But in spite of the beacons provided by enlightened leaders, here we are—twenty years beyond the first calls for change and well into the first decade of a new millennium, still hearing that cultural transformation is needed to give assessment its rightful place as a powerful tool in the service of continuous improvement in higher education. And if we can't convince a major portion of faculty to engage in scholarly assessment, there is little hope that we can make significant progress in the scholarship of assessment (see the Preface for the distinctions we have made between these terms).

Why So Little Progress Toward Transformation?

Just as the taxpayers in many major cities have not experienced sufficient frustration in commuting to pursue new, or even to utilize existing, mass transit systems, many faculty members have not seen a need to change their approaches or methods. They still have students in their classes and support for their scholarly activity. They may have heard that there is increasing competition for students and that student retention is a growing concern, but they see these as problems for others to solve: *Let someone else improve the services that will attract and retain students. That's not my job,* they mutter.

While resistance to changing something that seems successful keeps many faculty from assessment, many others are sincerely interested because they see it as a means of improving their teaching and student learning—matters about which they care deeply. But they are discouraged from trying assessment because they feel they don't know enough about it and don't have time to learn. Moreover, they don't think they would have the time in their over-loaded schedules to accommodate the extra time that assessment would take. Finally, they perceive that time spent on assessment to improve teaching and learning is not recognized by their peers or rewarded in the promotion and tenure process.

Even the term *assessment* is offensive to some. Although the term was coined in the 1980s to distinguish a process aimed at *improving programs* (assessment) from *evaluation*—in the minds of many faculty the process of reviewing their accomplishments for recognition and reward—an early and often lingering perception is that assessment ultimately will be used as a tool for evaluating individual faculty performance, ultimately abridging the cherished right to academic freedom.

Finally, assessment is fundamentally a collaborative process, and collaborative skills are not a hallmark of those who choose careers in academe. Assessment requires agreement on essential knowledge and skills for the major, on appropriate assessment methods and tools, on the interpretation of findings, and on the nature of appropriate improvement actions. Yet we study alone to make the grades required for graduate school, in graduate school we develop our knowledge of a narrow area as individuals, then we are hired as faculty members on the basis of our area of special-ization, we teach and conduct much of our research alone, and ultimately we are rewarded primarily for our individual achieve-ments. We thus are not well prepared for the collaborative work that effective assessment of outcomes requires.

What Strategies Might Move Us Toward Transformation?

As much as scholars like Dary Erwin and Steven Wise would like to focus the scholarship of assessment on the very important and valuable work of solving psychometric problems with our instru-ments and extending our knowledge of cognitive and psychoso-cial development (see Chapter Four), we must first address the problem of engaging a critical mass of faculty on each campus in cultural transformation that relies on assessment to provide direction for continuous improvement. What are some strategies for doing this that we might test by using scholarly approaches?

Although we do not routinely collaborate in our work with faculty in other disciplines, or even with faculty in our own departments whose areas of disciplinary interest do not intersect with ours, we do tend to interact more with colleagues at other institutions who share our area of specialization. We engage in self-reflection, share our observations with these close colleagues, design systematic studies to collect objective data to support or refute our subjective hunches, share these findings and compare alternative interpretations at professional meetings and in publications, and then take some responsive action, either to improve practice or to design another, more focused, study. This sounds very much like the sequence of steps involved in scholarly assessment. Both Gary Pike and Peter Gray (in Chapters Seven and Three, respectively) liken good assessment practice to the process of conducting scholarly work in one's discipline. We need studies to tell us if introducing assessment as a process similar to disciplinary scholarship is effective in drawing faculty into assessment.

Gray also suggests connecting assessment, as a form of systematic inquiry, with the scholarship of teaching. He believes that assessment can be introduced to faculty members as a tool for gathering evidence to answer practical questions about teaching and learning. Gray supports this position with a quotation from Peter Ewell: "It is extremely difficult to argue as a responsible academic that it is wrong to gather information about a phenomenon, or that it is inappropriate to use the results for collective betterment" (1989, p. 11). The effectiveness of this approach to engaging faculty members in assessment should also be tested through research.

Another approach to test is that proposed by Tom Angelo in Chapter Ten. He suggests several steps, including involving from the outset opinion leaders from the principal faculty groups that should be involved in assessment throughout its history and focusing assessment on its primary purpose—improving student learning. He also suggests starting with familiar concepts and making connections, for example, helping faculty turn students' grades into a more meaningful summary of student competence. He recommends providing support and developmental experiences, not only for novices but also for colleagues who are at an intermediate stage and would like some guidance about using a new method. Angelo would have us insist on clear criteria and high standards for quality in assessment, employing peer evaluation against agreed-upon, meaningful criteria for performance.

Finally, I have offered in Chapter Fourteen another model for engaging faculty that deserves testing: that of Michael Quinn Patton's utilization-focused program evaluation (1997), which emphasizes preparing and encouraging faculty and other stakeholders to *use* the results of assessment and program evaluation to improve instruction, curricula, and student services. Patton believes that the driving force for program evaluation—often used interchangeably with the term *assessment* in higher education—should be a commitment to using its findings in ways that are specified from the outset. Considering in advance who the recipients of assessment findings should be and how these stakeholders might use the findings should be employed to shape decisions about which evaluation design and data-collection methods will be used.

Beyond Faculty Engagement

While I believe that finding effective ways to engage faculty in cultural transformation that encompasses assessment as an indispensable tool in the process is the first topic on which we should focus the scholarship of assessment, my colleagues in the development of this volume have identified at least three other areas that merit systematic study. Those engaged in assessment practice think immediately of studies that would tell us more about which *methods of assessment* work best under what circumstances. Speaking more broadly, there are aspects of *organizational behavior and development* that could advance the practice of assessment if they were understood at a deeper level. Finally—and this brings us back to the ever-present issue of engaging faculty—there is the area of developing *shared reflective practice.*

Methods

In Chapter Four, Erwin and Wise provide a rich assortment of suggestions for future research, beginning with the need to develop better instruments for measuring content knowledge at more complex cognitive levels—looking at critical thinking and problem solving in one's discipline, for example. Assessing affective aspects of development is a further challenge, along with determining how to motivate students to learn and to take assessment seriously. At yet another level of complexity, Erwin and Wise call for research on the effects of educational interventions; that is, what combinations of learning strategies produce changes in outcomes? In this same vein, Kuh, Gonyea, and Rodriguez (in Chapter Six) remind us that we have not solved the psychometric problems associated with measuring changes in learning that occur over time.

Shermis and Daniels (in Chapter Eight) call attention to scholarship that employs technology to pose questions and grade responses using instruments as diverse as questionnaires and portfolios. Erwin and Wise discuss research on new formats for test questions and responses, including the use of artificial intelligence to develop assessment methods matched to each of the many ways in which students learn.

Erwin and Wise broach the issue of demonstrating the validity of locally developed instruments. Ewell mentions the difficulties faculty members encounter in forging consensual judgments about the quality of student performances. In Chapter Five, Mentkowski and Loacker call for more work on how to design feedback for students and opportunities for self-assessment so that these activities provide information to help faculty improve their teaching effectiveness and the validity of their assessment instruments.

Organizational Behavior and Development

Ewell believes that assessment must be fused with other systemic changes under way in institutions—focused and sustained faculty development, for example—that are aimed at changing the environment for teaching and learning. Alternative strategies for doing this need to be implemented and their effects studied. Pike, Peterson and Vaughan, and Erwin and Wise suggest looking broadly at organizational behavior, such as methods of interinstitutional communication, for patterns that promote and sustain assessment. In Chapter Nine, Borden discusses methods of providing and managing assessment information that should be tried and evaluated. The paramount issue for Black and Kline (in Chapter Twelve) is how to incorporate assessment data effectively in institutional program review and how to ensure that all the pertinent information from the review process will be used to improve academic programs and services.

Ewell and Erwin and Wise are concerned about the impact of public policy related to accountability on institutional behavior. Can we determine the effectiveness of various combinations of performance indicators in promoting improvement on campuses while at the same time satisfying the accountability demands of external stakeholders?

Shared Reflective Practice

Ewell concludes his chapter on an optimistic note, stating that "assessment will gradually become an integral part of each faculty member's reflective practice, documented through the scholarship of teaching. . . . And faculty will increasingly collaborate in this work, reflecting their growing assumption of collective responsibility for learning."

In Wright's conclusion, cited earlier in this chapter, she also emphasizes the importance of self-reflection, sharing insights about successful practice, and collaborating across institutions to ascertain what works in which settings. Mentkowski and Loacker advocate a "joint scholarship of assessment" that is characterized, among other things, by "integrating ways of knowing about assessment . . . and developing methods from points of coherence within a diversity of disciplines and practices." Gray urges us to conduct metaevaluations of various approaches to assessment in order to identify the qualities and characteristics that make the process meaningful.

Palomba (in Chapter Eleven), as well as the chapter authors just cited, believes in the power of sharing experiences, or case studies, of assessment, particularly under the auspices of professional organizations such as disciplinary and regional accrediting associations. Consortia of institutions also can provide the forum for shared reflective practice. In Chapter Six, Kuh, Gonyea, and Rodriguez add collaboration among academic and student affairs professionals to the mix and suggest that leaders of several national assessment programs, such as those situated at the University of

California, Los Angeles, and Indiana University, join forces to educate faculty across the country about analyzing and using data derived from their surveys in combination with campus-specific data from other sources.

Taken together, all of these suggestions for further study constitute a full agenda for at least two more decades of sustained work. While scholarly assessment is becoming more widespread in institutions of all sizes and types, the scholarship of assessment is just beginning.

References

Adelman, C. (ed.). *Assessment in Higher Education: Issues and Contexts* (Report No. OR 86–301, pp. 47–62). Washington, D.C.: U.S. Department of Education, 1986.

Adelman, C. *A Parallel Postsecondary Universe: The Certification System in Information Technology.* Washington, D.C.: OERI, U.S. Department of Education, 2000.

Altschuld, J. W. "The Certification of Evaluators: Highlights from a Report Submitted to the Board of Directors of the American Evaluation Association." *The American Journal of Evaluation,* 1999, *20*(3), 481–493.

Alverno College Faculty. *Assessment at Alverno College.* Milwaukee, Wis.: Alverno Productions, 1979.

Alverno College Faculty. *Student Assessment-as-Learning at Alverno College.* Milwaukee, Wis.: Alverno College Institute, 1979/1994 (Original work published 1979, revised 1985 and 1994).

Alverno College Faculty. (G. Loacker, ed.). *Self Assessment at Alverno College.* Milwaukee, Wis.: Alverno College Institute, 2000.

American Association for Higher Education. *American Association for Higher Education Research Forum: Research Agendas.* Documents created at the 1987–1993 annual meetings of the American Association for Higher Education, Chicago, Ill. Washington, D.C.: American Association for Higher Education, 1987–1993.

American Association for Higher Education. *Principles of Good Practice for Assessing Student Learning.* Washington, D.C.: American Association for Higher Education, 1992.

American Association for Higher Education. *CQI 101: A First Reader for Higher Education.* Washington, D.C.: American Association for Higher Education, 1994a.

American Association for Higher Education. "American Association for Higher Education Testimony to the Joint Committee on the Standards for Educational and Psychological Testing." Testimony presented by M. Mentkowski, AAHE adviser to the joint committee, at the Open Conference on the Test Standards Revision Project, Crystal City, Va. Complete set of documents submitted by AAHE to the Joint Committee available by e-mail from ere@alverno.edu. Oct. 1994. (1994b)

American Association for Higher Education. *Learning Through Assessment: A Resource Guide for Higher Education.* Washington, D.C.: American Association for Higher Education, 1997.

American Association for Higher Education Research Forum. *Mapping a Decade of Change.* (3rd ed.) Milwaukee, Wis.: Alverno College Institute, 1996. Brochure.

American College Personnel Association. *The Student Learning Imperative: Implications for Student Affairs.* Washington, D.C.: American College Personnel Association, 1994.

American College Testing Program. *Collegiate Assessment of Academic Proficiency (CAAP).* Iowa City, Iowa: American College Testing Program, 2000.

American Educational Research Association, American Psychological Association, and National Council on Measurement in Education. *Standards for Educational and Psychological Testing.* (Rev. ed.) Washington, D.C.: American Educational Research Association, 1999.

American Productivity and Quality Center. *Measuring Institutional Performance Outcomes: Final Report.* Houston, Tex.: American Productivity and Quality Center, 1997.

American Productivity and Quality Center. *Benchmarking Best Practices in Assessing Learning Outcomes: Final Report.* Houston, Tex.: American Productivity and Quality Center, 1998.

Anderson, R. D., and DeMars, C. E. "Differential Item Functioning (DIF): Investigating Item Bias." Unpublished manuscript, James Madison University, 2000.

Angelo, T. A. (ed.). *Classroom Research: Early Lessons from Success.* New Directions for Teaching and Learning, 1991, no. 46. San Francisco: Jossey-Bass, 1991.

Angelo, T. A. (ed.). *Classroom Assessment and Research: An Update on Uses, Approaches, and Research Findings.* New Directions for Teaching and Learning, no. 75. San Francisco: Jossey-Bass, 1998.

Angelo, T. A., and Cross, P. *Classroom Assessment Techniques: A Handbook for College Teachers.* San Francisco: Jossey-Bass, 1993.

Antons, C. M., Dilla, B. L., and Fultz, M. L. "Assessing Student Attitudes: Computer Versus Paper-and-Pencil Administration." Paper presented at the annual meeting of the Association for Institutional Research, Orlando, Fla., 1997.

Aper, J. P. "Higher Education and the State: Accountability and the Roots of Student Outcomes Assessment." *Higher Education Management,* 1993, *5,* 336–376.

Arns, R. G., and Poland, W. "Changing the University Through Program Review." *Journal of Higher Education,* 1980, *51,* 268–284.

Association of American Colleges. *Integrity in the College Curriculum: A Report to the Academic Community.* Washington, D.C.: Association of American Colleges, 1985.

Astin, A. W. *Four Critical Years.* San Francisco: Jossey-Bass, 1977.

Astin, A. W. "Student Involvement: A Developmental Theory for Higher Education." *Journal of College Student Development,* 1984, *40*(5), 518–529.

Astin, A. W. *Achieving Educational Excellence: A Critical Assessment of Priorities and Practices in Higher Education.* San Francisco: Jossey-Bass, 1985.

Astin, A. W. *Four Critical Years.* (2nd ed.) San Francisco: Jossey-Bass, 1987.

Astin, A. W. *Assessment for Excellence.* Old Tappan, N.J.: Macmillan, 1991.

Astin, A. W. *What Matters in College? Four Critical Years Revisited.* San Francisco: Jossey-Bass, 1993.

Atkinson, D., Morten, G., and Sue, D. *Counseling American Minorities: A Cross-Cultural Perspective.* Madison, Wis.: Brown & Benchmark, 1993.

Baird, L. L. "Value Added: Using Student Gains as Yardsticks of Learning." In C. Adelman (ed.), *Performance and Judgment: Essays on Principles and Practice in the Assessment of College Student Learning.* Washington, D.C.: U.S. Government Printing Office, 1988.

Ballou, R., Bowers, D., Boyatzis, R. E., and Kolb, D. A. "Fellowship in Lifelong Learning: An Executive Development Program for Advanced Professionals." *Journal of Management Education,* 1999, *23*(4), 338–354.

Banks, J. A. "The Cannon Debate, Knowledge Construction, and Multicultural Education." *Educational Researcher,* 1993, *22*(5), 4–14.

Banta, T. W. "Use of Outcomes Information at the University of Tennessee, Knoxville." In P. T. Ewell (ed.), *Assessing Educational Outcomes.* New Directions for Institutional Research, no. 47. San Francisco: Jossey-Bass, 1985.

Banta, T. W. "Summary and Conclusion: Are We Making a Difference?" In T. W. Banta and Associates (eds.), *Making a Difference: Outcomes of a Decade of Assessment in Higher Education.* San Francisco: Jossey-Bass, 1993.

Banta, T. W. "The Power of a Matrix." *Assessment Update,* 1996, *8*(4), 3–13.

Banta, T. W. "What's New in Assessment?" *Assessment Update,* 1999, *11*(5), 3, 11.

Banta, T. W., and Associates. *Making a Difference: Outcomes of a Decade of Assessment in Higher Education.* San Francisco: Jossey-Bass, 1993.

Banta, T. W., Lund, J. P., Black, K. E., and Oblander, F. W. *Assessment in Practice: Putting Principles to Work on College Campuses.* San Francisco: Jossey-Bass, 1996.

Banta, T. W., and others. "Estimated Score Gain on the ACT COMP Exam: Valid Tool for Institutional Assessment?" *Research in Higher Education,* 1987, *27,* 195–217.

Banta, T. W., and Pike, G. R. "Methods for Comparing Outcomes Assessment Instruments." *Research in Higher Education,* 1989, *30,* 455–469.

Banta, T. W., Rudolph, L. B., Van Dyke, J., and Fisher, H. S. "Performance Funding in Tennessee Comes of Age." *Journal of Higher Education,* 1996, *67*(1), 23–45.

Barak, R. J. *Program Review in Higher Education: Within and Without.* Boulder, Colo.: National Center for Higher Education Management Systems, 1982. (ED 246 829)

Barak, R. J., and Breier, B. E. *Successful Program Review: A Practical Guide to Evaluating Programs in Academic Settings.* San Francisco: Jossey-Bass, 1990.

Barr, R. B., and Tagg, J. "From Teaching to Learning—a New Paradigm for Undergraduate Education." *Change,* 1995, *27*(6), 12–25.

Baxter Magolda, M. B. *Knowing and Reasoning in College: Gender-Related Patterns in Students' Intellectual Development.* San Francisco: Jossey-Bass, 1992.

Bean, J. P. "Assessing and Reducing Attrition." In D. Hossler (ed.), *Managing College Enrollments.* New Directions for Higher Education, no. 53, San Francisco: Jossey-Bass, 1986.

Bean, J. P., and Bradley, R. "Untangling the Satisfaction-Performance Relationship for College Students." *Journal of Higher Education,* 1986, *57,* 293–312.

Bennett, R. E., and others. "Using Multimedia in Large-Scale Computer-Based Testing Programs." *Computers in Human Behavior,* 1999, *15,* 283–294.

Bennett, W. J. *To Reclaim a Legacy: A Report on the Humanities in Higher Education.* Washington, D.C.: National Endowment for the Humanities, 1984.

Bers, T. H., and Seybert, J. A. *Effective Reporting.* Resources in Institutional Research, no. 12. Tallahassee, Fla.: Association for Institutional Research, 1999.

Birnbaum, M. H. *Introduction to Behavioral Research on the Internet.* Englewood Cliffs, N.J.: Prentice Hall, 2001.

Birnbaum, R. *Management Fads in Higher Education: Where They Come From, What They Do, Why They Fail.* San Francisco: Jossey-Bass, 2000.

Blimling, G. S. "Uniting Scholarship and Communities of Practice in Student Affairs." *Journal of College Student Development,* 2001, *42*(4), 381–396.

Bloom, B. S. (ed.). *Taxonomy of Educational Objectives: The Classification of Educational Goals. Handbook I: Cognitive Domain.* New York: Longmans, Green, 1956.

Boland, D. L., and Laidig, J. "Assessment of Student Learning in the Discipline of Nursing." In C. A. Palomba and T. W. Banta (eds.), *Assessing Student Competence in Accredited Disciplines: Pioneering Approaches to Assessment in Higher Education.* Sterling, Va.: Stylus Publishing, LLC, 2001.

Borden, V.M.H., and Banta, T. *Using Performance Indicators to Guide Strategic Decision Making.* New Directions for Institutional Research, no. 82. San Francisco: Jossey-Bass.

Borden, V., Massa, T., and Milam, J. "Technology and Tools for Institutional Research." In R. D. Howard (ed.), *Institutional Research: Decision Support in Higher Education.* Resources for Institutional Research, no. 13. Tallahassee, Fla.: Association for Institutional Research, 2001.

Borden, V., and Zak Owens, J. *Measuring Quality: Choosing Among Surveys and Other Assessments of College Quality.* A joint publication of the Association for Institutional Research, Tallahassee, Fla., and the American Council on Education, Washington, D.C., 2001.

Bowen, H. R. *Investment in Learning.* San Francisco: Jossey-Bass, 1977.

Boyatzis, R. E., and Kolb, D. A. "Assessing Individuality in Learning: The Learning Skills Profile." *Educational Psychology: An International Journal of Experimental Educational Psychology,* 1991, *11*(3–4), 279–295.

Boyer, C. M., Ewell, P. T., Finney, J. E., and Mingle, J. R. "Assessment and Outcomes Measurement: A View from the States." *AAHE Bulletin,* 1987, *39*(7), 8–12.

Boyer, E. L. *Scholarship Reconsidered: Priorities of the Professoriate.* Princeton, N.J.: Carnegie Foundation for the Advancement of Teaching, 1990.

Breivik, P. S. *Student Learning in the Information Age.* American Council on Education, Series on Higher Education. Phoenix: Oryx Press, 1998.

Brennan, R. *Elements of Generalizability Theory.* Iowa City, Iowa: American College Testing Program, 1983.

Burke, J. C. "The Assessment Anomaly: If Everyone's Doing It, Why Isn't More Getting Done?" *Assessment Update,* 1999, *11*(4): 3, 14–15.

Burke, J. C., Modarresi, S., and Serban, A. M. "Performance: Shouldn't It Count for Something in State Budgeting?" *Change,* 1999, *31*(6), 17–23.

Carnegie Council on Policy Studies in Higher Education. *Three Thousand Futures: The Next Twenty Years for Higher Education.* San Francisco: Jossey-Bass, 1980.

Carnegie Foundation for the Advancement of Teaching. *The Control of the Campus: A Report on the Governance of Higher Education.* San Francisco: Jossey-Bass, 1982.

Carpenter, S. "Student Affairs Scholarship(re?)Considered: Toward a Scholarship of Practice." *Journal of College Student Development,* 2001, *42*(4), 301–318.

Chaffee, J. *The Thinker's Way.* New York: Little, Brown, 1998.

Chickering, A. W. *Education and Identity.* San Francisco: Jossey-Bass, 1969.

Chickering, A. W., and Gamson, Z. F. "Seven Principles for Good Practice in Undergraduate Education." *AAHE Bulletin,* 1987, *39*(7), 3–7.

Clark, B., and others. *Students and Colleges: Interaction and Change.* Berkeley: University of California, Center for Research and Development in Higher Education, 1972.

Clark, M. J. "Academic Program Evaluation." In N. P. Uhl (ed.), *Using Research for Strategic Planning.* New Directions for Institutional Research, no. 37. San Francisco: Jossey-Bass, 1983.

Cleveland, W. S. *Visualizing Data.* Murray Hills, N.J.: AT&T Bell Laboratories, 1993.

Cohen, M. D., and March, J. "Leadership in an Organized Anarchy." In M. W. Peterson (ed.), *Organization and Governance in Higher Education.* ASHE Reader Series. Needham Heights, Mass.: Ginn Press, 1991.

Cohen, R. J., Swerdlik, M. E., and Phillips, S. M. *Psychological Testing and Assessment.* Mountain View, Calif.: Mayfield, 1996.

Cole, J.J.K., Nettles, M. T., and Sharp, S. *Assessment of Teaching and Learning for Improvement and Accountability: State Governing, Coordinating Board and Regional Accreditation Association Policies and Practices.* Ann Arbor: University of Michigan, National Center for Postsecondary Improvement, 1997.

Conrad, C. F., and Blackburn, R. T. "Program Quality in Higher Education: A Review and Critique of Literature and Research." In J. Smart, (ed.), *Higher Education Handbook of Theory and Research.* Vol. 1. New York: Agathon Press, 1985.

Conrad, C. F., and Wilson, R. F. "Academic Program Reviews: Institutional Approaches, Expectations, and Controversies." *ASHE/ERIC Higher Education Reports,* no. 5. Washington, D.C.: Association for the Study of Higher Education, 1985.

Consortium for the Improvement of Teaching, Learning, and Assessment. *High School to College to Professional School: Achieving Educational Coher-*

ence Through Outcome-Oriented, Performance-Based Curricula. Final report to the W. K. Kellogg Foundation. Milwaukee, Wis.: Alverno Productions, 1992.

Cook, C. E. "FIPSE's Role in Assessment: Past, Present, and Future." *Assessment Update,* 1989, *1*(2), 1–3.

Core Institute. *Core Alcohol and Drug Survey.* Carbondale: Southern Illinois University, Center for Alcohol and Other Drug Studies, 1994.

Corrallo, S. "Critical Concerns in Assessing Selected Higher Order Thinking and Communication Skills of College Graduates." *Assessment Update,* 1991, *3*(6), 5–6.

Craven, E. "Evaluating Program Performance." In *Improving Academic Management.* New Directions for Improving Institutional Research, no. 27. San Francisco: Jossey-Bass, 1980.

Creamer, D. G., and Janosik, S. M. "Academic Program Approval and Review Practice in the United States and Selected Foreign Countries." *Educational Policy Analysis Archives,* 1999, *7*(23). [http://epaa.asu.edu/epaa/v7n23/].

Creswell, J. W. *Qualitative Inquiry and Research Design: Choosing Among the Five Traditions.* Thousand Oaks, Calif.: Sage, 1997.

Cross, K. P. "Teachers as Scholars." *AAHE Bulletin,* 1990, *43*(4), 3–5.

Cross, K. P., and Angelo, T. A. *Classroom Assessment Techniques: A Handbook for Faculty.* Ann Arbor, Mich.: National Center for the Improvement of Postsecondary Teaching and Learning, 1988.

Cross, K. P., and Steadman, M. H. *Classroom Research: Implementing the Scholarship of Teaching.* San Francisco: Jossey-Bass, 1996.

Cross, W. E., Strauss, L., and Fhagen-Smith, P. "African American Identity Development Across the Life Span: Educational Implications." In R. Sheets and E. Hollins (eds.), *Racial and Ethnic Identity in School Practices.* Mahwah, N.J.: Lawrence Erlbaum Associates, 1999.

Deming, W. E. *The New Economics for Industry, Government, Education.* (2nd ed.) Cambridge, Mass.: MIT Press, 1993.

Denzin, N. K. *Interpretive Biography.* Thousand Oaks, Calif.: Sage, 1989.

Denzin, N. K., and Lincoln, Y. S. *Handbook of Qualitative Research.* Thousand Oaks, Calif.: Sage, 1994.

DeZure, D. *Learning from Change: Landmarks in Teaching and Learning in Higher Education from Change Magazine 1969–1999.* Washington, D.C.: American Association for Higher Education, 2000.

Diamond, R. M. *Preparing for Promotion and Tenure Review: A Faculty Guide.* Bolton, Mass.: Anker Publishing, 1995.

Dreyfus, H. L., and Dreyfus, S. E. *Mind Over Machine: The Power of Human Intuition and Expertise in the Era of the Computer.* New York: Free Press, 1986.

Eaton, J. S. "Regional Accreditation Reform: Who Is Served?" *Change,* 2001, *33*(2), 38–45.

Eder, D. "Accredited Programs and Authentic Assessment." In C. A. Palomba and T. W. Banta (eds.), *Assessing Student Competence in Accredited Disciplines: Pioneering Approaches to Assessment in Higher Education.* Sterling, Va.: Stylus Publishing, LLC, 2001.

Edirisooriya, G. *Information Management in Higher Education Administration: A Slow Drive on the Information Superhighway.* Hershey, Pa.: Idea Group Publishing, 2000.

Education Commission of the States. *Challenge: Coordination and Governance in the '80s. A Report on Issues and Directions in Statewide Coordination and Governance of Postsecondary Education in the 1980s. Report No. 134.* Denver: Education Commission of the States, 1980.

Education Commission of the States. *Making Quality Count in Undergraduate Education.* Denver: Education Commission of the States, 1995.

El-Khawas, E. "New Directions for Academic Programs." *Campus Trends, Higher Education Panel Report No. 85.* Washington, D.C.: American Council on Education, 1995.

Embretson, S. E. "A Cognitive Design System Approach to Generating Valid Tests: Application to Abstract Reasoning." *Psychological Methods,* 1998, *3*(3), 380–396.

Embretson, S. E. "Cognitive Psychology Applied to Testing." In F. T. Durso and others (eds.), *Handbook of Applied Cognition.* New York: Wiley, 1999.

Emery, J. C. *Management Information Systems: The Strategic Imperative.* New York: Oxford University Press, 1987.

Engelkemeyer, S. W., and Landry, E. "Negotiating Change on Campus: Lessons from Five Years of AAHE's Summer Academy." *AAHE Bulletin,* 2001, *53*(6), 7–10.

Enthoven, A. C. "Measures of the Outputs of Higher Education: Some Practical Suggestions for Their Development and Use." In G. B. Lawrence, G. Weathersby, and V. W. Patterson (eds.), *Outputs of Higher Education: Their Identification, Measurement, and Evaluation.* Boulder, Colo.: Western Interstate Commission for Higher Education, 1970.

Erwin, T. D. *Assessing Student Learning and Development: A Guide to Principles, Goals, and Methods of Determining College Outcomes.* San Francisco: Jossey-Bass, 1991.

Erwin, T. D. *The NPEC Sourcebook on Assessment, Volume 1: Definitions and Assessment Methods for Critical Thinking, Problem Solving, and Writing.* Washington, D.C.: Postsecondary Education Cooperative, 2000.

Erwin, T. D., and Delworth, U. "An Instrument to Measure Chickering's Vector of Identity." *NASPA Journal,* 1980, *17,* 19–24.

Evans, N. J., Forney, D. S., and Guido-DiBrito, F. *Student Development in College: Theory, Research, and Practice.* San Francisco: Jossey-Bass, 1998.

Ewell, P. T. *The Self-Regarding Institution.* Boulder, Colo.: National Center for Higher Education Management Systems, 1984.

Ewell, P. T. "Implementing Assessment: Some Organizational Issues." In T. W. Banta (ed.), *Implementing Outcomes Assessment: Promise and Perils.* New Directions for Institutional Research, no. 59. San Francisco: Jossey-Bass, 1988.

Ewell, P. T. "Hearts and Minds: Some Reflections on the Ideologies of Assessment." In *Three Presentations from the Fourth National Conference on Assessment in Higher Education.* Washington, D.C.: American Association for Higher Education, 1989.

Ewell, P. T. "To Capture the Ineffable: New Forms of Assessment in Higher Education." *Review of Research in Education,* 1991a, *17,* 75–126.

Ewell, P. T. "Assessment and Public Accountability: Back to the Future." *Change,* 1991b, *23*(6), 12–17.

Ewell, P. T. "The Role of States and Accreditors in Shaping Assessment Practice." In T. W. Banta and Associates, *Making a Difference: Outcomes of a Decade of Assessment in Higher Education.* San Francisco: Jossey-Bass, 1993.

Ewell, P. T. "Strengthening Assessment for Academic Quality Improvement." In M. W. Peterson, D. D. Dill, L. A. Mets, and Associates (eds.), *Planning and Management for a Changing Environment: A Handbook on Redesigning Postsecondary Institutions.* San Francisco: Jossey-Bass, 1997a.

Ewell, P. T. "Accountability and Assessment in a Second Decade: New Looks or Same Old Story?" In American Association for Higher Education, *Assessing Impact, Evidence and Action.* Washington, D.C.: American Association for Higher Education, 1997b.

Ewell, P. T. "Organizing for Learning: A New Imperative." *AAHE Bulletin,* 1997c, *50*(4), 10–12.

Ewell, P. T. "Assessment of Higher Education Quality: Promise and Politics." In S. J. Messick (ed.), *Assessment in Higher Education: Issues of Access, Quality, Student Development, and Public Policy.* Mahweh, N.J.: Lawrence Erlbaum Associates, 1999.

Ewell, P. T., Finney, J. E., and Lenth, C. "Filling in the Mosaic: The Emerging Pattern of State-Based Assessment." *AAHE Bulletin,* 1990, *42,* 3–7.

Ewell, P. T., and Jones, D. P. "The Costs of Assessment." In C. Adelman (ed.), *Assessment in American Higher Education.* Washington, D.C.: U.S. Government Printing Office, 1986.

Ewell, P. T., and Jones, D. P. *Indicators of "Good Practice" in Undergraduate Education: A Handbook for Development and Implementation.* Boulder, Colo.: National Center for Higher Education Management Systems, 1996.

Facione, P. A. *Executive Summary of Critical Thinking: A Statement of Expert Consensus for Purposes of Educational Assessment and Instruction. "The Delphi Report."* Milbrae, Calif.: The California Academic Press, 1990.

Facione, P. A. *California Critical Thinking Skills Test.* Millbrae, Calif.: California Academic Press, 1992.

Feldman, K. A., and Newcomb, T. M. *The Impact of College on Students.* San Francisco: Jossey-Bass, 1969.

Firestone, J. M. "Basic Concepts of Knowledge Management." *DSstar* (on-line serial), 2000, *4*(46). Available at [http://www.tgc.com/dsstar/00/1114/102381.html]. Nov. 14, 2000.

Fischer, K. W. "A Theory of Cognitive Development: The Control and Construction of Hierarchies of Skills." *Psychological Review,* 1980, *87,* 477–53.

Flateby, T. L., and Metzger, E. "Instructional Implications of the Cognitive Level and Quality of Writing Assessment." *Assessment Update,* 2001, *13*(1): 4–5, 11.

Foltz, P. W., Kintsch, W., and Landauer, T. K. "The Measurement of Textual Coherence with Latent Semantic Analysis." *Discourse Processes,* 1998, *25*(2&3), 285–307.

Forrest, A. W., and Steele, J. M. *College Outcomes Measures Project.* Iowa City, Iowa: American College Testing Program, 1978.

Fowler, J. W. *Stages of Faith: The Psychology of Human Development and the Quest for Meaning.* San Francisco: Harper San Francisco, 1981.

Fox, M. F. "Publication, Performance, and Reward in Science and Scholarship." In J. C. Smart (ed.), *Higher Education: Handbook of Theory and Research.* Vol. 1. New York: Agathon Press, 1985.

Gainen, J., and Locatelli, P. *Assessment for the New Curriculum: A Guide for Professional Accounting Programs.* Sarasota, Fla.: American Accounting Association, 1995.

Gardiner, L. F. *Redesigning Higher Education: Producing Dramatic Gains in Student Learning.* Washington, D.C.: George Washington University, 1994.

Gardiner, L. F., Anderson, C., and Cambridge, B. L. *Learning Through Assessment: A Resource Guide for Higher Education.* Washington, D.C.: American Association for Higher Education, 1997.

Gilligan, C. *In a Different Voice: Psychological Theory and Women's Development.* Cambridge, Mass.: Harvard University Press, 1982.

Glassick, C. E., Huber, M. T., and Maeroff, G. I. *Scholarship Assessed: Evaluation of the Professoriate.* An Ernest L. Boyer Project of the Carnegie

Foundation for the Advancement of Teaching. San Francisco: Jossey-Bass, 1997.

Goldman, G. "Community College Strategies: Simulated Performance Assessment in a Community College Nursing Program." *Assessment Update,* 1999, *11*(3), 12–13.

Goldstein, G., and Hersen, M. *Handbook of Psychological Assessment.* New York: Pergamon Press, 1984.

Gray, P. J. "A Conceptual Framework for Statements of Educational Objectives." Thesis presented to the faculty of the Graduate School of Cornell University for the degree of Master of Science, Aug. 1975.

Gray, P. J. "Viewing Assessment as an Innovation: Leadership and the Change Process." In P. J. Gray and T. W. Banta (eds.), *The Campus-Level Impact of Assessment: Progress, Problems, and Possibilities.* New Directions for Higher Education, no. 100. San Francisco: Jossey-Bass, 1997.

Gray, P. J. "Campus Profiles: Assessment at Youngstown State University: 2000 and Beyond." *Assessment Update,* 1999a, *11*(2), 8–9, 14.

Gray, P. J. "Campus Profiles." In T. W. Banta (ed.), *Assessment Update: The First Ten Years.* Boulder, Colo.: National Center for Higher Education Management Systems, 1999b.

Gray, P. J. "Campus Profiles: Assessment and Learning Communities: Three Examples." *Assessment Update,* 2000, *12*(2), 10–11, 15.

Griffin, E. *A First Look at Communication Theory.* (4th ed.) New York: McGraw-Hill, 1999.

Grunert, J. *The Course Syllabus: A Learning-Centered Approach.* Bolton, Mass.: Anker Publishing, 1997.

Guba, E. G., and Lincoln, Y. S. *Effective Evaluation: Improving the Usefulness of Evaluation Results through Responsive and Naturalistic Approaches.* San Francisco: Jossey-Bass, 1981.

Guba, E. G., and Lincoln, Y. S. *Fourth-Generation Evaluation.* Thousand Oaks, Calif.: Sage, 1989.

Hall, G. E., Loucks, S. F., Rutherford, W. L., and Newlove, B. W. "Levels of Use of the Innovation: A Framework for Analyzing Innovation Adoption." *Journal of Teacher Education,* Spring 1975, 52–56.

Hammersley, M., and Atkinson, P. *Ethnography: Principles in Practice.* (2nd ed.) New York: Routledge, 1995.

Hanson, G. R. "Critical Issues in the Assessment of Value Added in Education." In T. W. Banta (ed.), *Implementing Outcomes Assessment: Promise and Perils.* New Directions for Institutional Research, no. 59. San Francisco: Jossey-Bass, 1988.

Harris, J. W., and Sansom, D. L. *Discerning Is More Than Counting.* Washington, D.C.: American Academy for Liberal Education, 2001.

Harvey, L., and Knight, P. T. *Transforming Higher Education.* London: Open University Press, 1996.

Hatfield, S. "Assessment in the Major: Tools and Tips for Getting Started." Paper presented at the 1997 Assessment Conference, Indianapolis, Ind., Nov. 1997.

Hatfield, S., and Yackey, B. "New Directions in Assessment: Leveraging Technology in the Quest for Quality." In Susan E. Von Kollenburg (ed.), *A Collection of Papers on Self-Study and Institutional Improvement.* Chicago: North Central Association of Colleges and Schools Commission on Institutions of Higher Learning, 2000.

Hausser, D. "Comparison of Different Models for Organizational Analysis." In E. E. Lawler III, D. A. Nadler, and C. Cammann (eds.), *Organizational Assessment: Perspectives on the Measurement of Organizational Behavior and the Quality of Work Life.* New York: Wiley, 1980.

Havemann, E., and West, P. *They Went to College.* Orlando, Fla.: Harcourt Brace, 1952.

Heath, D. H. *Growing Up in College: Liberal Education and Maturity.* San Francisco: Jossey-Bass, 1968.

Hedden, C. An Automated Data Collector for the Study of Human-Computer Interaction. *Computers in Human Behavior,* 1997, *13*(2), 205–227.

Heffernan, J. M., Hutchings, P., and Marchese, T. J. *Standardized Tests and the Purposes of Assessment.* Washington, D.C.: American Association for Higher Education, 1988.

Herman, J. L., Klein, D.C.D., and Abedi, J. "Assessing Students' Opportunity to Learn: Teacher and Student Perspectives." *Educational Measurement: Issues and Practice,* 2000, *19*(4), 16–24.

Higher Education Research Institute. *The Cooperative Institutional Research Program.* Los Angeles: University of California, Los Angeles, 1966.

Hill, I. B. "The Use of Assessment in Organizational Learning." *Assessment Update,* 1999, *11*(6), 1–2, 10–11.

Hirschborn, L., and May, L. "The Campaign Approach to Change: Targeting the University's Scarcest Resources." *Change,* 2000, *32*(3), 30–37.

Holland, J. L. *Making Vocational Choices: A Theory of Careers.* Englewood Cliffs, N.J.: Prentice Hall, 1973.

Holland, J. L. *Vocational Preference Inventory (vpi): Professional Manual.* Odessa, Fla.: Psychological Assessment Resources, 1985.

Holland, J. L. *The Self-Directed Search (sds): Professional Manual.* Odessa, Fla.: Psychological Assessment Resources, 1994.

Hood, A. B. *The Iowa Student Development Inventories.* Iowa City, Iowa: Hitech Press, 1986.

House, E. R. "Assumptions Underlying Evaluation Models." *Educational Researcher,* 1978, *7*(3), 4–12.

Hoyle, R. H. (ed.). *Structural Equation Modeling: Concepts, Issues, and Applications.* Thousand Oaks, Calif.: Sage, 1995.

Huba, M. E., and Freed, J. E. *Learner-Centered Assessment on College Campuses: Shifting the Focus from Teaching to Learning.* Needham Heights, Mass.: Allyn & Bacon, 2000.

Hutchings, P. "Principles of Good Practice for Assessing Student Learning." *Assessment Update,* 1993, *5*(1), 6–7.

Hutchings, P. *Making Teaching Community Property: A Menu for Peer Collaboration and Review.* Washington, D.C.: American Association for Higher Education, 1996.

Hutchings, P., and Shulman, L. S. "The Scholarship of Teaching: New Elaborations, New Developments." *Change,* 1999, *3*(5), 11–15.

"Inventory of Institutional Support for Student Assessment." For the Research Program on Institutional Support for Student Assessment. Project 5.2, National Center for Postsecondary Education, University of Michigan, [http://www.umich.edu/~ncpi/52/ISSA.pdf].

Jacob, P. E. *Changing Values in College: An Exploratory Study of the Impact of College Teaching.* New York: HarperCollins, 1957.

Joint Committee on the Standards for Educational and Psychological Testing. "Oral Testimony Summaries." Paper presented at the Open Conference on the Test Standards Revision Project, Crystal City, Va., Oct. 1994.

Jones, E. A., Voorhees, R. A., and Paulson, K. *Defining and Assessing Learning: Exploring Competency-Based Initiatives. A Report of the National Postsecondary Education Cooperative.* Washington, D.C.: U.S. Department of Education, National Center for Educational Statistics, 2001.

Jones, V. A. "Attitudes of College Students and Changes in Such Attitudes During Four Years in College." *Journal of Educational Psychology,* 1938, *29,* 14–35.

Kaplan, D. *Structural Equation Modeling: Foundations and Extensions.* Thousand Oaks, Calif.: Sage, 2000.

Karlowicz, K. A. "The Value of Student Portfolios to Evaluate Undergraduate Nursing Programs." *Nurse Educator,* 2000, *25*(2), 82–87.

Katz, A. M., and Gangnon, B. A. "Portfolio Assessment: Integrating Goals and Objectives with Learner Outcomes." *Assessment Update,* 2000, *12*(1), 6–7, 13.

Katz, J., and Korn, H. A. *No Time for Youth: Growth and Constraint in College Students.* San Francisco: Jossey-Bass, 1968.

Kerlinger, F. N. *Foundations of Behavioral Research.* (3rd ed.) Austin, Tex.: Holt, Reinhart and Winston, 1986.

King, P. M., and Howard-Hamilton, M. F. *Becoming a Multiculturally Competent Student Affairs Professional*. Final report submitted to the National Association of Student Personnel Administrators, Washington, D.C., 1999.

King, P. M., and Kitchener, K. S. *Developing Reflective Judgment: Understanding and Promoting Intellectual Growth and Critical Thinking in Adolescents and Adults*. San Francisco: Jossey-Bass, 1994.

Kohlberg, L. *The Philosophy of Moral Development: Moral Stages and the Idea of Justice*. San Francisco: Harper San Francisco, 1981.

Kraemer, H. C., and Thiemann, S. *How Many Subjects? Statistical Power Analysis in Research*. Thousand Oaks, Calif.: Sage, 1987.

Krilowicz, B., Garcia, R., Oh, D., and Goodhue-McWilliams, K. "An Interdisciplinary Capstone Course for Science Program Assessment." Paper presented at the American Association for Higher Education Assessment Conference, Charlotte, N.C., June 2000.

Kuh, G. D. *The College Student Report*. National Survey of Student Engagement, Center for Postsecondary Research and Planning. Bloomington: Indiana University, 1999.

Kuh, G. D. "Assessing What Really Matters to Student Learning: Inside the National Survey of Student Engagement." *Change*, 2001a, *33*(3), 10–17, 66.

Kuh, G. D. "College Students Today: Why We Can't Leave Serendipity to Chance." In P. Altbach, P. Gumport, and B. Johnstone (eds.), *In Defense of the American University*. Baltimore: Johns Hopkins University Press, 2001b.

Kuh, G. D., Hu, S., and Vesper, N. "'They Shall Be Known by What They Do': An Activities-Based Typology of College Students." *Journal of College Student Development*, 2000, *41*, 228–244.

Kuh, G. D., Schuh, J. H., Whitt, E. J., and associates. A. *Involving Colleges: Encouraging Student Learning and Personal Development Through Out-of-Class Experiences*. San Francisco: Jossey-Bass, 1991.

Kuh, G. D., and Stage, F. K. "Student Development Theory and Research." In B. R. Clark and G. Neave (eds.), *Encyclopedia of Higher Education*. New York: Pergamon, 1992.

Kuhn, D. "A Developmental Model of Critical Thinking." *Educational Researcher*, 1999, *28*(2), 16–26.

Lambert, N. M., and McCombs, B. L. (eds.). *How Students Learn: Reforming Schools Through Learner-Centered Education*. Washington, D.C.: American Psychological Association, 1998.

Lawler, E. E. III, Nadler, D. A., and Cammann, C., (eds.) *Organizational Assessment: Perspectives on the Measurement of Organizational Behavior and the Quality of Work Life*. New York: Wiley, 1980.

Lazerson, M. Wagener, U., and Shumanis, N. "What Makes a Revolution? Teaching and Learning in Higher Education." *Change*, 2000, *32*(3), 13–19.

Learned, W. S., and Wood, B. D. *The Student and His Knowledge.* New York: Carnegie Foundation for the Advancement of Teaching, 1938.

Lenning, O. T., Beal, P. E., and Sauer, K. *Retention and Attrition: Evidence for Action and Research.* Boulder, Colo.: National Center for Higher Education Management Systems, 1980.

Lenning, O. T., Lee, Y. S., Micek, S. S., and Service, A. L. *A Structure for the Outcomes of Postsecondary Education.* Boulder, Colo.: National Center for Higher Education Management Systems, 1977.

Light, R. J., Singer, J. D., and Willett, J. B. *By Design: Planning Research on Higher Education.* Cambridge, Mass.: Harvard University Press, 1990.

Lindblom, C. E. "The Science of Muddling Through." *Public Administration Review,* 1959, *19*, 79–88.

Loacker, G., Cromwell, L., and O'Brien, K. "Assessment in Higher Education: To Serve the Learner." In C. Adelman (ed.), OERI, *Assessment in American Higher Education: Issues and Contexts.* Washington, D.C.: OERI, U.S. Department of Education, Report No. OR86-301, 1986.

López, C. L. *The Commission's Assessment Initiative: A Progress Report.* Chicago, Ill.: North Central Association of Colleges and Schools, 1997.

López, C. L. *A Decade of Assessing Student Learning: What We Have Learned; What's Next?* Chicago: North Central Association of Colleges and Schools Commission on Institutions of Higher Education, 1999.

Madaus, G. F., and Kellaghan, T. "Models, Metaphors, and Definitions in Evaluation." In D. L. Stufflebeam, G. F. Madaus, and T. Kellaghan (eds.), *Evaluation Models: Viewpoints on Educational and Human Services Evaluation.* (2nd ed.) Norwell, Mass.: Kluwer, 2000.

Madaus, G. F., and Stufflebeam, D. L. "Program Evaluation: A Historical Overview." In G. F. Madaus, T. Kellaghan, and D. L. Stufflebeam (eds.), *Evaluation Models: Viewpoints on Educational and Human Services Evaluation.* (2nd ed.) Norwell, Mass.: Kluwer, 2000.

Madison, R. E., Fullner, N., and Baum, P. "The Assessment Outcomes Program at California State University, Northridge: A Model for Program Improvement." *Assessment Update,* 1999, *11*(5), 4–5, 7.

Manktelow, K. *Reasoning and Thinking.* Hove, U.K.: Psychology Press, 1999.

Marchese, T. J. "Third Down, Ten Years to Go." *AAHE Bulletin,* 1987, *40*(4), 3–8.

Marchese, T. J. "Undergraduate Reform." *Change,* May/June 2000.

May, B. A., and others. "Critical Thinking and Clinical Competence: A Study of Their Relationship in BSN Seniors." *Journal of Nursing Education,* 1999, *38*(3), 100–109.

McClain, C. J. *In Pursuit of Degrees with Integrity: A Value-Added Approach to Undergraduate Assessment.* Washington, D.C.: American Association of State Colleges and Universities, 1984.

McClain, C. J., and Krueger, D. W. "Using Outcomes Assessment: A Case Study in Institutional Change." In P. T. Ewell (ed.), *Assessing Educational Outcomes.* New Directions for Institutional Research, no. 47. San Francisco: Jossey-Bass, 1985.

McClellan, S. A., Cogdal, P. A., Lease, S. H., and Londono-McConnell, A. "Development of the Multicultural Assessment of Campus Programming (MAC-P) Questionnaire." *Measurement and Evaluation in Counseling and Development,* 1996, *29,* 86–99.

McConnell, T. "Changes in Scores on the Psychological Examination of the American Council on Education from Freshman to Senior Year." *Journal of Educational Psychology,* 1934, *25,* 66–69.

McLaughlin, G. W., Howard, R. D., Balkan, L. A., and Blythe, E. W. *People, Processes, and Managing Data.* Resources in Institutional Research, no. 11. Tallahassee, Fla.: Association for Institutional Research, 1998.

Mentkowski, M. "Higher Education Assessment and National Goals for Education: Issues, Assumptions, and Principles." In N. M. Lambert and B. L. McCombs (eds.), *How Students Learn: Reforming Schools Through Learner-Centered Education.* Washington, D.C.: American Psychological Association, 1998.

Mentkowski, M., and Associates. *Learning That Lasts: Integrating Learning, Development, and Performance in College and Beyond.* San Francisco: Jossey-Bass, 2000.

Mentkowski, M., Astin, A. W., Ewell, P. T., and Moran, E. T. *Catching Theory Up with Practice: Conceptual Frameworks for Assessment.* Washington, D.C.: The American Association for Higher Education Assessment Forum, American Association for Higher Education, 1991.

Mentkowski, M., and Chickering, A. W. "Linking Educators and Researchers in Setting a Research Agenda for Undergraduate Education." *The Review of Higher Education,* 1987, *11*(2), 137–160.

Mentkowski, M., and Rogers, G. P. *Establishing the Validity of Measures of Student Outcomes.* Milwaukee, Wis.: Alverno Publications, 1988.

Merwin, J. C. "Historical Review of Changing Concepts of Evaluation." In R. L. Tyler (ed.), *Educational Evaluation: New Roles, New Means.* The Sixty-Eighth Yearbook of the National Society for the Study of Education, Part II, Chicago: University of Chicago Press, 1969.

Messick, S. *Meaning and Values in Test Validation: The Science and Ethics of Assessment.* Princeton, N.J.: Educational Testing Service, 1988.

Messick, S. "Validity." In R. Linn (ed.), *Educational Measurement.* (3rd ed.) Phoenix: Oryx Press, 1993.

Messick, S. "The Interplay of Evidence and Consequences in the Validation of Performance Assessments." *Educational Researcher,* 1994, *23*(2), 13–23.

Mets, L. A. "Program Review in Academic Departments." In R. J. Barak and L. A. Mets (eds.), *Using Academic Program Review.* New Directions for Institutional Research, no. 86. San Francisco: Jossey-Bass, 1995.

Mets, L. A. "Planning Change Through Program Review." In M. W. Peterson, D. D. Dill, L. A. Mets, and Associates, *Planning and Management for a Changing Environment: A Handbook on Redesigning Postsecondary Institutions.* San Francisco: Jossey-Bass, 1997.

Micek, S. S., and Arney, W. R. *Inventory of Institutional Environment Variables and Measures.* Boulder, Colo.: National Center for Higher Education Management Systems, 1974.

Miller, D. W. "Scholars Say High-Stakes Tests Deserve a Failing Grade." *Chronicle of Higher Education,* Mar. 2001, pp. A14–A16.

Moos, R. H. *Evaluating Educational Environments.* San Francisco: Jossey-Bass, 1979.

Moos, R. H., and Brownstein, R. *Environment and Utopia: A Synthesis.* New York: Plenum, 1977.

Moos, R. H., and Gerst, M. *University Residence Environment Scale Manual.* Palo Alto, Calif.: Consulting Psychologists Press, 1976.

Moos, R. H., and Insel, P. M. *Issues in Social Ecology: Human Milieus.* Palo Alto, Calif.: National Press Books, 1974.

Moos, R. H., and Trickett, E. *Classroom Environment Scale Manual.* Palo Alto, Calif.: Consulting Psychologists Press, 1976.

Morey, A. J. "Using Classroom-Based Assessment in General Education." *Assessment Update,* 1999, *11*(5), 1–2, 14–15.

Morse, J. M. "Designing Funded Qualitative Research." In N. Denzin and Y. Lincoln (eds.), *Handbook of Qualitative Research.* Thousand Oaks, Calif.: Sage, 1994.

Moskal, B. M., Knecht, R., and Pavelich, M. J. "The Design Report Rubric: Assessing the Impact of Program Design on the Learning Process." *Journal on the Art of Teaching,* forthcoming.

Moustakas, C. "Phenomenological Research Methods." In R. S. Valle and S. Halling (eds.), *Existential-Phenomenological Perspectives in Psychology.* New York: Plenum, 1994.

Myers, I. B., and Myers, P. B. *Gifts Differing: Understanding Personality Type.* Palo Alto, Calif.: Davies-Black, 1995.

National Center for Education Statistics. *The National Assessment of College Student Learning: Identification of the Skills to be Taught, Learned, and Assessed.* Washington, D.C.: Office of Education Research and Improvement, U.S. Department of Education, 1994.

National Center for Postsecondary Improvement. "Revolution or Evolution? Gauging the Impact of Institutional Student Assessment Strategies." *Change,* 1999, *31*(5), 53–56.

National Center for Public Policy and Higher Education. *Measuring Up 2000: The State-by-State Report Card for Higher Education.* Washington, D.C.: National Center for Public Policy and Higher Education, 2000.

National Commission on Higher Education Issues. *To Strengthen Quality in Higher Education.* Washington, D.C.: American Council on Education, 1982.

National Education Goals Panel. *The National Education Goals Report.* Washington, D.C.: National Education Goals Panel, 1991.

National Governors' Association. *Time for Results: The Governors' Report on Education.* Washington, D.C.: National Governors' Association, 1986.

Newcomb, T. M. *Personality and Social Change.* Orlando, Fla.: Dryden Press, 1943.

Nichols, J. O. *Institutional Effectiveness and Outcomes Assessment Implementation on Campus: A Practitioner's Handbook.* New York: Agathon Press, 1989.

Nichols, J. O. *A Practitioner's Handbook for Institutional Effectiveness and Student Outcomes Assessment Implementation.* (2nd ed.) New York: Agathon, 1995.

North Central Association. "Academic Quality Improvement Project (AQIP)." [http://www.aqip.org]. See also http://www.aqip.org/allabout.htm, http://www.aqip.org/criteria.html, and http://www.aqip.org/members.html.

O'Banion, T. *A Learning College for the 21st Century.* Washington, D.C.: Phoenix: Oryx Press, 1997.

Olsen, D. R., Wygant, S. A., and Brown, B. L. "Electronic Survey Administration: Assessment in the Twenty-First Century." Unpublished manuscript, Brigham Young University, 2000.

O'Sullivan, P. S., Blevins-Stephens, W. L., Smith, F. M., and Vaughan-Wrobel, B. "Addressing the National League for Nursing Critical Thinking Outcome." *Nurse Educator,* 1997, *22*(1), 23–29.

Pace, C. R. *Measuring the Outcomes of College.* San Francisco: Jossey-Bass, 1979.

Pace, C. R. *Achievement and the Quality of Student Effort.* Washington, D.C.: National Commission on Excellence in Education, 1982.

Pace, C. R. *The Undergraduates: A Report of their Activities and Progress in the 1980s.* Los Angeles: University of California, Los Angeles, Center for the Study of Evaluation, 1990.

Pace, C. R., and Kuh, G. D. *College Student Experiences Questionnaire.* Bloomington, Ind.: Center for Postsecondary Research and Planning, 1998.

Palmer, P. J. "Good Talk About Good Teaching: Improving Teaching Through Conversation and Community." *Change,* 1993, *25*(6), 8–13.

Palomba, C. A., and Banta, T. W. *Assessment Essentials: Planning, Implementing, and Improving Assessment in Higher Education.* San Francisco: Jossey-Bass, 1999.

Palomba, C. A., and Banta, T. W. (eds.). *Assessing Student Competence in Accredited Disciplines: Pioneering Approaches to Assessment in Higher Education.* Sterling, Va.: Stylus Publishing, LLC, 2001.

Parsons, M. J. *How We Understand Art: A Cognitive Developmental Account of Aesthetic Experience.* New York: Cambridge University Press, 1987.

Pascarella, E. T. "Are Value-Added Assessments Valuable?" In *Assessing the Outcomes of Higher Education, Proceedings of the 1986 ETS Invitational Conference.* Princeton, N.J.: Educational Testing Service, 1987.

Pascarella, E. T., and Terenzini, P. T. *How College Affects Students: Findings and Insights from Twenty Years of Research.* San Francisco: Jossey-Bass, 1991.

Patton, M. Q. *Qualitative Evaluation and Research Methods.* (2nd ed.) Thousand Oaks, Calif.: Sage, 1990.

Patton, M. Q. *Utilization-Focused Evaluation: The New Century Text.* (3rd ed.) Thousand Oaks, Calif.: Sage, 1997.

Perkin, M. "Validating Formative and Summative Assessment." In S. Brown, P. Race, and J. Bull (eds.), *Computer-Assisted Assessment in Higher Education.* London: Kogan Page Limited, 1999.

Perry, W. G. *Forms of Intellectual and Ethical Development in the College Years: A Scheme.* Austin, Tex.: Holt, Rinehart and Winston, 1970.

Peters, R. "Some Snarks Are Boojums: Accountability and the End(s) of Higher Education." *Change,* 1994, *26*(6), 16–23.

Peterson, M. W. "The Organizational Environment for Student Learning." In J. S. Stark and L. A. Mets (eds.), *Improving Teaching and Learning Through Research.* New Directions for Institutional Research, no. 57. San Francisco: Jossey-Bass, 1988.

Peterson, M. W., and Augustine, C. H. "Organizational Practices Enhancing the Influence of Student Assessment Information in Academic Decisions." *Research in Higher Education,* 2000, *41*(1), 21–52.

Peterson, M. W., and Augustine, C. H. "External and Internal Influences on Institutional Approaches to Student Assessment: Accountability or Improvement." *Research in Higher Education,* 2000, *41*(4), 443–479.

Peterson, M. W., Augustine, C. H., Einarson, M. K., and Vaughan, D. S. *Designing Student Assessment to Strengthen Institutional Performance in Associate of Arts Institutions.* Stanford, Calif.: Stanford University, National Center for Postsecondary Improvement, 1999a.

Peterson, M. W., Augustine, C. H., Einarson, M. K., and Vaughan, D. S. *Designing Student Assessment to Strengthen Institutional Performance in Baccalaureate Institutions.* Stanford, Calif.: Stanford University, National Center for Postsecondary Improvement, 1999b.

Peterson, M. W., Einarson, M. K., Augustine, C. H., and Vaughan, D. S. *Institutional Support for Student Assessment: Methodology and Results of a National Survey.* Stanford, Calif.: Stanford University, National Center for Postsecondary Improvement, 1999a.

Peterson, M. W., Einarson, M. K., Augustine, C. H., and Vaughan, D. S. *Designing Student Assessment to Strengthen Institutional Performance in Comprehensive Institutions.* Stanford, Calif.: Stanford University, National Center for Postsecondary Improvement, 1999b.

Peterson, M. W., Einarson, M. K., Augustine, C. H., and Vaughan, D. S. *Designing Student Assessment to Strengthen Institutional Performance in Doctoral and Research Institutions.* Stanford, Calif.: Stanford University, National Center for Postsecondary Improvement, 1999c.

Peterson, M. W., Einarson, M. K., Trice, A. G., and Nichols, A. R. *Improving Organizational and Administrative Support for Student Assessment: A Review of the Research Literature.* Stanford, Calif.: Stanford University, National Center for Postsecondary Improvement, 1997.

Peterson, M. W., and Vaughan, D. S. "Planning a Multidimensional Strategy for Improving the Use of Student Assessment." *Planning for Higher Education,* 2002, *20*(2), 13–27.

Pettit, F. A. "Exploring the Use of the World Wide Web as a Psychology Data Collection Tool." *Computers in Human Behavior,* 1999, *15,* 67–71.

Pickering, J. W., and others. "The Effect of Noncognitive Factors on Freshman Academic Performance and Retention." *Journal of the Freshman Year Experience,* 1992, *4,* 7–30.

Pike, G. R. "Assessment Measures." In T. W. Banta (ed.), *Assessment Update: The First Ten Years.* Boulder, Colo.: National Center for Higher Education Management Systems, 1999.

Pike, G. R. "Assessment Measures: Methodological Issues in the Assessment of Learning Communities." *Assessment Update,* 2000a, *12*(2), 14–15.

Pike, G. R. "Rethinking the Role of Assessment." *About Campus,* 2000b, *5*(1): 11–19.

Pike, G. R. "Assessment Measures: The NSSE 2000 Report: National Benchmarks of Effective Educational Practice." *Assessment Update,* 2001, *13*(1), 8–9.

Pressy, S. L. "Changes from 1923 to 1943 in the Attitudes of Public School and University Students." *Journal of Psychology,* 1946, *21,* 173–188.

Prince, J. S., Miller, T. K., and Winston, R. B., Jr. *Student Developmental Task Inventory.* Athens, Ga.: Student Development Associates, 1974.

Program Assessment Consultation Team (PACT). *PACT Outcomes Assessment Handbook.* Bakersfield: California State University, Bakersfield, July 21, 1999.

Rice, E. "The New American Scholar: Scholarship and the Purposes of the University." *Metropolitan Universities,* 1991, *1*(4), 7–18.

Roberts, J. S. *GGUM2000 USERS Guide.* College Park, Md.: J. S. Roberts, 2000.

Roberts, J. S., Donoghue, J. R., and Laughlin, J. E. "A General Item Response Theory Model for Unfolding Unidimensional Polytomous Responses." *Applied Psychological Measurement,* 2000, *24*(1), 3–32.

Robinson, J. M. "Computer-Assisted Peer Review." In S. Brown, P. Race, and J. Bull (eds.), *Computer-Assisted Assessment in Higher Education.* London: Kogan Page Limited, 1999.

Rodgers, R. F. "Student Development." In U. Delworth, G. R. Hanson and Associates (eds.), *Student Services: A Handbook for the Profession* (2nd ed.) San Francisco: Jossey-Bass, 1989.

Rogers, E. *The Diffusion of Innovation.* (4th ed.) New York: Free Press, 1995.

Rogers, E. M. "The Communication of Innovations in a Complex Institution." *Educational Record,* Winter 1968, 67–77.

Rogers, G. "Measurement and Judgment in Curriculum Assessment Systems." *Assessment Update,* 1994, *6*(1), 6–7.

Rogers, G. M., and Chow, T. "Electronic Portfolios and the Assessment of Student Learning." *Assessment Update,* 2000, *12*(1), 4–5, 11.

Ruben, B. D. "We Need Excellence Beyond the Classroom." *Chronicle of Higher Education,* July 13, 2001, B15.

Sandmann, L. R., and others. "Managing Critical Tensions: How to Strengthen the Scholarship Component of Outreach." *Change,* 2000, *32*(1), 44–52.

Sanford, N. (ed.). *The American College: A Psychological and Social Interpretation of the Higher Learning.* New York: Wiley, 1962.

Satterlee, B. *Program Review and Evaluation: A Survey of Contemporary Literature.* Washington, D.C.: U.S. Department of Education, 1992. (ED 356261)

Schacter, J., and others. "Computer-Based Performance Assessments: A Solution to the Narrow Measurement and Reporting of Problem Solving." *Computers in Human Behavior,* 1999, *15,* 403–418.

Schilling, K. L. "The Electronic Campus: New Technologies for Assessing the Student Experience." *About Campus,* 1997, *2*(1), 26–28.

Schraw, G. "On the Development of Adult Metacognition." In M. C. Smith and T. Pourchot (eds.), *Adult Learning and Development: Perspectives from Educational Psychology.* Mahweh, N.J.: Lawrence Erlbaum Associates, 1998.

Schroeder, C. C., and Pike, G. R. "The Scholarship of Application in Student Affairs." *Journal of College Student Development,* 2001, *42*(4), 342–355.

Schulte, J., and Loacker, G. *Assessing General Education Outcomes for the Individual Student: Performance Assessment-as-Learning. Part I: Designing and Implementing Performance Assessment Instruments.* Milwaukee, Wis.: Alverno College Institute, 1994.

Scott, R. A. "Program Review's Missing Link." *The College Board Review,* 1980, *118,* 19–21.

Sedlacek, W. E., and Brooks, G. C. *The Development of a Measure of Racial Attitudes.* College Park, Md.: University of Maryland, Counseling Center, 1967.

Sedlacek, W. E., and Brooks, G. C. *Racism in American Education: A Model for Change.* Chicago: Nelson-Hall, 1976.

Seymann, R. G. "Assessing Honors Programs." Paper presented at the Virginia Assessment Group Conference, VI, Nov. 2000.

Seymour, D. T. *On Q: Causing Quality in Higher Education.* New York: ACE/Macmillan, 1991.

Shadish, W. R. and others. *Guiding Principles for Evaluators.* New Directions for Program Evaluation, no. 66. San Francisco: Jossey-Bass, 1995.

Shaw, J. D. "Applicability of Baxter Magolda's Epistemological Reflection Model to Black and Latino Students." University of South Florida, Dissertation Abstracts, 2000.

Shermis, M. D. *Automated Essay Grading for Electronic Portfolios.* Washington, D.C.: Fund for the Improvement of Postsecondary Education, 2000.

Shermis, M. D., and Averitt, J. "Where Did All the Data Go? Internet Security for Web-Based Assessments." Paper presented at the annual meeting of the National Council on Measurement in Education, New Orleans, La., Apr. 2000.

Shermis, M. D., Koch, C. M., Page, E. B., Keith, T. Z., and Harrington, S. "Trait Ratings for Automated Scoring." *Educational and Psychological Measurement,* 2002, *62*(1), 5–18.

Shermis, M. D., Mzumara, H. R., Olson, J., and Harrington, S. "On-line Grading of Student Essays: PEG goes on the World Wide Web." *Assessment and Evaluation in Higher Education,* 2001, *26*(3), 247–259.

Shermis, M. D., Stemmer, P. M., Jr., Berger, C. F., and Anderson, G. E. *Using Microcomputers in Social Science Research.* Needham Heights, Mass.: Allyn & Bacon, 1991.

Shulman, L. S., "Teaching as Community Property." *Change,* 1993, *15*(6), 6–7.

Silva, F. *Psychometric Foundations and Behavioral Assessment.* Thousand Oaks, Calif.: Sage, 1993.

Silverman, D. *Doing Qualitative Research: A Practical Handbook.* London: Sage, 2000.

Sloan Commission on Government and Higher Education. *A Program for Renewed Partnership.* New York: Ballinger, 1980.

Smith, D., and Eder, D. "Assessment and Program Review: Linking Two Processes." *Assessment Update,* 2001, *13*(1), 1, 14–15.

Smith, M. C., and Pourchot, T. (eds.). *Adult Learning and Development: Perspectives from Educational Psychology.* Mahweh, N.J.: Lawrence Erlbaum Associates, 1998.

Smith, M. K., Bradley, J. L., and Draper, G. F. *Annotated Reference Catalog of Assessment Instruments, Catalogs A–G.* Knoxville: University of Tennessee, Assessment Resource Center, 1994.

Stake, R. *The Art of Case Study.* Thousand Oaks, Calif.: Sage, 1995.

Stanley, L. S. "The Development and Validation of an Instrument to Assess Attitudes Toward Cultural Diversity and Pluralism Among Preservice Physical Educators." *Educational and Psychological Measurement,* 1996, *56,* 891–897.

Stanovich, K. E., and West, R. F. "Discrepancies Between Normative and Descriptive Models of Decision Making and the Understanding/ Acceptance Principle." *Cognitive Psychology,* 1999, *38*(3), 349–385.

Stanovich, K. E., and West, R. F. "Individual Differences in Reasoning: Implications for the Rationality Debate?" *Behavioral and Brain Sciences,* 2000, *23*(5), 645–726.

Steele, J. M., Malone, F. E., and Lutz, D. A. *Second Report of ACT's Research on Postsecondary Assessment Needs.* Iowa City, Iowa: American College Testing Program, 1997.

Stemmer, P. "Electronic Portfolios: Are They Going to Be the Very Next Craze." Paper presented at the Michigan School Testing Conference, Ann Arbor, Mich., Feb. 1993.

Stern, G. G. *People in Context.* New York: Wiley, 1970.

Strail, M. L. *College Student Inventory.* Coralville, Iowa: Noel/Levitz Centers, 1988.

Strange, C. "Implementing and Assessing the Voice Project." Paper presented at the annual meeting of the American College Personnel Association, Boston, Mar. 2001.

Strange, C. C., and Banning, J. H. *Educating by Design: Creating Campus Learning Environments That Work.* San Francisco: Jossey-Bass, 2001.

Strauss, A., and Corbin, J. *Basics of Qualitative Research: Grounded Theory Procedures and Techniques.* Thousand Oaks, Calif.: Sage, 1990.

Student Learning Initiative (A. Doherty, T. Riordan, and J. Roth, eds.). *Student Learning: A Central Focus for Institutions of Higher Education.* Milwaukee, Wis.: Alverno College Institute, 2002.

Study Group on the Conditions of Excellence in American Higher Education. *Involvement in Learning: Realizing the Potential of American Higher Education.* Washington, D.C.: U.S. Department of Education, National Institute of Education, Oct. 1984.

Stufflebeam, D. L. (ed.).*Evaluation Models.* New Directions for Evaluation, no. 89. San Francisco: Jossey-Bass, 2001.

Stufflebeam, D. L., and others. *Educational Evaluation and Decision Making.* Itasca, Ill.: Peacock, 1971.

Sue, D. W., and Sue, D. *Counseling the Culturally Different: Theory and Practice.* (2nd ed.) New York: Wiley, 1990.

Tallman, G. D., Jacobs, E. L., and Jacobs, N. W. "Developing Course Learning Outcomes." Paper presented at the AACSB Outcome Assessment Seminar, Clearwater Beach, Fla., Feb. 1999.

Teeter, D. J., and Lozier, G. (eds.). *Pursuit of Quality in Higher Education: Case Studies in Total Quality Management.* New Directions for Institutional Research, no. 78. San Francisco, Jossey-Bass, 1993.

Terenzini, P. T. "Assessment with Open Eyes: Pitfalls in Studying Student Outcomes." *Journal of Higher Education,* 1989, *60* (Nov.–Dec.), 644–664.

Terenzini, P. T., Pascarella, E. T., and Lorang, W. "An Assessment of the Academic and Social Influences on Freshman Year Educational Outcomes." *Review of Higher Education,* 1982, *5,* 86–109.

Terkla, D. G., and Armstrong, K. J. "Beyond Commencement: Using Alumni Research in Outcomes Assessment." *Assessment Update,* 1999, *11*(1), 10–12.

Thelwall, M. "Open-Access Randomly Generated Tests: Assessment to Drive Learning." In S. Brown, P. Race, and J. Bull (eds.), *Computer-Assisted Assessment in Higher Education.* London: Kogan Page Limited, 1999.

Thibodeau, S. J. "Portfolios as Assessment of Prospective Teachers for Licensure." *Assessment Update,* 2000, *12*(5), 6–7.

Thomas, S. L., and Heck, R. H. "Analysis of Large-Scale Secondary Data in Higher Education: Potential Perils Associated with Complex Sampling Designs." *Research in Higher Education,* 2001, *42*(5), 517–540.

Thompson, S. "Lessons Learned in Implementing the Scholarship of Teaching and Learning." *The National Teaching Forum,* 2001, *10*(5), 8–10.

Thornton, G. C., and Byham, W. C. *Assessment Centers and Managerial Performance.* Orlando, Fla.: Academic Press, 1982.

Tinto, V. "Dropout from Higher Education: A Theoretical Synthesis of Recent Research." *Review of Educational Research,* 1975, *45,* 89–125.

Tinto, V. *Leaving College: Rethinking the Causes and Cures of Student Attrition.* (2nd ed.) Chicago: University of Chicago Press, 1993.

Travers, R.M.W. *How Research Has Changed American Schools: A History from 1840 to the Present.* Kalamazoo, Mich.: Mythos Press, 1983.

U.S. Department of Education, National Commission on Excellence in Education. *A Nation at Risk: The Imperative for Educational Reform.* Washington, D.C.: U.S. Government Printing Office, 1983.

Upcraft, M. L., and Schuh, J. H. *Assessment in Student Affairs: A Guide for Practitioners.* San Francisco: Jossey-Bass, 1996.

Wainer, H. "Measurement Problems." *Journal of Educational Measurement,* 1993, *30,* 1–21.

Wainer, H. "Using Trilinear Plots for NAEP State Data." *Journal of Educational Measurement,* 1996, *33*(1), 41–55.

Wainer, H. "Improving Tabular Displays, with NAEP Tables as Examples and Inspirations." *Journal of Educational and Behavioral Statistics,* 1997, *22*(1), 1–30.

Walvoord, B. E., and Anderson, V. J. *Effective Grading: A Tool for Learning and Assessment.* San Francisco: Jossey-Bass, 1998.

Warren, J. "The Blind Alley of Value Added." *AAHE Bulletin,* 1984, *37*(1), 10–13.

Wechsler, H. *The Harvard Alcohol Survey.* Boston: Harvard School of Public Health, 1999a.

Wechsler, H. *The College Alcohol Study.* Boston: Harvard School of Public Health, 1999b.

Weinstein, C., Palmer, D., and Schulte, A. *LASSI: Learning and Study Strategies Inventory.* Clearwater, Fla.: H&H Publishing, 1987.

Weiss, C. H. "Have We Learned Anything New About the Use of Evaluation?" *American Journal of Evaluation,* 1998, *19*(1), 21–33.

Wheatley, M. J. *Leadership and the New Science. Learning About Organization from an Orderly Universe.* San Francisco: Berrett-Koehler, 1992.

White, R. W. *Lives in Progress.* Orlando, Fla.: Dryden Press, 1952.

Widick, C., Knefelkamp, L., and Parker, C. "Student Development." In U. Delworth, G. Hanson, and Associates (eds.), *Student Services: A Handbook for the Profession.* San Francisco: Jossey-Bass, 1980.

Willson, V. L. "Performance Assessment, Psychometric Theory, and Cognitive Learning Theory: Ships Crossing in the Night." *Contemporary Education*, 1991, *62*(4), 250.

Winston, R. B., Jr. "The Student Developmental Task and Lifestyle Inventory: An Approach to Measuring Students' Psychosocial Development." *Journal of College Student Development*, 1990, *31*(2), 108–120.

Wolf, L. F., and Smith, J. K. "The Consequence of Consequence: Motivation, Anxiety and Test Performance." *Applied Measurement in Education*, 1995, *8*, 227–242.

Wolf, L. F., Smith, J. K., and Birnbaum, M. E. "Consequence of Performance, Test Motivation, and Mentally Taxing Items." *Applied Measurement in Education*, 1995, *8*, 341–351.

Wolff, R. A. "Assessment and Accreditation: A Shotgun Marriage?" In *Achieving Institutional Effectiveness Through Assessment. A Resource Manual to Support WASC Institutions*. Oakland, Calif.: Western Association of Schools and Colleges, 1992.

Wood, P. "Inquiring Systems and Problem Structure: Implications for Cognitive Development." *Human Development*, 1983, *26*, 249–265.

Wood, P., and Conner, J. "Assessment Measures: Deciding How Many Participants to Use in Assessment Research." *Assessment Update*, 1999, *11*(4), 8–9, 11.

Worthen, B. R., and Sanders, J. R. *Education Evaluation: Alternative Approaches and Practical Guidelines*. White Plains, N.Y.: Longman, 1987.

Worthen, B. R., Sanders, J. R., and Fitzpatrick, J. L. *Program Evaluation: Alternative Approaches and Practical Guidelines*. (2nd ed.) White Plains, N.Y.: Longman, 1997.

Wright, B. D. "Evaluating Learning in Individual Courses." In J. G. Gaff, J. L. Ratcliff, and Associates (eds.), *Handbook of the Undergraduate Curriculum: A Comprehensive Guide to Purposes, Structures, Practices, and Change*. A publication of the Association of American Colleges and Universities. San Francisco: Jossey-Bass, 1997.

Zlatic, T. D. "Redefining a Profession: Assessment in Pharmacy Education." In C. A. Palomba and T. W. Banta (eds.), *Assessing Student Competence in Accredited Disciplines: Pioneering Approaches to Assessment in Higher Education*. Sterling, Va.: Stylus Publishing, LLC, 2001.

Name Index

Subject Index